# MY RIOT

## AGNOSTIC FRONT, GRIT, GUTS & GLORY

# ROGER MIRET

WITH JON WIEDERHORN

Post Hill
PRESS

A POST HILL PRESS BOOK

ISBN: 978-1-64293-197-6

ISBN (eBook): 978-1-64293-198-3

My Riot:

Agnostic Front, Grit, Guts & Glory

© 2019 by Roger Miret and Jon Wiederhorn

All Rights Reserved

Published by arrangement with Overamstel Publishers, Inc.

Post Hill Press

New York • Nashville

posthillpress.com

Published in the United States of America

For Nadia, Emily, Havi and Desi —**RM**

To my mother, Nancy Irene Wiederhorn, who always believed in me —**JW**

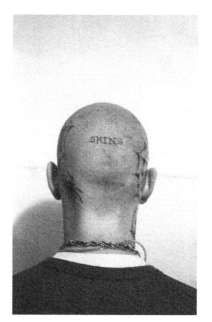

1983

# MY RIOT!

By Roger Miret and The Disasters

I was a teenage war
Punk rocker
An urban outlaw

Couldn't care at all
No feelings, back off!
Destroyed it all

This is my riot! My war—my hate!
This is my riot! My war—my hate!
This is my war! My hate!
Hate and war! This is my riot!

I was no disco bore
Punk rockin'
Loud, fast and raw

My riot!

Spray painted the walls! My riot!
Smashed bottles, pissed off! My riot!
I fought the law! My riot!

Walking down these dark streets of New York City
Reminiscing on yesterday and now today
This riot in me never ever seems to fade away

Never an end to my war or my hate!

# TABLE OF CONTENTS

# FOREWORD 1

## A Lesson Well Learned:
## Evolving Beyond Feuds and Living in Unity

**Al Barr of the Dropkick Murphys**

It was 1984, and the first wave of hardcore was going on, which felt like the second wave of punk. I'd been entrenched in it for almost three years, but I wasn't in a big city where the action was. I was living with my folks in New Hampshire.

When I saw Agnostic Front for the first time, I was 15. My buddy Keith Eaton invited me, and I thought we were just going to a punk concert. That show was a life changer.

Agnostic Front started the show with a wild bassline and then guitar and drums. There was a mic stand but no singer. Then out of nowhere, this guy flew in, grabbed the microphone, sprung up into the air and started screaming. When he went into the chorus of "Victim In Pain," "Why am I going insane?" he ripped his shirt off and I saw his tattoo of a crucified guy with a gas mask. He was muscular but lean. When he ripped off his kerchief, I saw he had a Mohawk. I thought, *Fuck! He has the same look as me!*

Keith and I went to the front and watched Agnostic Front from a few feet away. There was a rift between Boston and New York and this was a Boston crowd with a grudge, so they wanted to make a statement. Almost everyone was standing against the wall with their arms folded. AF was onstage ripping from one song to another, and no one was dancing!

Keith and I couldn't believe that they weren't blown away by all of AF's energy. I had never seen anything like this division at a show. There had always been a feeling of unity: Everybody danced and shared in an us-against-the-world mentality. Something was weird that Keith and I didn't understand. That's because we weren't part of the city politics.

We later became aware of the rift between New York and Boston. Some bands from Boston had gone to CBGB, said some disparaging things about New York and gotten their asses beaten. In response, these Boston kids were giving AF attitude. At some point AF stopped playing. The drummer, Dave Jones, made a speech about how they had driven six-plus hours to get there. "Where's the love, Boston?" he asked. "What the fuck is this?"

The band continued playing, but the tension grew. Eight or nine New York skins started bouncing through the crowd and beating the shit out of everybody. A young Dicky Barrett (later of the Mighty Mighty Bosstones) got punched in the face by Jimmy Gestapo from Murphy's Law. It was a knock-down, drag-out fight. Chairs were hoisted and swung at people.

Intimidated by the violence, my friend and I left early, but not before I learned about the power of NYHC. Roger taught me all about furious, sincere facial expressions, and he leapt around the stage like an acrobat. During the slower parts he was the master of that New York stage stomp that his brother Freddy later perfected in Madball.

The first time I met Roger was in 1988. My band The Bruisers played a show with Agnostic Front at Man Ray in Cambridge, Massachusetts. Anticipating AF's performance made us more energetic during our set. When they went on they were explosive. When we started doing shows together I briefly feared Roger. They had come up to New England, and they stayed in New Hampshire on a day off. Roger wanted to go to some bike stores. Then I sent the band down a seacoast road, which was a beautiful drive that went directly to the club. When we got to the show the next day, Roger had just found out that his squat had burned down. Freddy was in the hospital with smoke inhalation. I went up to him not knowing anything had happened.

"Hey, man!" I said. "What'd you think of the shops and isn't that ride to the coast amazing? Did you like it?"

"I don't fuckin' like anything!" he yelled.

He had a crazy temper. I didn't know what to think until someone told me his living space had gone up in flames. Any fear I had of Roger dissipated. We did a bunch of shows together over a couple months, then they gave us a song they had never recorded but had always sound-checked with called "Iron Chin." We recorded it in 1993 for our first full-length, *Cruisin' for a Bruisin'*. It became known as a Bruisers song and our fans loved it. This legendary group Agnostic Front gave a band from the sticks their song. And it wasn't some shitty leftover track. They didn't have to do that.

Once I became friends with Roger, he was like a big brother. He was someone I could talk to and look up to. On my first tour with Dropkick Murphys we opened for Agnostic Front, and I knew Roger better than the guys in my band. We were friendly, but friendships develop over time. Suddenly I was on a three-month U.S. tour with people I hardly knew followed by a month in Europe. Every day, there was a time when Roger and I talked about life.

Even though I had been in the punk scene and singing in bands for 15 years, I struggled to find where I fit in with the Dropkicks. There was a learning curve, but I had to learn fast since we were on the road. Everyone in the band was frustrated, including me. Roger was encouraging, and that boosted my confidence. I could be in a shitty mood, and we'd go have coffee, complain and laugh. Suddenly everything didn't seem so stressful.

I've become even closer with Roger over the years. The world finally caught up with Roger and Vinnie Stigma. They're the elder statesmen of hardcore. Roger feels that admiration from the community, and that makes him happy.

Roger is still an amazing performer. He's still making great music. It's loud and pissed off, but he's in a much happier place.

They don't come any more real than Roger. He has the heart of a lion, he's as ferocious as a bear and he's a stand-up guy. I love the dude and I always will.

CBGB, 1984. This photo was originally set to be the cover of *Victim In Pain*.

# FOREWORD 2

## The Voice of a Generation: There Is No Other
**Jamey Jasta of Hatebreed**

On my 14th birthday, I saw Agnostic Front's record *One Voice*, which shows Roger Miret's tattoo on the back cover. I thought, *What type of person would be that crazy to have this wild tattoo? I need to get this album.*

I was just getting into hardcore. I liked the metallic edge of AF's music. Roger, guitarists Vinnie Stigma and Matt Henderson, bassist Craig Setari and drummer Will Shepler sounded great, and the songs spoke to me.

I asked the kid at the record store about Agnostic Front's other albums and worked my way backwards. I learned the history of the band—the crossover fury of *Cause For Alarm* and the raw, in-your-face energy of *Victim In Pain*.

I couldn't wait to see them live. I had heard nightmare stories from kids at my high school: "Oh, they beat up punk rockers at their shows. Watch out for the skinhead guys and the crazy hardcore dudes. They bring chains and bats!" The reputation for violence made me want to see them more. I thought, *This is great! It sounds like ECW wrestling!*

There was an AF show near Yale University, but I wasn't able to go. I heard afterwards that there was a crazy fight, which made me regret missing the concert. I vowed to see them the next time they came through town.

Then I heard that they broke up and I was so bummed.

For the next few years, I kept listening to AF and learned their catalog inside-out. I would go to a friend's house and watch VHS tapes of Agnostic Front in Europe. I studied the way Roger swung the mic, whipped his hair and dove into the crowd. It was all so compelling. I thought, *Wow, I want to do that! It looks like so much fun!* The energy Roger gives off when he comes into a room is so powerful. I could feel it through the television.

Over the next couple of years I started Hatebreed and booked shows for the band. I told promoters, "If AF comes back, please let us play the shows. I'll do anything."

In 1996 we played two shows with them at a narrow, divey New York sweatbox club called Wetlands. It was life-changing.

Even though you're not supposed to be a rock star in hardcore punk, Roger was a star. When he walked in, the room lit up. I was nervous when we met. When you're a teenager in a band and you get to open up for a legend that has a crazy reputation, it's intimidating. The jitters quickly wore off as he was cool, friendly and easy to talk to.

We left the show freaking out, going, "Oh, my God! I can't believe we did that. We fuckin' played with Agnostic Front!"

Getting on a New York stage with such a legendary band helped us build buzz and get noticed by labels and promoters. Becoming friends with Roger and Stigma was great because I booked Agnostic Front in Connecticut and Hatebreed got to open. We did shows with AF and The Business, Warzone and H2O.

Agnostic Front liked giving groups a platform to reach the next level. Roger put together the Unity Tour, which gave Dropkick Murphys their first big boost. In the mid '90s, metal was still in a real dip, but punk, hardcore and metal were melding in different scenes and subgenres. AF is one of those bands you can like if you're a metalhead, a punk rocker or a straight edge guy, because of their energy, power, anthems and message of unity.

When I had the opportunity to give back to Roger and produce a record for Agnostic Front, I was excited to do so. I worked on the band's 2004 album, *Another Voice*. Their previous album, *Dead Yuppies*, came out around 9/11 and wasn't their best-received record. We had to change the perception of the band. New kids were coming into the hardcore scene and were willing to accept a classic band, and a great record would draw them in. I had some pull at MTV2 and Hatebreed had two records out on a major label, so people listened to what I had to say.

Being a fan of *One Voice*, I thought it would be cool for Agnostic Front to revisit a more metallic sound. Working in the studio with Roger was a blast. We had a great schedule with producer Zeuss. We stayed in a double room in the Econo Lodge. Every morning we'd get eggs and hash browns and talk about what we were would work on.

I was proud to work with them on that record because I'm a big fan. AF have been through it all and come out the other side. They went through eras when it was tough to be a punk rocker and a hardcore guy. They persevered and helped make it cool. Roger Miret is a warrior. The stuff he's been through and bounced back from is unbelievable. There is no other.

# PROLOGUE: URBAN DECAY

The CBGB that became famous in the '70s with Television, Blondie, Talking Heads and the Ramones—the trendy club that was the subject of a feel-good movie starring Alan Rickman as Hilly Kristal—is not the CBGB that my brothers and I in the New York Hardcore (NYHC) community grew up around in the '80s. Our CBs was right in the middle of gang territory and below a homeless shelter. Once in a while, some demented bums would come down and bother our girls or try to steal our wallets.

One day I was inside CBs and I saw a bunch of them stumbling around like zombies from *The Walking Dead*. I said, "This shit's gotta end." We had a few baseball bats. I rounded up some guys and said, "Come with me. Watch my back." I went up to their place and cracked a few heads. Our guitarist, Vinnie Stigma, called it social justice. I saw it as doing what had to be done.

As bad as the Bowery neighborhood used to be and as crappy as CBGB was, it played a major role in spreading the word about NYHC. Today, CBGB is gone, as are the other great shitholes that promoted hardcore—A7, Max's Kansas City and Two Plus Two Annex, to name a few. Even though there were places to play shows, the entire Lower East Side was a fucking cesspool. It was totally unsafe and riddled with degenerates from all walks of life. Even the clubs were full of violence.

During a Cavity Creeps show at the Sin Club, which was on Third Street and Avenue C, a girl named Polly was attacked by a Puerto Rican gang member. Between sets we were hanging outside when a girl named Cynthia, who used to date Johnny Ramone, got into an argument with this Hispanic chick. Polly stepped in and then this dude

14

came up to her. He was cross-eyed and grinning. Cavity Creeps singer Steve Poss, one of the younger kids in the NYHC scene shouted, "There's a knife!" Then the dude stuck his blade right between Polly's ribs. Some of us picked her up and brought her backstage to clean her up. The cut was deep and her side was ripped open. She was bleeding badly, but the knife didn't hit any organs or arteries. We called an ambulance and the paramedics were able to close the wound. Once we made sure she was going to be okay, we went after the guy who had stabbed her but he was nowhere in sight.

That was not unusual in Alphabet City, but the hardcore community wasn't total anarchy. Some people think we were all lowlifes who wanted to kick the shit out of each other. That couldn't be further from the truth. We were united. We hung out together and supported each other. The more popular bands helped get gigs for groups that were less well known, and some helped other bands put out their own records.

Most of the fights we got into were with organized Hispanic gangs that thought we were trying to take over their turf. And there were a lot of them: the Hitmen, the Alleyway Boys, the Forsyth Boys, The Ghost Shadows. These guys wanted to protect their territory, and it just so happened that the clubs courageous enough to book us were right in their backyard.

It wasn't hard to tell the punks from the gangs. Hardcore kids were mostly white. As a Cuban, I was a rare exception. A lot of us had pins in our jackets, boots or Converse shoes and weird hair or shaved heads. The gang dudes usually had on jeans, cheap T-shirts, a vest with their insignia on it and Pro-Keds—which only cost a few dollars, as opposed to Converse, which were about $13. When you're living in poverty, you wear what you wear.

These guys spray-painted graffiti on the sides of buildings not to create cool art, but so you would know whose neighborhood you were in. They had control of certain parks, and there was a mutual respect between them. Nobody crossed turfs. Then we moved in and the gangsters didn't understand what all the weird-looking white people were doing in their neighborhood, going wherever they pleased. Their only thoughts were: "What's this big party? Why is it going on in our neighborhoods? How can we stop it so it doesn't interfere with our drug business?"

Being one of the few punks who spoke Spanish, I mediated between the gang members and the hardcore guys. There was a big misconception that hardcore kids were part of a rival gang because we hung out together and dressed funny. A lot of us lived together, and in a lot of ways, we behaved like a big family—kind of like a gang.

We did a lot together: We drank, did drugs, went to shows, partied, moshed, ate, fought and fucked. The gangs that were selling drugs and doing other illegal shit, such as setting up dog fights and gambling rings, felt threatened and wanted us out. But we weren't going anywhere. A lot of us enjoyed the feeling of community that came from being together. We felt accepted for the first time ever, and all the threats and fights in the world weren't going to make us pack up and leave.

Whenever we'd see these Latinos coming, I would try to talk to them and chill them out so they wouldn't enter our clubs and go off on us. Sometimes it worked, and sometimes it didn't.

Once, in front of the Two Plus Two Annex, I was explaining in Spanish to a few members of the Lower East Side gang The Alleyway Boys that we were *not* a gang. We were just a bunch of bands playing music and we didn't mean any disrespect. I thought I could be a peacemaker and prevent a huge brawl with this group of Puerto Ricans who didn't understand punk or hardcore.

It was bad timing. Social Distortion and Youth Brigade were in town for the Another State of Mind Tour, which Social D was shooting for a film. Without warning, their singer and guitarist, Mike Ness, whipped a beer bottle at us from across the street. He was bombed out of his mind and didn't know what the fuck he was doing. He saw us standing in front of the club and thought it would be funny. When I saw the bottle in mid-air, I pushed one of the punk rock girls, Angelica, out of the way to keep her from getting hit.

The bottle hit Vinnie Stigma in the left knee. Crash! Shards of glass split Vinnie's knee wide open. Blood spilled down his leg and splashed on the sidewalk.

We worried that we would set off the gang guys, but when they saw our own guys turning against us they must have figured we were crazy. They muttered to them-selves and walked off. A bunch of us, including our friend John Nordquist, ran across the street to beat Mike's ass. We beat him so bad he shit his pants! I was angry, not just because Mike fucked up Vinnie's knee but because what he did was totally disre-spectful. We were a pretty lawless group of kids, but there was a street code. Fucking with someone who was trying to keep a gang fight from happening wasn't cool.

Mike knew that shit because he came from L.A., which was Gang Central—way worse than New York. Social Distortion were gonna play this club and then split. But we had to live there and deal with the fallout. A lot of times when people start something it causes a chain reaction, and ten seconds later everybody's fighting. Ness was in another state of mind at the time. Today he's sober, and he and Vinnie are good friends.

It took Social Distortion a long time to come back to New York. By then John Nordquist was dead. Not long after he contributed to Mike Ness's beatdown, he got beaten to a pulp by some guys in a local gang in his hometown of Nutley, New Jersey. They left him on the train tracks. He was so bashed up he couldn't get up. Then he heard a train coming. He waved his arms to try to stop it, and the conductor saw him at the last minute and hit the brakes. He couldn't stop the train in time.

In the '80s, CBGB became the eye of the hardcore hurricane. The club staged Sunday matinees, which helped establish us and numerous other bands, including Murphy's Law, Warzone, Cro-Mags, Sheer Terror, Youth of Today, Gorilla Biscuits and Sick of It All. Even before the matinees, we did hardcore shows there with Death Before Dishonor, The Abused, Antidote, Urban Waste, Reagan Youth, Cause For Alarm and The Mob—basically anybody who would be on the same bill as us.

At one concert, a guy was standing in front of CBGB and started harassing one of our girls. I went up to ask him what the fuck was going on, and he pulled out a big knife and was about to stab me. Vinnie was standing a few feet away and saw what was happening. He threw a bottle as hard as he could into this guy's face. It exploded, as did the dude's forehead. The flesh around his eye turned to mush and the sharp glass severed his optic nerve. He dropped the knife and held his hands to his face, trying to hold his eye in the socket. His eyeball dropped to the ground and Vinnie stomped on it with his combat boot. He squashed it like a water bug. That led to a pretty big fight. I don't know if this cyclops was homeless, but suddenly all the people who lived in a shelter above CBs came after us. It turned into a huge battle between us and the bums, junkies and crackheads. We swept the floor with all of them.

The one good thing about New York street warfare back then was that most guys in gangs and bands only had knives, bats, brass knuckles and homemade weapons.

Hardly anyone carried a gun, which kept the body count down. If you look at all the old hardcore photos from back then, we all wore chain belts. That was one of our favorite weapons: Take the chain belt off, wrap it around your fist and let's go! The Cro-Mags' bassist, Harley Flanagan, with whom I was good friends, liked to fill a sock with rocks, billiard balls or whatever he could find and swing it at anyone who fucked with us—or anyone he felt like fucking with.

We were wild, punked-out, drugged-up, tattooed kids. We lived fast; there were only so many hours in the day. Everything was crazy—our music, our lives. We didn't expect to make it to 30, and we didn't care. We lived for the moment and fed off the energy, adrenaline and attitude we generated. For about five years no one could touch us. The shows got bigger as all these heavy metal people—including guys in Metallica, Exodus and Anthrax—got inspired by what we were doing. Before long we were touring the world, playing on bills with bands like Slayer, Voivod, Motörhead, and Death Angel. I felt like I was on top of the world and nothing could get in my way. Then something did, at least for a while.

In 1987, I got busted for transporting drugs and went to prison for 22 months. Afterward, Agnostic Front got back together, and Vinnie and I rebuilt the entire band. Since then we've put the group on hold a couple times, but we've always gotten back together regardless of how popular hardcore was with the general public. Whether we've been firing on all cylinders or trying to figure out how to keep our lineup together, hardcore has continued to thrive in the underground. And that's how it should be.

Hardcore started out as angry outcast music birthed by people who walked out of step with mainstream culture and needed to scream out and be heard, even if there were only a handful of people listening. It has never mattered to me whether we were playing a festival or a small club; I've gone all out and performed with every ounce of strength and energy. Hardcore is in my blood. It's what keeps me feeling alive. It's what I piss, sweat and bleed. It's the way I make sense of the world. Even though I'm more than a half-century old and Vinnie has got almost a decade on me, it's what keeps us feeling young and as relevant as we did in 1983 when we released our debut EP, *United Blood*.

Vinnie came up with the name Agnostic Front in 1982, a year before I joined the band. He told me later that he chose "Agnostic" because it meant "in doubt of the absolute truth." It wasn't a religious reference. It was about questioning authority and society. Our motto was *Don't believe in anything unless you see it with your own eyes*. He went with "Front" because he thought it sounded bigger than "band." It sounded more like a movement, which is what it became. Everyone in hardcore loved the music, but NYHC was more than a sound or style. It was a way of life. Some bands were way different than other bands because hardcore is more about attitude and individuality than what music you play—or even knowing how to play. Having survived more than three decades of hardcore, there are a few things I've noticed from one generation to the next.

Each new scene has its own style, its own look, its own way of slamming in the pit and its own perspective on subjects like self-empowerment, government corruption, police brutality and family. At the same time, everything is tied together by the same tattered cloth. Most of these kids need hardcore to define them, to establish who they are and what they *don't* want to be. And many—not as many as when I first discovered the music but still a lot—have experienced major trauma in their lives. Whether it's sexual abuse, foster home neglect, domestic violence or childhood bullying, this trauma has caused them to reach out to hardcore for strength and unity. That's how it was for Vinnie and me and most of the people we hung out with. We were all fucked up in the head, but hardcore pumped us up and made our young adult years wild, hysterical, dangerous and fucking unforgettable.

# PART I

## From Cuba with Love:
## The Struggle of an Immigrant in a World of Hate

# CHAPTER 1

My mind is like *The Wizard of Oz*. My earliest memories are in black and white. Later they turn vivid and colorful. But some of my happiest recollections are the least distinct, like an old, flickering silent movie filmed before the age of high-definition images and dazzling special effects. The first thing I remember is being with my dad, Rogelio, on a rocky beach in Havana in the late '60s. We lived in a two-story house with a balcony, and I was running up and down the sand with my sheepdog, Chuchi. We were surrounded by towering cliffs. The sand was white and the buildings were gray. Those were happy days. They didn't last. Once the technicolor kicked into my brain a couple years later, life was a battle.

Everyone on my father's side left Cuba because they felt threatened by the Castro regime. My uncle Leo married an American woman, my aunt Betty, and was the first relative to go to the United States. My mother, Alicia, married my father when she was 15. I was born on their one-year anniversary on June 30, 1964, in a birthing clinic in Havana called Clinica Hija de Galicia. By the time my mom was 20, she had three kids—me, my brother Rudy, who is two years younger, and my sister Mayra—who was born a year after Rudy.

I came to America on April 30, 1968, when I was four and Mayra was only a few months old. We flew in on one of the Freedom Flights that were organized by the U.S. government to help get people out of Cuba. The flights began as part of America's Cuban Refugee Resettlement program in 1967, and you had to sign up on a list because they could only accept a certain number of people. About 1,000 Cubans flew into Miami each week, but the list was long. You had to wait for the U.S. government

Cuba, 1967.

to contact you, and then you had to pack up and go right away. My mother signed up and one day they called her name. We dropped everything and rushed to the airport. We left my father behind since he was in the Cuban military and couldn't leave. I was scared. I had never been on a plane.

We weren't old enough to know why we were leaving Cuba; we went wherever my mother took us. We had no idea we were heading for America or what would happen when we got there. We just knew we were moving away from home. We got on this old Pan-Am airplane and the pilot pinned little blue wings onto our shirts. That eased my fears somewhat. I looked out the window and saw the clouds, which was incredible. Today, hundreds of flights later—to and from Europe, South America and Australia—I'm not as impressed by fluffy white clouds.

The first stop for my family back in 1968 was Miami International Airport. We debarked and took a bus to a processing center at Opa-Loca Airport, which was like a refugee camp. We waited for hours to be processed, then flew to Kennedy Airport in New York. We were free—from Cuba, at least.

My uncle Leo picked us up in his 1963 four-door Buick and drove us to his thirty-eight–story building in Elmhurst, Queens. I had never seen anything so tall, even on television. It looked like it went straight to heaven. All the buildings seemed huge. Nothing in Havana was more than a few stories high. The skyscrapers were so tall I thought there must be giants living in them.

Once we washed up and ate, we drove to East Paterson, New Jersey, and met my father's side of the family. Since Leo was married to Aunt Betty, an American, he was able to bring his brothers and sisters over. The other relatives who greeted us were my grandfather Rafael, my grandmother Josephina, Aunt Clara, Uncle Ralph, Aunt Margarita, Aunt Amparito, Uncle Miguel and my cousins Betty Ann, Leonard, Clara, Sheila, Ralph Jr., Alex and Olguita. There were a lot of people in the room, and I was kind of freaked out—partially since I expected those giants to walk out at any minute. At the time, I didn't even know New York had a football team called the Giants! Everyone in my family was friendly and welcoming, but they overwhelmed us with questions.

Weeks later we were still figuring out what to make of our situation. (By that point, I realized there weren't any giants.) Around that time, my dad got shot by anti-Castro freedom fighters. He and my uncle Albert weren't on duty, but they were wearing their military fatigues and were in the wrong place at the wrong time. A gunman burst into a bus and opened fire. My dad and uncle were hurt pretty bad. They both survived, but I think my dad suffered from post-traumatic stress disorder. He was never the same.

In New Jersey, I spent a lot of time with my grandfather Rafael, who was a gentle and loving man. He was a Freemason and told us stories about their symbols and rituals. He showed me a book about the Freemasons with his name inside. Apparently, he was the first or second of the higher-ups in the movement, and although I didn't know it, when we came to America we were under investigation by the CIA because there was a lot of misunderstanding about what the Freemasons represented. They thought we might be communists, especially since we came from Cuba. That was my first exposure to politics. I was just a kid, and I didn't know anything about Castro so he was never a threat to me. But everyone on my dad's side of the family was anti-Castro—definitely not communist.

My mom's side included a lot of guerillas that supported the revolution and the

Castro regime. My mom was the only one in her family to leave Cuba. She came from a family of six kids. Her mother, Esperanza, was a guerilla insurgent, as was her husband. Since they were always on some secret mission or in hiding, my mom was raised by her sister Julia, whom we called Grandma because we never knew Esperanza. One of my mom's brothers, Filiberto Jr., became a famous model in Cuba and one of her sisters, Dulce Maria, was a successful actress. Maybe performing was in my blood. In contrast with a lot of my mom's family, neither Dulce Maria nor Filiberto Jr. were political and they weren't fighters. Decades later I became a little bit of the former and a whole lot of the latter.

It's weird that almost everyone from my mom's side of the family is still in Cuba and my dad's side is all here. I find it strange that American Cubans don't like the native Cubans. I always viewed everyone as the same growing up, though other people definitely saw *me* as Cuban. I kept my Cuban citizenship until 2006, when I became an American citizen.

As a little kid, New York seemed strange and wild to me. One time when we were driving through the City with my mom and Uncle Leo, I saw two men passionately kissing. They were really going at it.

"Look, mom! Look, look, look!" I said.

"Don't look! Don't look!" she replied, then covered my eyes. That was my first exposure to homosexuality. She wasn't about to explain it to me.

Growing up in the slums of New Jersey towns like Passaic and Paterson was a struggle. We never had any money. My mom worked at a local meat packing plant since she wasn't trained to do anything else. Before my dad came to America, she was all alone. Even though she had a job she could never afford the rent. Once or twice a year we'd get evicted, then we'd have to pack up and move. Because I never planted roots I didn't have any real friends. I was a shy kid, so I wouldn't make friends until my brother Rudy, who was more social, met kids. I tried to make friends with his friends, but by then we were usually moving again. After that happened a few times, I became closed off and introverted. Life was pretty shitty. My memories from this point on are more focused, in high-definition color and as sharp and harsh as could be.

We lived on welfare. We had food stamps and federal assistance because my mom was 20 years old and raising three kids by herself. She was embarrassed about taking money from the government, but we needed it. That's why I still believe in the system when it works. She had to feed us and the government helped make that happen. Say what you will about how corrupt and intrusive the government is, but we wouldn't have gotten by without the welfare system.

We didn't own much, not even a toaster. If we wanted toast, we'd light the stove, put bread on it and then flip it over so both sides were cooked. We'd put some sugar on the toast if it got burnt. We couldn't throw it away and get another piece of bread because there was barely enough to go around. We scraped off the burnt crumbs and made it taste as good as possible. There was no waste in our house.

No one on my mother's side of the family was into music. No one played an instrument or sang. I didn't listen to much music when I was really little—not even the radio. My father came to live with us two years after we arrived, and he was infatuated with Mexican music. He didn't care about Cuban music, but he'd blast classic rock and Mariachi. My dad was obsessed with anything Mexican. When he died in 1994 I put a Mexican sombrero in his coffin. He would have liked that.

Even though my dad had family around when we were growing up, he wasn't happy. The military got the best of him. He had insomnia, and when he was able to sleep he had horrible nightmares. He drank a lot, became an alcoholic and was abusive. Sometimes at night I'd pretend to be sleeping and I'd hear yelling, then the banging sounds of him pushing my mom against the wall. *Smack!* She'd cry or something would crash, and she'd fall to the floor with a thump. Then silence.

I can't condone what my dad did to my mom. I fucking hated it. But he never physically abused my siblings or me. He took all his anger out on her. I think she purposely shielded us from him by becoming the target of his violence.

Shortly after my dad joined us in New Jersey, he got a job at the factory where my mom worked. They hired as many immigrants as they could and paid them next to nothing. One day my dad had an accident while working with a machine that chopped up chickens. He wasn't paying attention. The blade came down on his hand and cut off four of his fingers. He shook his forearm and blood spurted from his mangled hand like water from a sprinkler. It splashed on the metal machine, and crimson rivulets ran down the chopping blade. Someone got a towel and wrapped my dad's hand in it. He held it tightly as the white cloth turned red, but he didn't scream or freak out. Either he was in shock or he didn't care too much about losing a few fingers. He went to the infirmary, got stitched up and went home. Maybe somebody got four fingers in their wrapped package of deboned chicken breasts that week.

Since he was an immigrant, he didn't get worker's compensation and as soon as his hand healed he went right back to the plant. The place was dirty, it stank and it was hazardous. There were no safety regulations, and employees who got hurt were replaced by the next desperate people in line. That's the way life was for new immigrants. My dad hated the factory, and he didn't work there for long. It wasn't because he quit. My mom left him.

She met a Colombian man who also worked at the plant. He put on the charm and she fell for him. Soon after my mom started seeing him, my dad lost it. I don't know how long it took for him to catch on, but one day he walked in on the two of them. My future stepfather climbed out the window and ran away while my dad went nuts. He stormed into my sister's room and yanked the carpet. All the furniture went flying. The noise didn't stop; it sounded like he was trashing the room. He wouldn't stop screaming and swearing in Spanish. Then he grabbed my mom by the throat, choked her and banged her head against a metal heat pipe until she was unconscious. He kept yelling, but when he realized he might kill her, he let go and tossed her aside like a broken mannequin. Her forehead was cut and her nose was broken and bloody. The black eye didn't appear until the next day. The neighbors upstairs called the police.

When my mom regained consciousness, she refused to press charges, but the police took my dad away in a paddy wagon anyway. There was a law that if the police showed up at a domestic violence scene, they had to arrest somebody. That was the last time I saw him for a while. I think my dad wanted to make up afterwards, but my mom had had enough. He moved to Florida and I briefly thought that might eliminate the crazy drama in our lives. We had a better chance of outrunning our shadows.

Violence was often part of the picture one way or another. I almost killed my brother one afternoon when we were hanging out in an apartment in Passaic, New Jersey, and my mom was out shopping. Rudy and I used to wrestle and play-fight. I'd pin him and rub his face against the ground. I was bigger and stronger, and that infuriated him. One time we were fighting and he was so mad that he started chasing me around the house. I ran out and slammed the storm door behind me, and he went through it with a horrifying crash. It sounded like someone had taken a bat to a giant window. Pieces of glass ripped open his neck, arms and legs. He lay on the ground screaming as blood poured out of dozens of wounds and gushed from a huge gash in his throat. A neighbor across the street saw what happened and told me to call 911.

While we waited for the ambulance to arrive, the neighbor tore up pieces of cloth and tied them like a tourniquet around Rudy's neck. I was terrified because my mom wasn't home. I thought, *Oh, my God! If she comes home and sees all this blood I'm going to be in so much trouble!*

The police took Rudy to the hospital, and his heart stopped while the doctors worked on him. They were able to revive him with a defibrillator, but he almost bled out. If it wasn't for our neighbor, Rudy would have died. He needed stitches inside his neck and across the carotid artery, which had ripped open. But he survived.

Not long after Rudy recovered, my mom married my stepfather, which planted the seeds for a garden of new scars. My stepdad wasn't as mentally unstable as my father, but he was a lot meaner, especially when he was drinking—and he liked to drink. I guess my mom saw something in him—mainly the fact that he wasn't my father and he wasn't beating her . . . yet.

With my mom and her new husband both working, our financial situation improved, but we still lived in a ghetto. The thing is, I didn't know how poor we were. To me, that life was normal. It's what I knew. I was with my family, and I had a roof over my head. Everything seemed okay. As a kid, you only know what you've experienced, so even when my stepfather started smacking all of us around, I didn't realize that most people didn't live like that.

The first time I realized I grew up in a ghetto was when I was older and I went back to visit. Driving through the dodgy streets and looking around and at the crumbling buildings, I thought, *Holy shit! I lived here?*

# CHAPTER 2

Since we barely had enough money for food, my stepfather introduced a plan to reduce our food bills. We went to the park and put down metal nets made out of twisted clothing hangers with T-shirts sewn around them. I threw bits of bread or crackers on top of them, and pigeons came over and ate them. When there were as many birds in there as I could get, I closed the contraption, which trapped the birds. I brought them home, pecking and wriggling, and my stepdad bashed them against the ground to kill them. Most of them died from broken necks. My mom cut off their heads, cleaned them and boiled them to disinfect them and remove the feathers. Then we had pigeon soup. It wasn't as good as chicken soup, but she cooked it with carrots, celery and chicken broth and seasoned it with enough salt and pepper to make it edible. Even though they both worked at a factory that packaged chicken, if they wanted to bring home meat they had to pay for it and they didn't have that kind of money. So we ate pigeons instead!

Struggling was a part of life. Sleeping on the floor, eating peasant food and getting physically abused by my stepfather were the norm. I didn't like it, but I got used to it and nothing surprised me.

For a lot of kids, school is an escape, especially if their home environment is dysfunctional. For me, school meant more humiliation and frustration. None of the teachers spoke Spanish, and on my first day of kindergarten I was terrified because everyone else spoke English and I had no idea what they were saying. I cried and no one did anything.

By the time I was in class for a week, a Middle Eastern kid came in. I knew he was from that region because he was reading books backwards. The teacher was trying to teach us to read left to right and he read the other way. I thought that was the coolest shit in the world. I wanted to read the other way, too. I wanted to be his friend even though we couldn't understand each other. I liked that he went against the norm and, like me, was different.

Going to school was my first public experience of being out of step with society, but I always knew I was a rebel. Growing up, I identified more with the outcasts than the popular kids, and that went for characters in TV shows and movies as well. When my brothers and I played Cowboys and Indians, I wanted to be the Indian. Even when we played military, I didn't want to be the good guy. I wanted to be the Germans—not that I knew anything about the horrors of Hitler or the Nazis. I just wanted to be the villain.

Since I couldn't speak English in school, the teachers put me in a special education class until I got up to speed. That was common back in the late '60s and early '70s. If you didn't speak English and the teachers didn't speak Spanish, how the hell were they gonna teach you? Looking back, it was harsh and it fucked me up because I felt like everyone else knew what they were doing while I was a complete outcast. I was nervous and scared, and moving from one apartment to another all the time made me more insecure.

When I was in fourth grade we went to Catholic school because my mom figured we would get a better education. Since there was still a language barrier, I became a class clown to make the other kids laugh, which was a questionable move. The nuns used to pull my tie and smack my hands with a ruler. Whatever they did, it was nothing compared to what was going on at home. The TV show *Happy Days* was cool at the time and I liked Fonzie, so I would imitate him, going, "Heeeeey!" and giving everybody the thumbs-up. The nuns didn't like that, but they never got the chance to punish me since Rudy, Mayra and I had to leave the school. My family couldn't afford to keep us there.

You didn't pay for Catholic school directly. You were supposed to put money in the collection tray every Sunday at church. When the priest found out we didn't have the money to make any donations, the school threw us out. Looking back, that seems hypocritical. One of the rules of Catholicism is to give to those in need. My siblings and I were in need of an education. It's not like we were holding back from paying the church because we were cheap. We were poor. Expelling us for that was fucking wrong. As I'd soon learn, there are a lot of things about organized religion that are wrong.

When I went back to public school the teachers kept me in remedial classes because my English still wasn't good enough. After a while I learned to speak well enough to be transferred into the regular class with the "normal" kids. I still wasn't fluent and I had to concentrate hard. It didn't seem fair because everybody else spoke naturally. To excel, I had to learn everything from them, but they didn't care about learning anything from me. They couldn't even say my name right. My real name is Rogelio, like my dad. No one could pronounce it, so my teacher started calling me Roger. I thought that was great because I finally had an identity that people could grasp. I wasn't being called "Rogilia, Rogalio or Ro-jelly-o." I was Roger. Of course, afterwards every stupid animal we read about or saw in cartoons was named Roger, so I got picked on. I couldn't win.

Those were mixed up times, and the constant physical and mental abuse slanted the way I viewed the world. It hardened me. Any given moment my stepdad would snap. Whenever he came home stinking of alcohol, my mom and everyone else would get nervous because that's when he was most likely to go on a rampage. But even when he was sober he was unpredictable—happy and funny one moment, vicious the next.

If my sister and I were arguing or if I dropped a fork at dinner, he might shift into attack mode. When he shoved his chair back from the table, stood up and came after us, my mom would get in the way and, most of the time, take the beatings so that we wouldn't have to. It was history repeating itself. Just like with my real dad, I'd sit up and listen to my mom scream while she got smacked around. Some of the shit my stepdad pulled was psychotic.

When I turned eight, my dad flew to New Jersey to visit. He gave me a big fluffy white rabbit as a birthday present. It had red eyes, nibbled at my fingers and wiggled its paws like a dog. I couldn't stop smiling and sat there petting it all day. The next day my stepfather took the rabbit and made me watch as he twisted its head between his gnarled hands. The animal's neck snapped like a breaking branch. Once the rabbit stopped twitching, he skinned it. It's horrific to see someone turn your pet inside-out. The rabbit's skin was shiny and wet with blood, and the meat looked like a red, uncooked clump of beef. My stepfather discarded the pelt and slit the rabbit open. He pulled out the organs and drained the blood in the sink. Then he cut it up, gave the pieces to my mom and made her cook it. That sick fuck felt he had to show my dad who was in charge, so he turned my pet into dinner and threatened me with a beating if I left any meat on my plate.

Even though I didn't see my dad often, I knew he loved me. He just had funny ways of showing it. One time I visited him in Florida and he gave me a little alligator. Back then you were allowed to travel with them on planes. I brought it home in a lizard carrying case. When my stepfather saw the alligator, he threw a fit and flushed it down the toilet. I don't blame him now, but at the time I was furious. I screamed in rage and ran straight to my room before he had a chance to take a swipe at me. Soon after, I saw a movie about all these alligators living in the sewers that would eat homeless people and kids who fell in the water. I used to play in the sewers, so that was very real to me.

"I'm never going back to the sewers again," I said. I was sure my alligator was down there waiting for me. I was afraid of sitting on the toilet because I thought he would climb up out of the sewer pipes and bite my balls off.

Looking back, shit like that is funny, but in the moment it was traumatic. There's a lot of other stuff that happened that scarred me to this day. When I was in primary school and we lived across the street from Passaic Park, my mom got pregnant. We were looking forward to having a new brother or sister in the house. One night my stepfather came home drunk and angry and beat the crap out of my mom. He hit her so hard in the belly that she lost the baby. She was crying hysterically and when I ran into the bathroom to see what he had done, there was blood all over the floor and on her legs and hands. She called the police and an ambulance took her to the hospital.

The cops came to the house and took a report, but unlike the time with my dad, they didn't take my stepfather away. They asked my mom if she wanted to press charges, and of course she didn't. The cops didn't give a fuck. That was just the nature of the relationship between my mom and my stepfather. It was extremely unhealthy and uncomfortable for my siblings and me.

# CHAPTER 3

After my mom lost the baby, she got pregnant again. That didn't end the drama or the beatings. My stepfather was just less aggressive with my mom. He wanted to have his own child. Before Freddy was born, my stepdad got into a bad car accident. Fortunately, it didn't hurt my mom or the baby, but it rattled us all.

There was just one lane leading to the shorefront, so traffic was stop-and-go. Someone who wasn't paying attention rear-ended us. I flew past the driver's seat and my head smashed into the windshield. My brothers and sister flipped over their seat and ended up in the front of the car. I was the only one who was hurt, and I was pretty much okay. But my stepdad told us all to let the paramedics take us to the hospital on little stretchers, and my mom said we should all act like we couldn't move our necks. They both saw it as an opportunity to make some bank, and a few years later, after hiring a lawyer and going after the other driver's insurance company, they came away with some solid cash.

Not long after the accident, my mom gave birth to my little brother, Freddy. He was 11 years younger than me, and it was amazing to see this little person who couldn't do anything. I wasn't jealous. I loved that kid from the start. Sometimes I'd lift him up and burp him after he ate or help rock him to sleep. Holding something that's helpless and reliant on you for survival is incredible. When he got a little older he started smiling, which made me laugh. A few months later he giggled when I played peek-a-boo with him. That was a trip. It was just about the only thing that made me happy. I thought it would make my stepdad happy, and in a way it did, but it didn't calm his temper. In fact, he became more abusive.

Eventually, my mom lost it. It was in the middle of the day. She was changing Freddy's diaper, and she started crying. She couldn't stop. She was shaking. She dropped to the ground and rolled up into a ball. Rudy and I were scared. We ran out and got my mom's friend Claudia, who took her to the hospital. By that time, she switched between crying and laughing, so they checked her into a mental institution. Freddy stayed with his aunt Omaira.

The rest of us flew to Florida to stay with my dad. That was weird but fairly uneventful. The most excitement came on weekends, when he took us out to lunch and a movie. When my mom was released from the hospital, she drove down to Florida with my stepfather to pick us up and bring us home. We were with my dad when my mom pulled up to the house where he was staying.

"We have to go. Now! We have to move!" she shouted.

We started getting into the car. When my dad realized what was happening, he ran out and grabbed my arm.

"No! Rogelito can stay with me!" he shouted.

He figured that I'd live with him and the rest of the family would go back with my mom.

"Rogelito, whom would you like to stay with?" my mom asked in a tense but measured tone.

It's not like I wanted to leave my dad, but I thought I should be with my brothers and sister, so I said I wanted to go with her, and that hurt my dad. I saw it in his face. He was heartbroken. I never got to tell him I was sorry or explain the situation to him. It wasn't a choice of whom I loved more or wanted to be with. I was surrounded by all this chaos, and being with my siblings meant we would get through it together, which was better than being alone.

Once we got back to New Jersey it was business as usual. My stepdad usually stormed out of the house after he was done smacking my mom around, but sometimes he came after us next. And sometimes my mom wasn't there when he went off.

When I was 12 he ordered me to paint the doors. I didn't know anything about painting, but I wasn't going to question him. I got a paint can and a brush, and I started stroking the wet brush against the door. I painted against the grain of the wood because I had never learned that you have to paint with the grain. When he saw what I was doing he took off his belt. I knew what that meant. He made me remove my shirt before he punished me since he didn't want his belt to rip my shirt. If that happened, I'd have to get another one. My back stung as the leather slapped against it. Then it started to burn, but not as much as my rage. It never occurred to my stepdad to sit down with me and explain how to properly paint a door. With him, there was just straight-up aggression and violence. And pain.

I was always wary of him and would sit in bed at night fuming and thinking about how this was going to end. I wanted to kill him and planned different ways to do it—a knife when he was sleeping, or maybe I'd poison his food. Whenever he gave me a black eye or left bruises from his fists or marks from his belt, I thought about what I would say at school. If I told them the truth it would get back to my stepdad and I would get a worse beating. I'd say I tripped and fell or got hurt playing sports. They must have thought I was the clumsiest kid in the school.

None of us escaped my stepfather's anger, not even my sister. When Freddy grew up, he got beatings, too. I fantasized about getting a gun and blowing my stepdad's brains out. I guess my mom did, too. One time she found out about him cheating on her with a woman at work. When he came home she acted like nothing was wrong. She casually removed a .22 from a drawer and shot him twice in the chest. She called 911 and said someone shot her husband. The ambulance came and rushed him to the hospital.

My mom went to visit him there, and when he saw her he started quivering, figuring she came to finish the job. She had every right to, but she didn't and he didn't tell anyone she shot him. She told the cops it happened in the street when he got caught in the crossfire of two criminals, and he confirmed the story. Since we lived in a bad neighborhood, the police believed them. They didn't care anyway. What was one more Hispanic gunshot victim to them? Just another load of paperwork.

When my stepdad came home from the hospital, he and my mom continued their dysfunctional life like nothing had happened. He even had the balls to get violent with her after he healed.

I'll never forgive my stepdad for his behavior, but when I was older I learned to understand it. He came to America from Colombia with his family in 1970, and his father beat the shit out of him. He paid it forward because that's what he was used to. It was socially acceptable to beat the shit out of your kids. But it wasn't healthy for anybody, and it took a toll on my psyche. Over the years, I've blocked out a lot of the details about what he did. I learned to lie about some of the incidents and hide others. It was my method of survival. I still can't vividly remember too many of the beatings, but the shit that's stuck in my head is pasted there like a poster on the side of a wall.

For my thirteenth birthday, my stepdad got me a five-speed green Apollo Chopper. We were living on Chadwick Street in a condemned industrial area of Paterson, New Jersey, and the bike was really nice. I rode it all over town. The wheels hugged the sidewalk, and it took bumps pretty well.

*Damn! This is the nicest thing he's ever done for me!* I thought.

He showed me how to chain it up to a tree or a telephone pole, then I went for a ride. With the wind whipping in my face, I felt like a biker. I thought I was a badass! Dumbass was more like it. When I got home I wrapped the chain around the seat instead of the frame, and the bike got stolen from right in front of our house. My stepdad was pissed. He yanked me into the car, and we drove all around Paterson, checking the alleys in between houses. Somehow we found the kids as they were stripping the bike down. He grabbed my half-stripped bike and another bike that wasn't mine, threw them into the car and sped away. When we got home he took out the belt. He made me drop my pants and take off my shirt, and he beat me until my back bled. Then he hit me one more time.

Since the kids who stole my bike picked it up outside our house, it wasn't too hard for them to figure out where we lived. They wanted to make my stepfather pay for humiliating them. Late one night, a girl from across the street knocked on our door. That was unusual, so my stepdad asked her what she wanted. When she didn't answer he opened up the door a crack and saw a bunch of the thug kids standing there with crowbars and knives. After he slammed the door in their face, they banged on it and scared the shit out of everyone. My mom and Freddy started crying and I wished my stepdad would just walk out there and let the kids kill him. Eventually they went away.

But they came back. This time they didn't try entering through the front door.

They figured out how to get in through the air ducts and broke in one night while we were at church. When we got back my dad opened the door, and it looked like the Tasmanian Devil had stormed through the place. These kids ransacked the house and even ate our food. Somehow they didn't find the bike, so they returned another night when we were home. We heard them scurrying behind the walls like rats. They burst through the heating vents and came into the house. Rudy and I kicked at them, and my stepdad swung a chimney poker and chased them off. The next day they surprised us outside the house. They had pit bulls on leashes and threatened to sic the dogs on us, so we ran inside. My stepdad got the hidden bike he stole, threw it at them and slammed the door.

We hoped that would end things; we were wrong. These kids enjoyed victimizing us. As I've learned through the years, payback isn't always an even trade. They kept returning to vandalize and terrorize us, and we wound up moving to get away from them. My stepfather was pissed. It was a major blow to his pride. He felt like he had lost, but his ego couldn't accept the blame. He said it was my fault and took out his anger on all of us, including my mom, who didn't have anything to do with the bike theft. It was around then that I learned how to turn off my pain receptors when the beatings came. Maybe that's what my mom had been doing all along.

We bounced from building to building within the Puerto Rican community, but we didn't fit in anywhere. We were Latin American, but we had our own cultural customs. Even the language is slightly different. Cubans, Puerto Ricans and Dominicans all speak Spanish, but they have different slang words. One time some ladies were yelling at my mom because she thought we were cursing and teaching the other kids bad words.

"What do you mean?" said my mom.

"They're using the word *bicho* around our kids!" replied one of the women.

To Cubans, a *bicho* is a bug, but to Puerto Ricans it's a dick. It was hard to say anything without offending somebody. My stepfather used to make a meal called *bollo*, which is a tasty Colombian bun made from corn, yucca or potato. But in Cuban, a *bollo* is a pussy. So we would all laugh when he said he wanted some *bollo*, and he would get pissed. I've already explained what happened when he got pissed.

# CHAPTER 4

Most of my early music memories come from being with my mom and my stepfather, who listened to a lot of cumbia, which was Colombian music, and salsa. Oddly enough, they were also into R&B, including Marvin Gaye, Al Green and Barry White. I liked that stuff, but once I started listening to the radio I got into disco, strangely enough. In the late '70s, the disco craze was everywhere and a lot of Latin people evolved from merengue and salsa music to full-on disco. Like everyone else, I listened to Donna Summer, Chic and Village People. Blasting that stuff got me through some harsh emotional times.

There were some funny moments in between the episodes of violence. When I was 14 my mom decided to advance her career, so she left the meat factory and went to cosmetology school. She asked me to babysit my siblings. I was supposed to supervise and feed them. One day I gave them Alpo dog food between two slices of bread and called it sloppy joe. Afterward I told them what they had eaten. They're still mad at me about that.

While my mom was in school, my stepfather was striving to better himself, too. He quit the meat plant and started a family business, Bulldog Gas, in Passaic, down the street from where we lived. Instead of hiring another employee, he made me pump gas and work on cars. He taught me how to change oil and make basic repairs, and I became a grease monkey. I may have had trouble painting a door, but I was a natural with cars. Still, I was more interested in motorcycles. I was in awe whenever a gang of guys on Harleys came into the shop. I thought their outcast culture was so cool. My stepdad didn't want me to be a sissy boy, so he was okay with me being into motorcycles. He appreciated that the guys who rode them were tough.

My stepdad was big on anything macho, and he believed in this heroic code. He rarely practiced what he preached, but he made sure I always had Rudy's back. As fucked up as his attitude was about domestic violence, he believed in family dignity, and that meant if Rudy was in a fight, I was in a fight, too. He would sit there and watch us duke it out with these neighborhood kids over the stupidest shit. Once a bunch of black kids came over and started fucking with Rudy because he looked white. They might not have messed with him if they had known he was Hispanic.

"Go out and help your brother. He's in a fight," my stepdad said.

I went into the street and Rudy and I started battling all these kids. We were doing well. It was like a video game or a martial arts film without the martial arts. I'd swing at one kid and feel that satisfying thud as my fist connected with his chest or face and he'd hit the ground. Then I'd turn around and throw a hook at another kid. There were 16 or 17 of them, and we were holding our own until they started throwing bricks at us. When one came too close to cracking open my skull, my father came outside and chased the kids away. The next day they invited us to ride bikes with them, and we were all friends.

"You see that?" my stepdad said. "They have respect for you now because you stood up for yourselves and showed them you weren't afraid."

He was right. That's the type of shit my stepdad taught us. He was also seriously into making sure we had a strong work ethic, which is hard to teach a kid who's 14 and wants to do his own thing. The main reason I didn't want to keep working on cars with him was because he forced me to do it. I wanted to be outside playing with the other kids. He wasn't having that.

When I started outgrowing my clothes he said I'd have to work overtime to buy new ones. I worked through the summer at his auto repair shop for slave's wages. Then when I was too big to button my pants, we went to the store, but he still wouldn't pay for the clothes! We picked out shirts, pants, socks and underwear and put them into a burlap sack. Then he distracted the store clerk while Rudy and I went over to a ladder. We climbed up, opened the hatch, went onto the roof and threw the sack full of clothes over the property's fence. Then we left the store and picked up the clothes.

If we wanted new shoes we tried on a pair we liked, left our old shoes in the changing room and walked out of the store wearing the new pair. Back then stores didn't have security tags on the clothes that set off alarms, so we always got away. But the fucker still made me work for him before he'd let me steal my own clothes.

The summer before I turned 15, I went to Florida to visit my grandma Cho-Cho and my dad. I spent a lot of time hanging out with my cousins, Albert and Clara, and Clara's boyfriend, Kiko. They played me Meatloaf and Led Zeppelin. I really liked Zep's "Fool in the Rain." There was a whistle near the end and it got really fast. The first time I heard the song, Kiko was driving a Ford Mustang Mach 1, Clara was in the front seat and I was in the back. I was already into Zeppelin, and I hadn't even heard "Stairway to Heaven," "Communication Breakdown" or "Whole Lotta Love" yet.

When I was in Kiko's car I'd listen to whatever he was blasting on the stereo: Zep, Foreigner, Bad Company. That was as close as I got to classic rock for a while. When I got back to New Jersey, I discovered bands like the Sex Pistols and The Damned. That was all thanks to my cousin Chuchi, who was into punk music and blasted it really loud in the house. Chuchi could do anything without getting in trouble since he was really ill. He had a kidney disease and the doctors thought he was terminal. He was an only child, so his parents gave him everything he wanted. He had this big Marshall amplifier stack and a guitar and went into the City to see shows any time he wanted. His parents thought he was living on borrowed time.

After numerous surgeries Chuchi miraculously recovered. Today he has half a lung, but he got into weight-lifting and strength training and wound up being Mr. Natural Universe in New Jersey. Eventually, he got a job with New Jersey law enforcement and is still working as a cop.

Back in 1978, Chuchi had a girlfriend named Barbara who lived on the street. She was a Blondie fanatic. Some people think of Blondie as a glossy pop band that played hits like "One Way or Another" and "Heart of Glass," but Blondie were a big part of the '70s CBGB scene and a portal between punk and new wave. They were fast and intense, and Debbie Harry could snarl like Johnny Rotten and sing like Joan Jett. I thought they were cool and liked that they were from New York

The first time I bought records was that summer I went to Florida when I was 14. My grandma Cho-Cho took me to Peaches in North Miami Beach and let me choose three records. I picked up Blondie's *Parallel Lines*, The Cars' self-titled debut and the

Ramones' *Rocket to Russia*. I loved them all, but the last one was a game-changer. I listened to it over and over. The blunt simplicity and buzzing heaviness of "Rockaway Beach" and "Sheena Is a Punk Rocker" was like nothing I had ever heard. The vocals were melodic like those of '60s girl groups, but with guys singing. It was fast and made me want to throw rocks through windows. I'd run around the house singing all the songs on the record until someone yelled at me to shut up.

While I was in Florida I spent most of my time with Cho-Cho and my aunt Clara. I had some private time with my dad, which was always weird. He didn't treat my mom well, but he loved her and was devastated when she married my stepfather. It took all the fight out of him, and he never recovered. When I chose to live with my mom instead of him, he went a little crazy.

"You want to meet my new girlfriend?" he asked me that summer.

"Yeah, what's she like?" I said.

"She's beautiful," he replied. "Let's go see her."

He took me to a strip joint. I was a kid at a nudie club, which was fucked up. He introduced me to one of the strippers, bought two drinks and handed her a few extra bucks.

"This is my new girlfriend, Lola," he said. And then he did shots of tequila with the dancer.

I was old enough to know she wasn't really *with* him, but what could I say?

"Okay, Dad. That's good. I'm glad you found someone."

I never got the chance to talk to him about a lot of real stuff, like dignity, self-respect and raising a family right. He wouldn't have understood any of that anyway. I never had any closure in our relationship when he died on September 10, 1994, from cirrhosis of the liver and lung cancer. He was only 54.

Chuchi and I had a blast listening to new music. He got me into the Sex Pistols, which was the gateway to Black Flag, the Dead Kennedys and the early New York shit like The Stimulators and The Mad. Chuchi went to Max's Kansas City to see all these bands and sometimes I went with him. He turned me onto this drug called rush, which came in little packets that you sniffed, kind of like airplane glue, but the effects were more like acid. He also got me into mescaline, which I loved and used regularly for a while. There were little pills called Purple Haze, which were stronger than the other types I've tried. It was similar to taking shrooms, but they didn't taste like dirt. It was kind of the same as acid, but not as strong. I hallucinated some crazy shit on that, like walls bleeding and roads cracking like I was in the middle of an earthquake. I've seen funny things, too, like people growing extra noses or mouths and food changing colors and breathing like it was alive.

The first time I took mescaline, we were in Chuchi's room and his mom walked in. We were cranking music and he was playing guitar, trying to keep up with the riffs on a Dead Kennedys record. We were tripping balls. I had a glass of water in my hand and my head was still tilted back swallowing a pill when she opened the door.

"Can you turn that music down?" she yelled reflexively over the sound of screaming vocals, raggedly strummed guitars and a hammering beat. Her eyes darted from the glass I was holding to a bag of pills on the table. Busted!

Chuchi didn't say anything. He just looked at her, so I burst in. "Uhhh, we were just . . ."

I tried to concentrate on what I was saying, but somewhere between the first and fourth word all I heard in my head was TV static. I started again. "We're listening to music," I spoke slowly—not so she could understand me but because that's as fast as I could talk.

"Okay, well, please just turn the stereo down."

She knew we were high as fuck, but she didn't care because we were inside and we were safe. I thought that was cool. Chuchi eventually formed a band called Barbed Wire Babies. It wasn't much, but I thought it was cool. They played a bunch of little towns in New Jersey and I stole my mom's car to drive out to one of their shows. Right after I joined Agnostic Front years later, Barbed Wire Babies opened for us at CBGB.

My mom didn't catch me the first time I took her car, so I took that as an open invitation to use it whenever I wanted to. I knew how to drive well because I had been parking cars for my stepdad for a while. We lived on Jackson Street between Passaic and Paterson, right behind an old venue called The Capitol Theatre, which was built in 1926 as a vaudeville joint. Later it became a porno theater before promoter John Scher took it over in the '70s and turned it into a music venue.

All these big rock shows came into town and I parked people's cars in our back-yard to make extra money. My stepfather put up a "Park Here" sign and charged concertgoers to use our rental property as a parking lot. We spent hours moving their cars. In the afternoon, before the crowd arrived, Rudy and I watched the backstage area of the venue open up. We could see the bands and people hanging out. We saw Talking Heads, The Tubes and the Ramones. One day there were a lot of Rastafarians hanging around. I didn't know anything about reggae or Rasta culture. I had never even heard a strong English accent until that day; it was March 8, 1980, and The Clash were headlining at the Capitol Theatre. Between the British accents and the Rasta talk I didn't know what the hell was going on. I listened to some of the music during their soundcheck, but I was more interested in the crazy accents.

I didn't find out about Rastafarians until years later because the only way for me to learn about history or culture was at school and they didn't teach about The Clash, the Sex Pistols or Bob Marley. They taught about the Constitution and the Bill of Rights—shit that seemed useless at the time but would prove invaluable when I was a young adult (especially the Fourth Amendment, which protects people from unreasonable searches and seizures).

I used to "borrow" my mom's car a lot to see concerts in New York. But I didn't drive all the way to the City. That seemed too risky. I drove to the Jersey City PATH station and then took the PATH train into Manhattan. When I was out on the town I was free to soak in the music and nightlife, and there were beautiful girls everywhere. I just didn't have the courage to talk to any of them. Still, I could do whatever I wanted. At home I felt like I was in a cage. And the violence in the clubs was nothing compared to the violence at home.

My stepdad was ruthless and the beatings never stopped. The memory of the swooshing sound when he took off that fucking belt still makes me queasy. Sometimes, for a change of pace, he smacked us with an untwisted clothes hanger. He was the man in the house. That was clear. My mom was the one who raised us and I couldn't understand how she allowed him to physically abuse her and us, especially after she had gone through it all with my real dad. I think it had something to do with her feeling inferior, as if she didn't deserve anything better. Who the hell wants a woman with four kids? That's baggage. She was trying to hold onto whatever she could, even though it was bad. I always felt like she should have shot him again and ended everyone's misery, but if she did that she probably would have wound up in prison and I didn't want that.

# CHAPTER 5

I was so excited by seeing The Clash behind the stage at the Capitol Theatre that I checked them out for real when they played a string of dates at Bond's International Casino in Times Square with Kraut in June 1981, supporting their *Sandinista* album. Later, I saw them at Shea Stadium on October 13, 1982, supporting *Combat Rock*. The headliner for the show was The Who. I recently sold the Clash shirt I bought that night and got some decent money for it. The New York Dolls' David Johansen opened the show, then The Clash went on and tore the place up. Then I left. I didn't want to see The Who. I was an ignorant punk rock kid. To this day I haven't seen The Who. I got into them when I was older and by then they were a shadow of their former selves. Hey, at least I got to see The Clash multiple times.

Around the time of the Bond's International Casino shows, I started dating my first real girlfriend, Elsie Blanco. She was a goth chick from New Jersey I met at a small concert. I liked her smile and the sound of her voice. Her eyes were riveting. She didn't have great taste in music. She introduced me to the music of Siouxsie and the Banshees, Bauhaus and Joy Division. I was never a big fan of that stuff, but I was happy to put up with it to be with her—especially since she let me get into her pants. She also introduced me to a bunch of her friends, which widened my social circle.

While I was getting lucky with Elsie, my family had a bit of good luck as well. The insurance companies finally settled the lawsuit with my stepfather's lawyer after we were rear-ended at the beach. We each got about $4,000, which allowed my mom to move the family to Florida.

The insurance company's attorneys put all of the money allocated for Rudy,

Mayra, Freddy and me in a trust that we couldn't touch until we were 18. But my mom and stepdad wanted to buy a house right away. She hired a lawyer to draft up papers that let us sign our shares over to her so she would have enough cash for the down payment. After all the beatings my mom had taken for me, I was happy to sign over my share of the money; I owed her that much. I didn't want to move with them to Florida, though.

The more independent I became, the worse life got at home. Home wasn't a home anymore. Maybe it never had been. The point of no return came when we were living on 11th Street in Union City, New Jersey, which is right on the other side of Manhattan. I was playing one-on-one basketball with my friend Jose. I had a curfew on weekdays and had to be home by 8 p.m. The game was really close. I was having fun and lost track of time. When I checked my watch I was already past my curfew.

"Fuck, man! I gotta go!"

I grabbed my ball and sprinted home. I walked in the door, short of breath. I bounced the basketball once on the floor and that set off my stepfather. He was holding something, but I didn't know what it was. Then I saw it was a broom and figured he had been cleaning up. I thought he was going to put it down and yell at me for being late. I turned around to walk away because I didn't want to hear it.

The next thing I knew, something hit my back. I heard a snapping noise and saw a broken broom handle fly across the room. It didn't hurt, so I shrugged it off. I didn't want to fight. I just wanted to go to my room and lie down. Then there was a sharper crack just to the left of my spine. My stepdad had dropped the useless broom, picked up a hammer and hit me with it—hard. I figured he had made his point, but he wasn't done. He raised the hammer and brought it down on my back. Again and again. While he was beating me I kept bouncing the basketball like I didn't care, and I really didn't feel anything. I didn't scream or cry. I just bounced that ball. *Thump, thump, thump.* Then I went numb and collapsed.

I was in bad shape, so they took me to the hospital. In the emergency room I told the nurse I fell and hurt myself playing basketball. My mom was crying. She made my stepdad apologize and he actually did; it was one of the only times he said he was sorry for anything. He knew he had gone too far.

Nothing was broken, just badly bruised. But I knew I had to leave the house. I was almost 17 and my life was changing. I had discovered a new world and needed to get out. I couldn't stand being in the house anymore. I couldn't take the beatings. And I couldn't stay there while everyone else was getting abused. It was too much to take without snapping. Sitting there in the emergency room was the breaking point for me. If I stayed in the house, someone was going to wind up dead and it probably would have been me.

My mom invited me to Florida and promised the new environment would calm my stepfather down, but I wasn't going. I felt bad for my brothers and sister since they had to go, which meant they had to keep putting up with the abuse. But I had finally made friends and found something I liked. I had to get the fuck out of the house right away.

# PART II

## Hardcore Born: Planting Roots and Establishing a Community on the Lower East Side

# CHAPTER 6

I moved in with Elsie and her parents, who lived in North Bergen, New Jersey. One day we were hanging out at a cheap neighborhood diner, and she just picked at her food while I devoured mine. While we waited for the check she told me she was pregnant. A rush of adrenaline flowed through me that was comparable to the way I felt when I heard a great band for the first time. But it came with a sweeping wave of fear. I had just left home. I didn't have my own shit together. How was I gonna raise a child?

Elsie and I got married because that's what you did when you got your girl pregnant. Since Elsie was 18 years old, my mom signed me over to her. Elsie wasn't only my wife, she was also my legal guardian, which was insane because she wasn't any more responsible than I was. Shortly afterward, she lost the baby.

I can't say that we really loved each other. Who the fuck knows what love is at 17? We tried to make it work.

We put together a goth band called Rabies that was kind of like Siouxsie and the Banshees. She sang and I played bass. When I was six years old my mom got me a beginner's bass, and there's a great picture of me posing with it like Dee Dee Ramone. I never learned to play it, but I figured that if I was in a band with Elsie I should get a higher quality instrument. I wanted to be Sid Vicious, so I went to a music store on 48th Street in Manhattan and bought the same bass that he played—a white Fender P-bass with a black pick guard—for $400. With the money I had left, I went to the Lower East Side and bought some pot from a bodega. There was a guy there in a booth, and he slid this little door open and sold weed like postage stamps. I bought a bunch of it and smoked it all. Then I did some mescaline. The mellow vibe I got from the weed combined with the trippy effect of the mescaline made me relaxed, giddy and uninhibited about being out in public.

I walked around the village carrying the bass. I looked at the case and felt like I had X-ray vision. I could see through it to the instrument nestled inside. I imagined it was resting comfortably and when it woke up, I would open the case, plug it in and fuckin' destroy. I thought of it as something I had to protect and concentrated hard on not losing it. That worked out for about two or three hours, then I went to a record store called Venus on West Eighth Street in Greenwich Village. I put the bass on the floor while I flipped through the punk albums. When I looked back down again it was gone. Someone had stolen it from right under my ass. I was crushed. It was like I had abandoned a friend. To console myself I stole some money from someone and got into a fight. I'll say I won, but the guy got a few shots in before I knocked him to the ground. I went home with swollen knuckles, a black eye and one of the lenses from my sunglasses missing.

"What the fuck?" Elsie snapped when I stumbled back into the house. She didn't even know about the bass I bought and lost.

"I got jumped," I told her. "There were, like, five of them. I'm lucky I got away."

She felt sorry for me and encouraged me to lie down. She came in later and we had sex, though I can't say I was at my best since my eye was throbbing and my hand felt like it had been crushed in a vice. Plus, I was probably still high. She didn't seem to mind, and afterwards we fell asleep.

Two days later, I went back to the music store to buy another bass. They didn't have the same one so I bought the opposite model, a black P-bass with a white pick guard. I decided to strip it down and make it white like the one that was stolen. I started working on it but I never finished it. I used that bass forever. I played in all my bands with that bass stripped down to the wood. Agnostic Front bassist Rob Kabula even played it on our first album, *Victim In Pain*.

At the time I bought the thing I didn't know how to play. I didn't have an amp because I spent all my money on the bass and I didn't feel like robbing someone else to get more gear. So I plugged the bass directly into my stereo and learned everything by ear, playing along with the music from my favorite records. Eventually I got to the point where I could imitate the bass lines for a lot of the songs, as long as they weren't too complicated. Elsie sang and I played what I could, but we never did a show. I wanted to do aggressive, hard-edged stuff and she was more into goth. Fuck that! I wanted to take mescaline and get into fights. But I liked her and, fuck, we were married, so I humored her.

Rabies rehearsed in the same practice spaces as other New Jersey bands, and we hung out with them and drank beer. I liked being with other musicians. It made me feel like we were a real band, but I didn't drink too much back then because I didn't want to be like my father or stepdad. I took to beer and booze later when I moved to the City, but that's the only part of my dad's character that rubbed off on me. No matter how violent I was, I never hit any of my girlfriends, wives or kids. I was determined not to continue that awful cycle.

I was borderline crazy, going out at night, taking mescaline and seeing shows. I had found other people to hang with and get high. I kept up the appearance of being a functional member of society for a little while. I stayed in school through eighth grade and then enrolled at Emerson High. I loved football, so I joined the team. I played fullback and practiced with the varsity squad the summer before my first semester started. Since I was on the team I got a varsity jacket when they won the state championship even though I had dropped out by then.

I stayed in high school for few months before I stopped going. I thought I could glide through it since I only took Spanish and cooking. I figured those were the two things I couldn't possibly flunk. I already knew Spanish and nobody failed cooking, not even degenerate, drug-abusing punks. By the time I was a verified high school dropout I had other things going on. And when I was in prison years later I got my GED. I also took some college level classes in there, but to quote *This Is Spinal Tap*, I wasn't exactly "university material."

I got my first tattoo when I was 16 and a half. I always wanted one, but I knew I had to wait until I moved out of the house or else I would have been beaten within an inch of my life. One night when I was living with Elsie and doing mescaline, I decided it was time to get that tattoo. I went to a biker tattoo shop in Jersey City on Kennedy Boulevard. There were a couple tattoo places in the city—including Spider Webs and Mike Perfetto's Tattoo Shop—but I hadn't discovered them yet. Back then it was illegal for anyone else to open a tattoo shop, so they weren't all over of the Village like they were a decade later.


When I showed the tattoo to Elsie, she freaked out. She ranted and raved about what an idiot thug I was.

Living with Elsie was way better than being with my stepfather, but we had our problems. At one point I was blasting the stereo and playing bass, and she grabbed the enlarged picture of me playing bass as a little kid, tore it off the wall and ripped it up.

"You're never going to be a musician. You're never going to be nothing!" she screamed.

That really upset me. I liked that picture. But I was more insulted than angry and I wanted to prove her wrong. I was determined to get in a band that played shows and had a following. I knew Rabies wasn't ever going to get there and I realized I didn't look like a musician. All the guys in bands I liked looked cool and mean, so I grew a giant red Mohawk like Wattie Buchan of The Exploited. I never thought about how a Mohawk might limit my chances of finding a job. Thinking like that wouldn't have been punk rock, but I have to admit it would have been practical. Even though I was a crazy punk rocker and I knew what I wanted to do with my life, I wasn't making any money and I needed to support Elsie and myself. I found a hardware store called Gorman Supply Company in North Bergen that agreed to hire me. I worked a lot and rarely got time off. Even if I had wanted to keep going to school, there was no way I could have fit it into my schedule.

The place was owned by a Jewish family who accepted that I wanted to be an individual. As long as I worked hard they didn't care what kind of music I listened to, what I did with my hair or that I had tattoos. I had no problem working hard. If I'm going to do something I'm going to do it with passion and dedication. That goes for making records, playing shows, working a cash register, fixing a motorcycle or putting in a ceiling fan. Maybe that's part of the work ethic I learned from my stepdad. Old Man Gorman appreciated my work ethic. I started as a stock boy and even though that was the bottom level position, nobody treated me like I was any less important than they were. They didn't care about my Mohawk or my shaved eyebrows.

I can't say the same for Elsie. She was upset when I came home with the Mohawk and my mom wasn't too happy about it either. One day she flew up from Florida to surprise me at the hardware store, and when she saw me she started crying. Before then, I had little black spiked hair and suddenly, in her eyes, I looked like this mutant freak. The hardware store might have sided with my mom if they knew I sold mescaline on the job, but they never found out. A lot of times I got home late because I got wasted and went to shows after I got off work. The people I worked for knew I was tired, but when you're a kid you can pull all-nighters without missing a beat. They could smell the booze on me, but I still did a good job, even when I was hungover, so it was okay.

They treated me well—better than my own family. One time, the owner, Mr. Gorman, invited me to his daughter Rachel's wedding. She was getting married to Dennis, one of the other guys that worked there and I was grateful to be invited. It was a traditional Jewish wedding. When I arrived they told me I had to wear a yarmulke. It's a little round beanie that Jews wear in temple to show their respect to God. I was fine with that, but it was hard to wear the little hat over my huge red Mohawk, so I propped it on just to the side. The wedding was pretty cool and the food was way better than anything I was used to. I felt included, which was nice.

The next day I took my yarmulke, drew a little swastika on it and wore it around. I thought I was being cool and rebellious. I wasn't anti-Semitic at all. I was anti-religion, anti-society, anti-conformity. I wore my swastika yarmulke while I worked and when the boss's son Ira saw it he flipped out.

"Why are you wearing this?" he demanded. "Did you know it represents the death of six million of my people?"

"Uhhh, no, I . . ."

"We invite you to a wedding and this is how you treat us?"

At the time, I was totally into chaos and rebellion. I had no idea that the swastika was a symbol of all this hatred and brutality. I thought it was a sign of the chaos that was part of punk culture, like the anarchy symbol, which I'd seen punks wearing on their clothes for years. I didn't know the details about the Holocaust or how many Jews were killed in concentration camps. I only knew about my own crazy world. I apologized to Ira and took off the yarmulke. I don't know if anyone else who worked at the hardware store saw me, but nobody said anything and life went on.

Work was okay, but living with Elsie was getting to be a drag. We were still kids, and I didn't want to be tied down or check in with someone before I went out. Remember, she was technically my fucking guardian. I wanted to party and do drugs and see shows. I wanted to play gigs and be with other girls. That couldn't happen as long as Elsie and I were still together.

We split up when I was 17.

St. Marks Place, 1983.

# CHAPTER 7

Despite my contempt for hate groups of any type, I had a small pin on my jacket modeled after the famous, controversial Sex Pistols "Destroy" symbol that Malcolm McLaren printed up on shirts he sold at his clothing shop, SEX. It had a little swastika as part of the design. One time I was going to Florida to visit my family, and a lady at the airport saw the pin. She said, "Do you know what that is?" I didn't want to argue with her, so I said something stupid.

"It's about chaos! It's punk!"

She pulled up her sleeve and showed me the numbered tattoo she was given when she was in a concentration camp in Europe. My stomach dropped into my balls and I felt terrible. I stammered an apology and told her I didn't mean to offend her. That was the last time I wore that pin or anything that had German symbols of hate. That's when it truly hit me that those images are hurtful and horrible for certain people to see.

*This poor lady*, I thought. *She's been through so much already. She was probably starved and forced to work in a labor camp or worse. She might have lost friends or family to the Nazis. This symbol isn't cool. It's not about chaos. It's about suffering.*

I grew up with so much respect for the elderly. In Cuba and even when I first came to America, I was raised to treat the elderly well and understand what they've been through. And there I was pissing on my moral code. I vowed it wouldn't happen again.

My head was really fucked up back then and I hoped being in Florida might help me clear my mind from my failed marriage. I missed my brothers and sisters. They were in Miramar, which is right outside of Miami and I figured I could always start a new band there. But as soon as I arrived, another crazy incident put the kibosh on that idea. My stepdad came in drunk and started beating up everybody. My brother and I had to tackle him. As we approached him from either side, I realized he was more of a danger to me than ever.

"Fuck, Rudy!" I screamed. "He's got a gun!"

He wasn't pointing it at us, but he had it in his right hand and when he heard me, he started to raise the weapon. Rudy and I went straight for his fingers and pried the gun away from him. Together, we pushed him towards the door. Rudy opened it and I shoved him out, then my brother slammed the door shut.

"That's it! He's not coming back!" I shouted. "I'm going to kill him if he comes back!"

My brother felt the same way. I realized being in Florida wouldn't work out for me even if my stepfather stayed away, which I knew wouldn't happen, so I went back to New Jersey. At least while I was down south I got to see the Misfits with the Necros at Finder's Lounge in Hallandale Beach. A few months earlier, I had caught them at Irving Plaza. The Beastie Boys opened the show. I loved the Misfits, so seeing them twice in one year was a real treat. When you're passionate about certain bands and the style of music they play, moments like that can become highlights of your life.

As soon as I got back to New Jersey I called my brother. Sure enough, my stepfather was back in the house. He was pounding booze and using cocaine, so the violence got even worse. He would black out and go on rampages. By then the damage was done. I felt bad about ditching my family, but I did what I had to to survive. If there's any consistency to my life it's that. I've always done what I needed to do in whatever situation I was in.

Since I was flying solo, I searched around and found a shitty apartment in North Bergen, New Jersey. That's where I met Elio Espana. He was the first traditional English skinhead I ever saw. I was hanging out on the street and he was on the other side. We sussed each other out, then I crossed the road and we started talking. How often do you see a guy with no eyebrows and a giant, red spiked Mohawk and a traditional skinhead walking down opposite sides of the street? It sounds like the beginning of a joke. I found out Elio played guitar, so he and I formed a band called Distorted Youth.

We totally sucked, but Elio later made his mark on New York hardcore in a big way, but not by playing in bands. He became an amazing tattoo artist.

At first, he wasn't that talented. He practiced his craft by tattooing all of the bands in the scene. I was his first guinea pig. He tattooed "Crucified Skin" on my forearm. It was cool in a prison tattoo sort of way. I introduced Elio to everyone in the hardcore scene and he did tattoos in Vinnie Stigma's kitchen. Since it was illegal to have a tattoo shop in New York, he had to keep it under the table. He learned fast and got really good and now has his own place, ADK Tattoos, in Constable, New York, where he does ink for clients that have to schedule appointments weeks in advance.

A former member of Distorted Youth, André Schlesinger, later formed the New York Oi! band The Press. They had a popular song called "21 Gun Salute," but while they were one of the most well-known Oi! bands, a lot of skins considered them reds because of their political lyrics. As many cool groups as there were in Jersey, most of them weren't accepted right away by the New York hardcore scene. Bands in the City were reluctant to have dudes from Jersey in their lineup, so the Jersey scene became very incestuous. The biggest Jersey group was the Misfits, who came from Lodi, a middle class suburb in Bergen County. They formed in 1977 and for as long as I can remember, they were always several cuts above any of the other local bands. Theatrical and charismatic, their songs and concerts mixed heavy punk rock with imagery from horror movies.

In the late '70s and early '80s, part of being a rebellious punk involved heckling or harassing the bands on stage, even if you loved them. Musicians got heckled or spat at, and even though it was gross, it was a gesture of respect. But there were lines to be drawn. At one Misfits show I went to with Distorted Youth's singer, Rob Rodrigues, on Christmas Eve 1981 in Hitsville, New Jersey, we were pressed up against the front of the stage and bassist Jerry Only kept coming over to where we were standing. Dave, in an effort to be a "punk," started razzing Jerry. He heckled him and reached up and grabbed his bass while Jerry was playing. After this happened a couple times, Jerry shot a warning glance Rob's way, but Rob was too caught up in the excitement to realize he was pushing his luck.

Rob reached up one more time and grabbed Jerry's bass. In one fluid motion, Jerry Only grabbed the body of the instrument with both hands and hit Rob with it. He wasn't trying to kill him or knock him out. It was more like a warning, but the nubbed part of Jerry's bass, where the strap hooks into the body of the instrument, made contact with the back of Rob's head. It was like he had been clubbed with a log. Rob went down, then got back up. I figured he was okay and that he had learned his lesson. But his eyes were rolling in his head. I looked at him when a spotlight hit him and there was blood streaming down his neck and T-shirt from a gash in his head. We went outside to get him cleaned up.

"Fuck, dude. That's what you get for messing with a dude when he's trying to do a show," I said as Rob held a cloth tightly against his head to stop the bleeding. It was an important lesson about how to treat bands and the danger you faced when you violated their space.

The Misfits were a band I crossed paths with and toured with years later, after vocalist Glenn Danzig started a solo career. I never hung out with them in my early Jersey days. I came to respect them later on when I was hanging on the steps of St. Marks Place with other punks. Glenn was always approachable and friendly.

Within the more insular, grassroots New Jersey hardcore scene, guys played in other guys' bands and spent a lot of time together. Dudes hooked up with other people's girlfriends, which caused an abrupt end to more than a few groups. But that wasn't what broke up Distorted Youth. We realized we weren't any good and we were doing the world a disservice by continuing. After the band broke up, Elio hooked up with Elsie. Eventually they got married and stayed together for 10 years. I didn't care. I just wanted to be with other girls, get crazy and make a bunch of noise.

Back when I was hanging out with Elio and listening to the Sex Pistols, The Clash and Sham 69, I didn't know that much about the New York punk scene beyond bands like The Stimulators and the Mad. Then we started listening to a pirate radio station that had a program called *Noise the Show*. They played stuff like Misfits, Necros, Heart Attack and Nihilistics. During one broadcast, the DJ said there was a big underground concert coming up at Max's Kansas City on December 11, 1981, but he didn't say who was on the bill.

"We should totally check that shit out," I said to Elio.

"I don't know, man," he replied. "It's probably going to be a bunch of shitty, no-name bands."

Since we had nothing better to do, we went and it turned out to be the Bad Brains and the Beastie Boys. This was back before the Beasties discovered rap. They did songs from *Poly Wog Stew*, their punk EP that came out on Rat Cage Records, which was the same label that put out Agnostic Front's *Victim In Pain.* But that wasn't the highlight. Bad Brains were absolutely mind-blowing!

They were incredible musicians and amazing performers. They played faster than anyone and still sounded tight and furious. HR was an unbelievable front man and singer with so much charisma. After you'd see them you'd feel like throwing all your amps and guitars in the garbage and giving up. They were that good. But at the same time they were inspiring. It was, like, "Well, hold on. We could work really hard and get somewhere near this good as well."

Bad Brains set the musical bar really high for the whole New York punk scene. Plus, they had this thing they called PMA: Positive Mental Attitude. It's about keeping your mind focused on your goals and achieving whatever you want in life by being persistent and staying optimistic. That helped a lot of people in the hardcore scene discard the shitty hands they were dealt before they found one another and NYHC.

A week after the Bad Brains show at Max's, we went back and saw Even Worse and Reagan Youth. Soon we saw The Mad, Headlickers and Misguided, which we had heard on *Noise the Show*. As the scene started to grow, all these great bands started playing A7 and Two Plus Two Annex. I felt like I was in the middle of something that was bigger than me and was flinging me around like a giant hardcore pit. In actuality, it was tiny. There were only 25 to 50 people at a lot of these shows. But that didn't matter. It was all great: the music, the people, the drugs. I was fucked up all the time, but hardly anyone knew it.

Some people get really extroverted when they're high. I was always the quiet guy in the back checking everything out, a Mohawked fly on the wall. I still wasn't a part of the inner circle. I was shy outsider. At the same time, I felt more at home with these people than I ever had with anyone else in my life. The danger that lurked all around the Lower East Side didn't even matter; it just went along with everything else.

Maybe the danger helped enhance the experience. The volatility mixed with all this creativity from these artists, most of whom were outcasts, encouraged people to go for broke and do exceptional things. This crazy life we all lived was about being authentic. We were true to ourselves. The scene didn't tolerate poseurs or people who were just there to be cool. And even if you were on the level, when you went to The Mudd Club, Max's Kansas City or A7 you always had to mind your Ps and Qs because anything could happen.

I'd get off the PATH train at the West Village stop at Christopher Street, start walking east, and pretty soon it looked like a warzone in a third world country. There were all these burned-out buildings and boarded-up apartments. One day you'd see people selling junk or shooting up in the street. Another day there were gangs brawling right in front of you, and you'd have to try to fade into the background if you didn't want to get involved. Sometimes you'd run across both in the same night. It was ugly, but I liked it. The turmoil and decay were inspiring. It made me feel like a character in *The Warriors*.

Back when I was trying to get my band with Elio off the ground, I met a girl named Chessie Huber. She was from Jersey and used to go out with Rob, the singer of Barbed Wire Babies. She lived a block from where I had lived with Elsie, was 16 and a cheerleader for Weehawken High School, but she was really into punk. Picture the cutest anarchist pom-pom girl in Nirvana's "Smells Like Teen Spirit," and that was Chessie. We hung out a lot at our rehearsal space. Eventually we clicked and started dating. I was into British and New York punk, and Chessie got me more into American hardcore like Black Flag, Minor Threat and Circle Jerks. We'd go to all the underground shows in the East Village that we'd heard about or saw flyers for. One day we were at Rat Cage Records on Avenue A under 171A Studio, and I saw an ad on a "Musicians Wanted" bulletin board: "Psychos seek bass player. Must be loud!"

I thought Psychos sounded like a cool name for a band, and I had no problem with the loud part. I tried out and they liked me and my Mohawk. Back then the band was a three-piece. Stu Psycho was the guitarist and vocalist, I played bass and did vocals and Billy Psycho was on drums. They were from New York and I was from New Jersey, but I was enough of a presence at New York shows by then that they were okay with me being part of the bridge and tunnel crowd. We wrote the songs together. We played a lot of crazy shows and Billy always got into fights with kids in the pit. We were all nuts, but Billy was the real psycho.

One time Billy and I were tripping on acid. We started smoking weed and sharing a 40-ounce of Old English. He took a big swig, and his tooth fell out and into the bottle. It was like a ghetto version of a mezcal worm, only there was no way I was gonna swig his tooth into my mouth, no matter how many hits of acid I had taken. To get to the tooth we had to finish the beer—we didn't want to waste the beer! I figured the tooth wouldn't come out until the liquid was just about gone, so I made sure Billy had the last swig. But the tooth didn't come out. It got stuck on the side of the bottle. We turned it upside-down, tapped it and shook it but it wouldn't come out. So I threw the bottle down in the street and smashed it. Billy picked his tooth up from the gutter.

"Put it in your pocket," I said. "We'll get some Krazy Glue and stick it back in your head later."

When we got back to my place I got the Krazy Glue and tried to put Billy's tooth back into the gap in his mouth. But I was still tripping really hard, so I got confused and put the tooth in backwards. He looked like a snaggletooth. He didn't get mad; he thought it was funny and kept it that way for a while. Typical Billy.

Once, he showed up all frantic at the place where I was living with Elio.

"Can I stay with you?" he asked. "Man, I really need to stay with you!"

"Okay, tell me, what's up?" I said.

At the time, Billy lived in a second-floor walk-up that looked like it hadn't been cleaned in a decade.

"I got into an argument with my landlord because I owed him rent and he came charging at me," Billy began, sounding as much like he was pleading with me as telling me a story. "I moved out of the way and the guy went right out the window. He didn't even scream. I think he's dead. I looked out the window and he didn't move, so I got the fuck out of there before someone could call the cops."

I figured that Billy might have been shitting me—that he had just gotten kicked out and needed a place to stay. But I looked at the newspaper the next day and there it was: a story about a landlord who was pushed out of a window to his death. The cops eventually caught Billy because he wasn't hard to find, but after his girlfriend corroborated his story, he was released.

Another time, Billy passed out drunk in some guy's doorway right near A7. He wouldn't move. The guy finally woke him up and told him to leave and Billy wouldn't go, so the guy shot him in the leg. When we heard from one of his friends what had

Playing bass with the Psychos at A7, 1983.

happened we went to Saint Vincent's Hospital, where he had been admitted.

The staff at the place eyed us suspiciously and asked, "Who are you here to see?

"Billy Psycho," I said.

"Who?"

"Uh, Billy . . . Oh, shit, I don't know his last name." No one in the hardcore community knew his real name, so none of us could visit him to see how he was doing.

I liked playing in the Psychos. Our songs could have been faster and heavier, but they were my first "real" band, even though we were held together with popsicle sticks and Elmer's Glue. I had some decent equipment, but everyone else played with whatever they could throw together. Billy's drums were made up from pieces of five or six different sets, and Stu had a cheap red guitar that didn't even have a brand name on it. Everybody played out of my amp, an Ampeg G4, which I had ponied up for when I joined the band. Whatever we lacked in professionalism we made up for in humor and insanity, both live and in the practice room.

Stu had false teeth and he'd take them out to play. He'd put them on top of the amp and they'd chatter from the vibrations, which was the most hardcore thing ever! Stu was one of the first guys to play in drop C. He'd tune the whole guitar down to D and then drop the low E string to C so he could play chords with one finger. He didn't need the other four fingers . . . or his teeth. In the early '90s that became standard practice. We were years ahead of our time! After I left the Psychos and joined Agnostic Front, Stu Psycho went to prison for being the infamous "Axe Man of Brooklyn." He held up random people in the street with a hatchet and eventually got taken down by the police.

# CHAPTER 8

The first time I saw Vinnie Stigma was on October 14, 1981, at the Peppermint Lounge. The Stimulators and The Professionals (which featured Sex Pistols' guitarist, Steve Jones) were playing, and Vinnie was a fucking maniac. I had no way of knowing how important he would be in my life over the next 35 years. Vinnie was on the floor doing this crazy dance, and I was standing at the top of the balcony looking down. I was flying on mescaline, which is why I wasn't down where the action was.

When I did mescaline I withdrew from the world and stayed within myself. I'd always feel worried, like something bad was about to happen. I don't know why the fuck I did it, but I did it a lot. Being high like that and acutely aware of my fears, I was looking for the scariest thing around, maybe as a defense mechanism. Whatever it was, I usually found it fascinating. At that moment Vinnie was the craziest, most outrageous thing in sight. He was dancing hard, going against the pit. Usually, guys in the pit rotate around with the flow of the circle like chunks of wood in a whirlpool. Vinnie was right there in the middle like a salmon swimming upstream. The pit was going one way and he was going the other, crashing his way through a wall of people, with a mad glint in his eye. He was with Big Paul, who was an American skinhead and a good dude.

In the U.K., a bunch of skinheads were messed-up motherfuckers. They were hateful and malicious, and a lot of them supported an ideology of white power. They'd go gay-bashing and beat up black people and other minorities. I wasn't oblivious to the messages in the music I liked. I thought about what bands were saying in their lyrics. I never liked racist or bigoted bands. I hated everything they and their followers stood for, and I wanted nothing to do with them. But sometimes things aren't so cut and dried.

Music is a funny thing; it can be blinding. If it's really good or catchy, you may overlook certain things like goofy lyrics or a mixed message. Especially when you're young, dumb and punk.

The shock value can also skew your logic. I mean, I've seen African-American punks with swastika pins. That's ridiculous, right? That being said, as soon as White Power became a clear-cut genre with a hateful agenda, most of us instantly boycotted it and the accompanying mentality. There were some guys who secretly—or not so secretly—continued to support that message, either as a fan or because of some sick ideological delusion.

In the early days, if you didn't disrespect people and minded your own business, people tended to let most things slide. But even that ultimately ceased. Our scene was evolving, and it was too multicultural for bigotry to be accepted or tolerated. The sympathizers took a more discrete approach. The rest took a more vocal and aggressive approach against it—rightfully so.

This new approach inspired me to write songs for our first full-length record, *Victim In Pain*. Songs like "United and Strong," "Fascist Attitudes" and "Your Mistake" focused on bringing kids together. Just read the lyrics!

Despite my efforts to bring unity instead of hate to our scene, there were those that had already formed an opinion, based on stories they heard instead of taking us at face value. They certainly didn't listen to *Victim In Pain*! They also didn't realize that I'm a Cuban immigrant. I was raised in multicultural neighborhoods in New Jersey and New York. I always had friends from all walks of life and still do.

In the late '80s, after a shit-ton of media attention was put on skins, wrongly identifying them all as White Power, there was an even stronger reaction against the White Power genre skins. People drew more definitive lines in the sand. It's a shame the media never paid as much attention to the multiracial side of things. But unity doesn't sell. Hate does.

My idea of being a skin came largely from American bands like Iron Cross and The Effigies. Obviously not all U.K. skinhead bands where messed up. If it wasn't for Sham

69, Cockney Rejects, The Business or The Last Resort, I probably wouldn't have channeled in such great working-class music and discovered the American skin bands.

Elio was the first person I knew who brought the European skinhead look to the New Jersey scene. He was British, kept a fresh buzzed #1 crop and wore Ben Sherman shirts, pressed slacks, braces and steel-toed oxblood Dr. Martens boots. We mostly wore American military boots, homemade T's of our favorite bands, ripped jeans and spiked bracelets. We had our own thing. It would be a while before I had to worry about fascists coming to my shows.

We were from New York and New Jersey. We grew up with different races, religions and colors, and that lent great diversity to the scene. We accepted everyone as long as they were into the same music. We didn't mind offending anyone. We loved it. It was great to insult people and be obnoxious, but we never set out to put down anyone's race and we never tolerated racism.

The Psychos were barely big enough to draw any type of crowd. Chessie came to all of our shows. She was one of the few chicks, along with Billy's girl, Kitty Hawk, from the band Killer Instinct and my cousin Tito's girl, Laurie. We'd get a few hardcore dudes, maybe a New York skin and a punk or two. There was a big division back then between the punk and hardcore scenes. I always liked both, but the punk scene was artsy, self-destructive and suicidal. A lot of the artists and fans were drug addicts and those that weren't shooting up were depressed all the time. It wasn't positive. Hardcore was violent, but it was a fun violence—a decadent celebration of destruction and chaos.

I didn't know anything about heroin at the time. Then on October 30, 1981, I went to see Misfits with a girl named Zoe, whom I had just started dating, and I got a firsthand introduction to the dangers of smack. The band was playing the Ukraine Hall with Necros and I was losing my mind for the whole show, jumping up and down while holding her shoulders. I figured she was just as stoked about the show as I was. Before the concert was over she excused herself to go to the bathroom. I figured she had to piss; we had been drinking a lot of beer. I needed to go also, but I didn't want to miss any of the show. After, I went to the bathroom and emptied my bulging bladder. I was pumped and in a great mood.

We went back to Zoe's car, and I could tell she was definitely out of it. I thought,

"Damn, jumping around at the concert took a lot out of her." Then I figured she got really bombed during the show and it had just hit her, because alcohol takes a little while to get into people's bloodstreams. I don't know why I thought she was okay to drive, but she got in the driver's seat. Before she turned the keys in the ignition, she slumped over.

I didn't realize she had overdosed. Since I hadn't experimented with hardcore drugs yet, I didn't know what people looked like when they were nodding off. I didn't see her shoot up. She must have done it in the bathroom, but when I nudged her she didn't move or make any noise. She had foamy spit running down the corner of her mouth, and I couldn't tell if she was breathing. We were right by St. Mark's Place and since the concert had just let out, there were some people on the street and police patrolling the area. I looked around desperately and ran up to a police officer.

"Hey, there's something going on! I just saw this girl in her car. I thought she was asleep, but she's not moving."

I acted like it was just something I saw because I wasn't sober and didn't want to get arrested. The cop came over to check Zoe out and then shouted something into his walkie-talkie. Before I could ask him what was happening, an ambulance arrived. Paramedics jumped out, scooped up Zoe and took her away.

I didn't know where they took her and I didn't hear from her afterwards. I didn't know if she had a seizure, a heart attack or a brain aneurysm. I contacted one of her friends, and she told me Zoe had overdosed. She was the first one I knew who did that. She wouldn't be the last. But the night went from a great experience to something horrific. Apparently, doctors revived her at the hospital and she lived. But she separated herself from the punk scene afterwards, or her parents made her stay away from the people she had been hanging out with. I never saw her again.

I hardly had time to take in what had happened on Halloween night when Fear played *Saturday Night Live.* John Belushi, who was a big fan of the scene, pushed the show's producer, Lorne Michaels, to have them on the show. Minor Threat vocalist Ian MacKaye and a bunch of kids from D.C. and Boston came up to Rockefeller Center, and we waited in line with them. Fear played six songs, two of which were filmed for broadcast. Organizers let us in as soon as the band started playing, but they brought us to a back room instead of to the audience. We were all fucked up and pissed off, so we trashed the place.

We pulled all the strings out of a piano and smashed the bathroom sinks because we were frustrated and wanted to get down there to see the band. Finally, they let us downstairs and into the studio for the last song, and we went off. Even before they started playing we were slamming into each other and diving into the audience. Then everyone started getting rough and throwing punches. The kids from D.C. and Boston were in our town acting tough, so we got right back in their faces and the show erupted into a big brawl. Security tried to break up the fights while the band was playing. We saw these pumpkins all over the set and started throwing them at each other and at the security guards. Finally, the NYPD came in with batons and started beating kids, so we split. Cops were chasing us down the halls, and we managed to get out of the studio and escape through the street.

It was sheer insanity—a Misfits show and an overdose, followed by Fear, a bunch of fights and escaping from the cops. For punks, living was like walking a 50-foot tightrope made of razor wire. It was as dangerous as it was fun, even on Halloween. A lot of the kids in the NYHC scene didn't expect to live long, but they didn't waste time thinking about dying. They were living in the moment and didn't worry what would happen down the road. We stayed out as long as we could, as if that would slow down the arrival of the next day.

On a typical night we went to the Mudd Club because they had punk nights downstairs and reggae upstairs. And when the night was over there, we went to A7, which didn't open until 2 a.m. and which also doubled as a reggae venue. Of course fights could erupt at any punk show at any time, but sometimes being at concerts kept us out of trouble. When nothing was going on and we were just fuckin' bored, that's when we acted like real degenerates, especially if we were too drunk or on speed or angel dust.

One time I was standing by a parked car outside the Mudd Club, where Fear and The Young and the Useless were playing, and Big Paul and Jimmy Gestapo from Murphy's Law came out looking for a fight. They broke the antenna off a car, snapped it in half and started beating on one guy. I didn't know who he was or why they were bashing him, but they got in a few good lashes. The guy's shirt tore with every stroke. It looked like a slow motion scene in a hardcore version of *A Clockwork Orange*. The antenna came down and made a sickening *thwack*. Then a long line of blood appeared; it started at one corner of the shirt tear and spread to the other end, as if some force was coloring all the gashes crimson—at least that's what it looked like on hallucinogens. I watched fascinated, but also kind of sickened because it reminded me of my stepdad and the punishments he dished out whenever he was in a bad mood—and sometimes when he was in a good mood and wanted to feel more empowered.

When I turned around I saw a group of people coming down the street straight towards me! I went, "Fuck. This is it!" I pulled off my chain belt and got ready to fight, but everyone ran right past me and started beating on Billy Psycho. Billy saved the day yet again.

Billy was always a target, but he loved it. He'd get in the pit and get knocked over and roughed up. Someone would kick him in the ribs and someone else would step on his head. He'd come out of every show limping and black and blue. Sometimes he'd have a broken nose or he'd have a fat lip or a black eye. The more abuse he took, the more fun he had.

Back when I was in the Psychos, I hung out a lot with Billy and Stu, but I didn't fit in with the rest of the New York scene. Since I had a Mohawk (which was more punk than hardcore) and I came from Jersey, most guys didn't go out of their way to befriend me. They didn't talk to me and I didn't talk to them. They respected my band, which was cool, but when I wasn't onstage I felt awkward, even though I was around people I had a lot in common with.

When the Psychos got a show at A7 it was a big deal, at least to me. Only about ten people were there—which was pretty good for us—and Vinnie Stigma was one of them. We talked after the show and discovered that we liked a lot of the same bands, even outside of punk. Vinnie was one of the main reasons I joined AF. He's always had my back and has been like a brother to me. Alex Kinon from Cause For Alarm and Jimmy Gestapo from Murphy's Law also liked the Psychos and slammed at our shows. We played on bills with Murphy's Law, The Mob, Abused, Major Conflict, Urban Waste, Cause For Alarm, Kraut, Rapid Deployment and Killer Instinct, and we tried to be crazier and more energetic than all of them so people would notice us. At first, we weren't accepted by the hardcore crowd. Even though we played hardcore music, we looked more punk than most other bands, who were adopting the new hardcore look. Everyone else had cropped hair, jeans and combat boots, and I still had a Mohawk and a leather jacket with studs on it. But we played so much it didn't take long for crowds to get into us, and our look quickly evolved, too.

As punk and hardcore spread, more venues booked bands and some were pretty unconventional. There was a place called 171A that screened movies and scheduled shows. I went there one day in 1982 to see *Shellshock Rock*, a 1979 documentary about the evolution of the punk scene in Belfast, Ireland. They also played The Outcasts' concert film *Self-Conscious Over You*, and between the two flicks the Stimulators performed. That's the night when I really clicked with their drummer, Harley Flanagan, whom I had briefly met previously at a show. He was 14 at the time and was playing drums for the Stimulators. He looked 12, and I was only 16. I went up and talked to him after the show. I was amazed at how approachable he and the rest of the Stimulators were. That's when I realized how genuine the NYHC scene was. Soon after, Harley went to Canada for a year so I didn't see him for a while. A year can seem like a lifetime when you're not yet 20.

A really solid bonding night for the developing New York hardcore scene happened on July 16, 1982, when Dead Kennedys played a show with D.O.A., SS Decontrol and Kraut at the Paramount Theater in Staten Island. The show was in an old art deco movie theater that had been converted into a concert hall. The whole New York crew took the Staten Island Ferry to the concert. And while the locals there had gotten used to concerts they had never seen a group of deviants like us invade their side of the New York Bay. The working class natives decided they didn't like the way we looked and were gonna keep us from coming back to their community by teaching us a lesson. They underestimated who they were up against. We were used to conflict and abuse. We were reckless and eager for an excuse to bust some heads. And we were hyped up by the volume and intensity of the concert.

Some of the locals tried to threaten and intimidate us at the show, but we weren't having it. Before Dead Kennedys finished their set, fists started to fly. All these Staten Island guys had to do was wait until the end of the show and we would have gotten on the ferry and gone back to the City. Either they weren't that patient or they weren't too smart. They thought we were criminals and wanted us out. They wanted us to flee with our tails between our legs. Not gonna happen! I hadn't fully come out of my shell yet, but I learned how to take a stand. As soon as the show let out, these goombahs started throwing punches and we fought back.

Agnostic Front's original bassist, Diego, took off his chain belt and started beating the shit out of these guys. They clearly weren't ready to take on anyone as crazy and amped up as our crew was that night. A Staten Island chick was hitting on our scene photographer, Ran-D, and her boyfriend pushed him away and slapped her. So Ran-D decked the guy. That enraged the guidos further. We battled our way back to the ferry. Lazar saw a pile of bricks on the ground, picked them up and threw them as hard as she could at anyone within range. She popped one of those idiots in the head and he collapsed. Between Diego's belt, which must have leveled a half-dozen people, Lazar's bricks and other punks who had spiked rings and studded bracelets, we wiped the floor with those guys right up to the point where we boarded the ferry. We celebrated the whole way back to New York, chanting and shouting lyrics from our favorite punk songs. On most summer evenings on the ferry, the air was hot and muggy and smelled like old socks. That night the smell of victory was in the air.

NYHC Troublemakers: Me, Harley Flanagan and Vinnie Stigma.

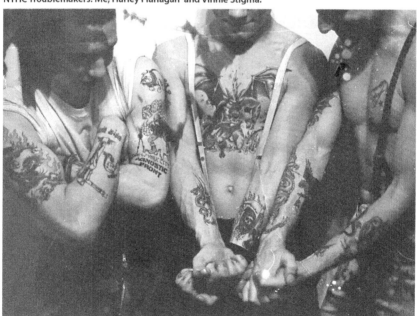

# CHAPTER 9

Even after the Psychos were accepted by New York punks, I still felt like a loner. I was living in New Jersey, so I'd do drugs by myself or with Elio. Whether it was because of the drugs or paranoia stemming from my childhood, I felt alienated from everyone around me. Even though I loved the music and wanted to hang out with people in the scene, I didn't put myself out there.

On April 3, 1983, I decided to shave my head—not to be accepted but because I wanted to. That night I put on combat boots and went to see Angry Samoans play at Great Gildersleeves, which was one of the bigger venues that booked punk and hard-core shows. To my surprise, when I stepped down to the floor, people gave me space and treated me with respect. I felt safer in the pit than ever just because I was buzzed down. I looked the part. I went crazy stagediving. It was like a hardcore baptism. I had undertaken a rite of passage and suddenly was an active member of this wild community. The scene was all about individualism and self-expression, but it wasn't until I did the "hardcore" thing that I was totally accepted—so much so that, after the show, I was invited to join Agnostic Front.

Their bass player at the time, Adam Mucci, and drummer, Raybeez, came up to me. Ray said, "Hey, we're looking for a singer." I was a little hesitant because I thought the Psychos were a better band. I was also reluctant to join because the Psychos were nuts but AF were fuckin' crazy.

The first time I saw Agnostic Front them was at the Two Plus Two Annex on August 14, 1982. When they first advertised the show, they called themselves The Zoo Crew. It was a dumb name, but anyone who told them that would have gotten their teeth

71

knocked out. Before the show happened, they changed their name to Agnostic Front.

The band were the original four members—John Watson on vocals, Diego on bass, Robbie CryptCrash on drums and Vinnie on guitar. They looked hard as fuck. They'd start a song and only make it halfway through, which isn't saying much since the songs were 40 seconds long. At the 20-second mark, the mic went down and John Watson dove in the pit. Diego dropped his bass and jumped in there and started swinging. Only Vinnie and Robbie were left onstage. John and Diego were hard dancers. Everybody had to dodge or duck when these guys swarmed through. They were like wrecking balls smashing through walls of people. Then they'd get back up onstage and do the whole thing again. It kept going like that throughout the whole set.

"Are these guys ever going to finish a song?" I thought. "This is awful—but fucking insane to watch."

The next time I saw AF was September 4 at a big, free show in Astoria, Queens. The show was at a center in the projects where Johnny Waste lived and it was at a party for his birthday. They were on a huge bill with Reagan Youth, Urban Waste, The Mob, Armed Citizens, Headlickers, Cavity Creeps and Shök. They did the same thing all over again and everyone loved it. Their M.O. was to be harder than anyone else and not worry about playing songs. As long as they looked fierce, played loud and left trails of destruction, everything was good.

When John Watson got arrested and went to Rikers Island, AF replaced him with Keith Burkhardt, later of Cause For Alarm, for a few shows. But Watson was back with them on November 2, 1982, when they played a legendary concert in a super-sketchy neighborhood in Camden, New Jersey, that became known as the Buff Hall show. It was Minor Threat, SS Decontrol, Agnostic Front, Flag of Democracy and Crib Death. Everyone came with their crews. There were people representing D.C., Boston, New York and New Jersey. I jumped in a car with the guys from the Psychos. Soon after we got there, someone in a car ran down Ian MacKaye and sped away. We all wondered if it was a hit or an accident, but Ian was okay and made it through the show. In addition to fans of the bands, members of Black Motorcycle Club and Ghetto Riders were there in big numbers and insisted on doing security. I wondered if it was going to turn into a situation like the show at the Altamont Speedway, where the Hell's Angels did security for The Rolling Stones and four people got killed. But aside from Ian MacKaye getting hit by a car, nothing else major happened and Agnostic Front were the best I'd seen them. They were the band New York sent to represent us and they came away with their heads held high.

Soon after the show, Watson bailed again and they invited a guy named Jimmy the Russian to join. (Jimmy later formed the hardcore punk band Virus, which released an album on Rat Cage Records after we did.) I saw Jimmy the Russian play with Agnostic Front on a bill with Black Flag and Minutemen on March 13, 1983, at Great Gildersleeves. That was about a month before they asked me to join. Apparently, having a new vocalist didn't calm their wild side. They sounded like an exploding airbase when they were onstage, trashed everything, stormed through the crowd and left the crowd shaking. It was intense, but I wanted to play in a band that finished songs and played a full set.

The night Raybeez asked me to join, I was torn. "I dunno, man," I said to Adam, who had replaced Diego. "I've never just been a singer. I've always had a bass to stand behind. This might be weird."

He was determined to get me in the band because he liked how crazed I looked onstage and dug my shaved head. Back then, AF chose new members by looking at the pit and seeing who looked the wildest. They didn't care if you could play an instrument or sing. I asked Chessie what she thought.

"Just do it!" she said.

I figured I could play with both bands, but the Psychos were mad as hell that I joined Agnostic Front because of some imaginary rivalry Billy and Stu felt existed between the two bands. Billy didn't care that they beat him up; he was mad because he felt I had crossed allegiances. AF were straight-up hardcore and the Psychos were hardcore punk. But I saw how insane they were onstage, and I thought that if they could generate that type of energy and finish their songs, they could be a really powerful band.

Vinnie also wanted guys who could play full shows, and he wanted some stability in the band. By the time I went to my first rehearsal, the original four were no more. But those guys' importance in the history of the band can't be overstated. One of the greatest characters of the original lineup was Robbie CryptCrash, who was a solid, charismatic drummer. He came from a band in Philadelphia called the CryptCrashers.

There was a rumor that he's a descendent of the Rockefellers, but he was disowned by the family because he devoted his life to punk rock and married his punk rock chick, Michelle CryptCrash, a Lower East Side girl that no one in the family liked. The family thought the two of them were like Sid and Nancy and were embarrassed by them, so he was excommunicated.

He left to play with vocalist Keith Burkhardt, bassist Rob Kabula and guitarist Alex Kinon in the newly formed Cause For Alarm. Interestingly, all four of the original Cause For Alarm guys were members of Agnostic Front at one point or another.

AF didn't take Robbie's departure personally and still hung out with him all the time. He remained part of the scene. The same went for John Watson, whom we raised hell with for years and who remains a good friend.

Things happened so fast that it was sometimes hard to keep track of who was coming and who was leaving. When I joined, Raymond "Raybeez" Barbieri was playing drums. He couldn't keep a beat, but at least he stayed behind the kit. He was a total character. We were great friends up until the day he died. No one raged like that guy. Back then he had an X on his hand, as if he was straight edge, but at the same time he'd be high on angel dust. A lot of times when it was cold, and even when it wasn't, he'd have gloves on and another pair of gloves with the fingers missing over the first pair. He'd wear three or four pairs of pants. Then he had a regular shirt on top of a t-shirt and a long-sleeve shirt over both. He used to walk around to the rehearsal studios with a bag of clothes.

Being in the band with Raybeez caused Chessie and I to break up. I liked her. It wasn't my choice. There were three rules for being in Agnostic Front:  1) Shave your head. 2) No girlfriends. 3) Dance hard. Raybeez was especially strict about rule number two. He thought anyone who had a girl couldn't possibly be devoted to the band, which was ridiculous. But that was the rule and I didn't have any leverage to argue it. Chessie was so pissed when I told her we couldn't stay together, especially since she had encouraged me to join. Raybeez was worried about girls trying to influence what we did with the band. He didn't want a hardcore Yoko Ono trying to call the shots. It was a stupid rule, and Raybeez was only in the band for a short while after Chessie and I broke up. It didn't matter. I was moving on.

My first show with Agnostic Front was April 16, 1983, at The Anthrax Gallery in

Stanford, Connecticut. We played with CIA. I wasn't seasoned yet, but I knew the punk rock ropes from the Psychos. I barked out the songs as best I could and no one complained. Then we prepared for the next show.

Two weeks later I was on television for the first time. On April 30, 1983, a TV program called *Monitor* filmed the concert for a segment they were doing on the New York hardcore scene. I had a good buzz, but I was still so nervous I was shaking. The fears I expressed to Adam were coming to light. I was used to standing behind a bass, and when you do that you automatically look like a musician. When you take the instrument away all you've got is the microphone. You have to be a *front man*.

Vinnie didn't care what I did onstage as long as I went nuts, screamed at the top of my lungs and got in the pit and danced. At one point I ducked down and Jimmy Gestapo got onstage and jumped over my head and back into the crowd. It couldn't have looked better if we had choreographed it. John Watson also took the mic and sang "It's My Life," which gave me a feeling of acceptance. He was doing his last bit and passing the torch to me.

The night the show aired we went to Vinnie's place in Little Italy, where he grew up. He had a TV and chairs set up, and his mom made us pasta. We were so excited about our big television debut that it was all we could talk about between slurps of spaghetti. As soon as the show started, the announcer defined hardcore and how it differed from regular punk. Then the program switched to footage of our show. It was so cool to see ourselves on TV, but right away we noticed something was wrong. We were slamming, but the song we were playing wasn't coming through the TV speaker. The producers of the show had dubbed the New York band Kraut over us. I was bummed out. It wasn't until later that I figured out we were playing so loud that night that the audio of the show was distorted and unusable. Since we didn't have any records out yet they went with another band's music.

It was just as well. We weren't at the top of our game back then. I was screaming away, sometimes not even forming real words. Vinnie was a little out of tune and sloppy, and Raybeez was struggling to keep up with Mucci's tempos. But it was *us* and it was hardcore. Suddenly the media started catching onto hardcore, and it provided a lot of exposure for the scene, even though a lot of the coverage was negative. Truthfully, it hadn't grown that big yet. Most of the concerts were still in small clubs, but it was controversial because it was explosive. Eventually all of the big talk show hosts, including Donohue, did segments on how hardcore turned healthy teenagers into raging psychopaths. At least when hardcore came to New York, it was the other way around.

I was still living in New Jersey with Elio for a while after I joined AF. We had an apartment right by the hardware store, where I was still working. But I became less reliable. I'd show up at work drunk or painfully hungover. Going back and forth between Jersey and New York became a drag. I decided to move to the Lower East Side since I spent so much time there anyway. I took over the lease on Apartment X at 188 Norfolk Street, which, at the time, was Keith Burkhardt from Cause For Alarm's place. I had previously purchased Keith's old Yamaha RD350 motorcycle to drive in and out of the City. Now I had his apartment. He was as happy about it as I was. He was tired of all the roaches and rats at Apartment X and decided to move to 6th Street between avenues B and C, so he signed over the place to me and I lived there for a totally event-packed year. The lease was symbolic since Apartment X was an illegal basement apartment that was falling apart. Unfinished drywall and hanging bed sheets divided the space. Shitty plumbing and lighting set the vibe for that muggy, moldy and dingy dungeon, yet everyone had their little compartment between the makeshift curtains. Every time it rained the place would flood and there'd' be up to a foot of water. But we made the best of it.

All the bands came over to hang, drink, get high and crash on the floor. We found mattresses on the street and brought them into the place. Some of the people who crashed there never left, so there were a bunch of us living there, including the LES (Lower East Side) Girls.

They were our original girls and they were family; we were like a bunch of Mormons on acid. The LES girls were: Kym (who was my girlfriend at the time), Michelle CryptCrash, Nancy Mohawk, Lisa Bat, Leigh Marie, Dawn, Linda, Manon, Lazar, Shelly and Lucy. Five of the chicks—Michelle, Kym, Linda, Lucy and Dawn—got LES girls tattoos to show how devoted they were to our crew.

Everybody staying there got crabs. It's impossible to tell if the crabs came from someone who was already infected or if they were living in the mattresses we dragged in from the street. All I know is these little buggers were resistant to any insecticide we used. They'd go away for a little while, but they kept coming back. They finally left for good after I visited my family in Florida and went swimming in the ocean. Maybe the salt water killed them. I used to joke that they swam away to hang out with real crabs underwater.

Lots of rats scurried inside the walls and ran through the apartment. Once, one came right out in the open while I was hanging out in my room. He didn't seem especially dirty or scary. He wasn't scared of me, and he seemed curious. I went towards him and he backed up a little, but he came right back. He seemed more like a dog you meet for the first time than a rat. I fed him some bread, and he stuck around and ate it. Then he looked up at me for more. I found a moldy hot dog, broke it up into pieces and fed it to him. He loved that. From that point on we were friends. I named him Simon and he became my pet. I could always tell him apart from the other rats that were uglier and nasty. Simon was gentle, almost friendly. While I was at Apartment X he'd scramble over to me and visit, and when I left the apartment I took him with me. I even took him on tour.

This is how I remember Apartment X from when I had the lease. We built our own spaces. I had a room in the back with Kym and I had two of the street mattresses on the floor. Raybeez had a front closet room that you saw when you first walked in, and he made himself a little loft. Poss had the other small room on the right, between the bathroom and the kitchen, and it was the room that always flooded. Kabula and Dawn had the other big room next to mine. Harley and Little Chris always crashed and slept in the living room on the beds we destroyed during the dust party, when we all smoked a half-ounce of dust, wrecked the place and chased Raybeez around because he had a gun.

We were castaways from mainstream society, and we formed our own demented commune. We all went to sleep at 6 or 7 a.m., so everyone woke up late. Depending on what night it was and who was playing, we'd go to one of a half-dozen or so clubs, sometimes hitting more than one. We didn't need a concert to have a party. Some days we kicked it off by cranking killer hardcore seven-inches before going into Tompkins Square Park to listen to punk albums. Day turned into night, as we smoked angel dust, took mescaline or dropped acid and drank Ray's Deli's famous egg creams. Then we'd have breakfast at Odessa or Leshko's. They were right across the street from the park,

Amy with Simon.

kitty-corner to the A7 club.

Since we spent our money on drugs, we'd sit outside in the afternoon and grub for change until we had enough to get breakfast. We'd usually send the girls and the younger punks like little Freddy (when he was visiting me) because they came back with the most cash. People had more sympathy for them than for degenerate punk rock teenagers whom they figured were just gonna use the money to drink and get high. They were right, but we had to eat, too.

My sister, Mayra, came to visit Apartment X once and had no idea what kind of squalor I was living in. She was only 14 and thought it would be a nice vacation. She was completely disgusted. My mom thought I was in a decent band making decent money. I never told her any different. Not long after we got to my room at Apartment X, Simon exited through a crack in the ceiling and came running down the wall. Mayra bugged out. I laughed.

"It's just Simon," I said. I tried to reassure her that it wasn't some rabid animal that was going to attack her.

"You name the rats?" she snapped at me once she got over her revulsion that I was now holding a fat, furry animal with a long, bare tail.

"No, most of the rats suck. Simon's my pet."

"You have a pet rat? That's just gross."

Mayra didn't enjoy her visit. I told her we were going to go out and eat. But first everyone had to go out in the street and grub for change, and she had to go with them to help make more money.

"What the fuck, Roger? I'm not going to beg for money," she said.

"C'mon, just do it so we can go eat," I laughed.

The restaurants we went to were Polish-owned and the people who ran them were polite to us. Maybe they couldn't afford to lose our business. When you're poor, any customer with money is a good customer. After we ate, we went back to Apartment X and did all the drugs we wanted—except Mayra. Then guys and girls hooked up for the night and everyone slept all day. We'd get up at 6 or 7 at night and start drinking to clear the cobwebs out of our heads. It wasn't the healthiest lifestyle, but being a degenerate was part of the program and we were all having a blast. Also, we protected our own. Once in a while, guys in local gangs would see our girls and try to win them over. We weren't having any of that. As soon as we saw them we pulled our chain belts off and started swinging.

"C'mon, motherfucker! Let's see you hittin' on our girls now!"

Most of these girls were close to us and we protected them like family, the way a big brother would stand watch over his little sister. A lot of the people in the hardcore scene in New York back then were runaways from abusive families or misfits that couldn't get by in ordinary society. They all filtered down to the Lower East Side and a lot of them found the same kind of acceptance that I found. We were a community. We were there for one another.

One time, one of the punk chicks got raped. She came into the A7 club sobbing and told us how it happened and who did it. I saw red. We all did. One of our sisters had been violently sexually violated. A lot of girls in the scene had been molested or abused in their youth, and we were damned if we were going to let it happen here. We went outside with bats, found the guy and threw a little boot party. We were swinging for the bleachers, and he was cowering on the ground. *Crack!* We heard his ribs break. *Crunch!* A quick golf swing and his jaw was shattered! It was a flurry

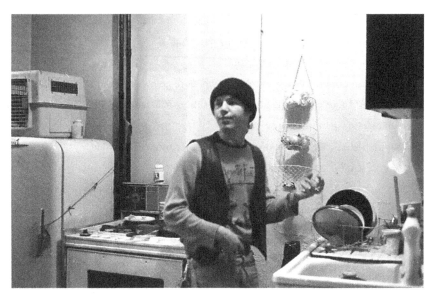
Our apartment above Robbie CryptCrash, 1983.

of mob violence because we were protecting our own and punishing a scumbag. We didn't care if we wrecked him. He deserved a beating. I don't know if the guy walked away. It was street justice, hardcore-style.

Back then, Avenue A was dangerous as fuck and the rest of Alphabet City was even worse. There would be a building that looked normal, and then there would be five more buildings that were destroyed and leveled. It was like someone's mouth was open and there were teeth missing. Everything was burnt out—entire streets. If you went between avenues C and D, all of 7th, 8th and 9th Street looked like they had been bombed. There were complete blocks where there was maybe one building standing. Everything else had crumbled. Whatever was left was covered with graffiti.

We had nicknames for all the streets. Avenue A was adventurous, B was bold, C was crazy and, if you wanted to get really nuts, Avenue D was deadly. That's where the heart of the projects were and where the serious gangbangers lived. People who weren't from the hood got stabbed or beaten up badly if they trespassed. But if you stayed in your place and stuck with your own, you had a good chance of making it through the night.

The area was infested with packs of wild dogs, stray cats, even wild roosters. All the abandoned buildings—even the places we considered safe—were used for selling drugs. Everything was on the menu, from heroin down to marijuana, though a lot of the heavier stuff got dealt on the street. If you were buying weed, you left the store and smoked it wherever you wanted. The junkies scoring smack wandered over to the shooting galleries on Avenue C.

Almost the entire East Village was a thrilling mixture of grit, grime and great art. Since it was underdeveloped, the area was affordable. Every storefront was occupied by artists, musicians and weed dealers. There was an abundance of creativity, and the streets teemed with life. Between the elements of danger, the creativity of the art community and the intensity of the musicians, it was a wild, dangerous, wonderful scene.

**Raybeez and Jimmy G, Lower East Side 1983.**

# CHAPTER 10

**S**ome kids in the NYHC scene got in too deep or mixed with the wrong element and wound up in mental institutions or worse. By far, drugs caused most of the breakdowns, arrests, illnesses and deaths. Once you start getting involved in drugs, they overwhelm you little by little, like an ocean current that carries you away when you stray too far from the shore. There was a time around 1982 when a lot of people in the punk scene were doing heroin because it was all around us. Our friends started dabbling and soon got hooked. They seemed to like it—at least at first.

I tried it, too. I started by snorting it, and it immediately numbed my entire nose. Then I threw up. It didn't make me feel good. It just made me nauseous. Even so, I shot it a couple times after that. I figured that snorting it might have made me sick because it didn't get into my system fast enough. Also, I felt pressured to do it because a good friend was using. I still hated it. It made me woozy and unable to speak, but at least I didn't puke.

The last time I shot heroin, there were five of us sharing a needle, which was incredibly stupid. It was me, Raybeez and three of the LES Girls. Back then, we didn't know how people got AIDS or hepatitis. Somehow everybody I shared that needle with, except Raybeez, is still alive and never caught anything. By the third time I shot up, I decided it wasn't the right drug for me. Maybe it's because I was never an addictive person. If I was addicted to anything, it was Quaaludes. Those, I liked. And I did cocaine, too, mostly because it was around and other people were snorting it. I didn't really enjoy it, and when I was too gakked up, I got cocky, talked too much and did some really stupid, violent things.

I would get angry at myself for doing coke because I knew it messed me up, so I'd be in a bad mood and get into fights. I'd pick fights with anyone. I didn't care. I thought I was on a path to destruction. Live fast, die young. That was fine with me. Maybe it was better that way. One of the guys who played with the Barbed Wire Babies, Gus Gross, was always shooting up, and it wasn't always narcotics. One time he shot Budweiser because he couldn't find any heroin or speed.

There were no straight-edge people living at Apartment X. That wasn't the nature of NYHC at the time. If we weren't high on dust, Quaaludes or dope, we were piss drunk. There were bodegas everywhere that were open all night and would sell anyone beer. We drank even more in the winter because alcohol helped keep us warm. For a quick shot of warmth we'd drink what we liked to call skin juice, which is cheap brandy. That was a trick we learned from the bums in the park.

We hung out on the street with homeless people and drank with them around their bonfires at night. We laughed together and they told us crazy stories about what they used to do. A lot of them were lifelong deadbeats or schizophrenics, but some were Vietnam vets who had amazing war stories, as well as discouraging tales about how they were discarded by society after they returned home. Others told us about successful careers they had in the past before something—drugs, booze, mental illness, a girl—turned their lives to crap. It was interesting to hear them talk. You just didn't want to get too close because they smelled like a combination of shit and rotting meat.

There were a couple kids who crashed with us in Apartment X that were under the age of 15: Little Chris, Eric Casanova and my brother Freddy, who was the youngest of them all. Freddy stayed with me for a few weeks for the first time when he was seven and he was on vacation from school. I wanted to get him away from the anger and violence at home in Florida, so I brought him into the anger and violence of the New York hardcore scene. My mom was okay with it because she thought I had a real apartment (Mayra hadn't told her otherwise) and I'd show Freddy the tourist sites of New York like the Empire State Building and the skating rink in Rockefeller Center. That was a laugh. Freddy loved the hardcore scene from the start and took to it like a pyromaniac to a blowtorch. We used to hide him in a drum case and sneak him into shows. Then he'd come onstage with us and sing the Animals' "It's My Life." That was the first song Freddy ever sang onstage, and it was at a show at Great Gildersleeves on July 17, 1983, when we opened for GBH. The crowd loved it.

I have pictures of Freddy sitting on Raybeez's shoulders at a Bad Brains show, and Vinnie used to put him on his shoulders and mosh around in the pit with him. That probably wasn't too smart, but Freddy loved it and I sheltered him as much as I could. I wasn't gonna let him take part in full-on gang fights, but he definitely got a taste for the NYHC lifestyle. Everybody loved him and treated him like a little brother. We used to send him down the street to the bodega to bring us back some 40s when we were too wasted to go. At first he was nervous about doing it, but it only took a couple trips before he was traveling those two blocks with pride. He would walk in, get 40s without a problem and come right back. When we played CBGB we'd stick Freddy into the drum case, just like we did at A7 and Great Gildersleeves. Raybeez would lug him in. When Karen, the wife of owner Hilly Kristal, heard there was a kid in the club, she tried to crack down. She'd spend the whole afternoon at a CBGB matinee looking for Freddy. She knew he was there, but we'd tell her he wasn't. When she went back to her desk, we nearly pissed ourselves laughing.

Since none of us had jobs or were getting paid to play music, cash was in short supply, especially when we needed large amounts of it to buy drugs. We had to get creative, which usually meant doing something illegal, whether it was breaking and entering, holding someone up or selling hot credit cards. When we needed angel dust and didn't have the cash, we robbed drug dealers. Some people think I was the kingpin of the Agnostic Front fuck-ups since I was the vocalist, but I was never the guy to plan this shit. It was always Raybeez, and his weakness was angel dust. We were always on *his* missions. He was the crazy guy who made the decisions, and for some reason a lot of people followed him. He had the kind of charisma that prevented you from second-guessing his stupid decisions. I always went along because I liked hanging out with him, and we never caught too much trouble. Lots of bad shit could have gone down. We were just lucky, time and time again.

This was our game plan for ripping off dealers. We wouldn't rob anyone in the Lower East Side because that's where we lived and people knew who we were. You don't shit in your own backyard. We went up to Harlem, where Raybeez used to live.

He knew who the drug dealers were up there. We went into the buildings where they worked and scoped out the places. The guys who had the best drugs had the guards with the biggest guns. If you spotted a dude with a semi-automatic gun you knew you were gonna wind up with some pretty bad-ass shit. We'd send one guy in as a buyer to negotiate for whatever drugs we wanted. While that was happening, the rest of us would navigate around the guys with semi-autos. Usually, a couple of our guys jumped in from a rear window or down a fire escape. One of our dudes used a meat hook and held it to these dealers' faces, and that got the point across that we meant business. Most of these thugs didn't even know they were getting robbed until we were out the door and running to the van. When we jumped in, we'd hear people shouting and sometimes there were gunshots, but we were gone before they could see us. Thank God none of us ever got beaten up or shot.

With elation and adrenaline pumping, we felt high as fuck, even without drugs coursing through our system. Next thing we knew, we'd be on our way to Connecticut to play a show, blasting music in the van. Our token meat hook guy would be slamming and waving the hook around that he had just held up to these dealers' faces. We got away with everything, and we knew that if we got caught by the cops they didn't give a shit. They turned a blind eye to whatever we were doing, and the one time I tried to come clean and confess a crime they told me to get lost.

The whole scene was supposed to be simple, but it was really ugly. I needed cash so I snatched a lady's purse, but she held onto the strap. As I ran down the street I dragged her along with me. Her knees scraped the cement and she screamed like I was ripping out her scalp before she eventually let go and I ran away. At least I had the cash I needed to score. After I came down from my high I felt so bad for what I had done that I turned myself in at the local police precinct. I told them I had taken a lady's purse and then bought drugs and they should arrest me. They laughed and told me to get the fuck out of their building. Of all the crazy, illegal shit I pulled in my youth, that's the one act that still haunts me.

It wasn't until later that I realized the cops didn't care because the politicians told them to ignore us. We were part of a political game we didn't even know was being played. They were using us as guinea pigs to see if they could gentrify the Lower East Side. There was even a patrolman named Officer Craig who would casually check in on our crazy asses to see how their experiment was going. We were violent, degenerate trash that they were using to help clean up the streets. They knew we were underage and they saw us hanging out and drinking. Maybe they saw us doing drugs, too. I was probably too high to notice. But they always left us alone because we were pawns in a police campaign called Operation Pressure Point, which was designed to squeeze out the drug dealers in Alphabet City. In the early '80s it wasn't as easy as when Mayor Giuliani turned Times Square from a porn and prostitute mecca into Disney Central. He had lawyers for that. Operation Pressure Point just had hardcore kids and other freaks living on the Lower East Side. Back then, you couldn't walk more than a block or two without seeing a line of people waiting to score. It was casual, like people waiting for tickets to a movie, only some of these dudes were twitching and rubbing their arms, desperate for a fix that would end their withdrawal symptoms for a little while.

The gangs selling drugs and the shooting galleries made the Lower East Side gross and seedy and prevented people with money from moving into the area. The establishment realized that if they wanted to gentrify the area, they needed to clean up the vermin, so they encouraged our loud, after-hours punk rock shows in areas where these gangs were trying to sell drugs. The gangs didn't want us there because we were drawing crowds and that was chasing away their customers. To the police, that was exactly the point. When really popular bands like Bad Brains or Circle Jerks played a show, it interfered with dope sales. And that upset the dealers. They didn't want any shows going on, and they were happy to stab, club or beat on hardcore kids to get their point across.

We flirted with death lots of times, even at places that were right in our backyard. One time something was going on right by the A7 club with one of the members of the Hitmen. I went out there to try to talk down this gangster. He didn't dig that I was out there. Either he didn't believe we were just there to see music or he didn't care. He pulled out a knife and started coming at us. I pulled out my chain and swung it at him. He dodged it and took a stab at me and I blocked it with my hand. The blade slashed across my palm right through the flesh, but it didn't hit bone. He didn't get a second try. A bunch of our guys jumped in and wrestled the knife out of his hand, but he managed to run away from a serious beatdown.

None of us were old enough to drink, but the A7 club let us work the door and decide  whom to let into the club. They let us run the place. Doug Holland, who played guitar in Kraut and later the Cro-Mags, was the bartender, and Jimmy Gestapo was the DJ. He also worked the door with Raybeez and me, which is a good thing because sometimes two or three of us would have to lean against the door while the gangsters on the other side were kicking it and throwing their full weight against it. Most of them were at least a few years older than us. We're lucky they never burst down the door, and we're lucky we didn't all die in street fights.

A few times when I was working the door at the A7 Club, I'd hear a knock, open the door, see a fucking knife coming right at me, close the door and hear the *thunk* as the knife stabbed the door. The same thing happened to Raybeez and Jimmy. We all had to be street smart, but we easily could have gotten the shit kicked out of us if a gang barged in and went to town on us.

Most of the dudes in the NYHC community were decent enough people. A lot of them would steal, fight without provocation and smash stuff to pieces when they were pissed off, but I got along with nearly everyone, and those who were too weird were kicked out of the circle. But with the hardcore scene growing almost by the hour I couldn't keep track of everyone. Over the years some dodgy dudes infiltrated the scene.

There was a guy who used to hang out named Daniel Rakowitz. He called himself the marijuana guru and carried a chicken on his shoulder. We knew he was weird and we usually kept our distance, but there were times we broke bread with him and shared our food, and he went to our shows. He had a soup kitchen and used to feed homeless people all over Tomkins Square Park, which seemed admirable. "Maybe he wasn't so creepy after all. Maybe he's a caring guy." Maybe not.

One night, Daniel killed his girlfriend, Monika Beerle, who was a Swiss woman studying dance and paying for her tuition by working in a titty bar. I don't know if he was upset that she was a stripper or what, but he cut her up, made soup out of her and fed it to everybody in the park.

Police found out he killed her at his tenement building on 9th Street and Avenue C and arrested him in September 1989. Cops later found Monika's skull at the Port Authority Bus Terminal sitting in a bucket of cat litter. Rakowitz probably deserved the death penalty, but he was found not guilty by reason of insanity and went to a maximum security psychiatric prison on Ward Island.

Another tragic story involved Dave Insurgent (Rubenstein), the singer from Reagan Youth. He was incredible to watch with his band and a good guy to hang out with. But he got heavily into drugs. His girlfriend, Tiffany Bresciani, was a prostitute who was murdered by the serial killer Joel Rifkin.

The police caught Rifkin on June 28, 1993, when he was driving his pickup truck without license plates on the Southern State Parkway. They tried to pull him over and he accelerated to get away from them. There was a high-speed chase, and Rifkin crashed into a telephone pole. The cops had no idea why this guy was trying to run away from them, so they approached his totaled car with weapons drawn. When they smelled the stench from the back of his trashed truck, they opened it up and found Tiffany's dead body. As if that weren't crazy enough, the pole the guy crashed into was right in front of the courthouse where he was eventually tried and found guilty. In 1994 he was sentenced to 203 years in prison.

Dave Insurgent was so out of it on drugs when he was with her that he didn't know she was a prostitute and didn't know she had been killed. He owed a dealer a lot of money and they beat the shit out of him, nearly killing him. Rumor has it that a week later, his father accidentally ran over his mother while backing up the car. She died. Dave loved his mother but hated his father. Even though the smack he was on numbed what he was feeling, when he found out Tiffany and his mother were dead he killed himself by taking a fatal overdose.

# CHAPTER 11

In 1983, when Harley Flanagan got back from Canada, he had a chest tattoo of a big demon bat with its wings spread. He was the first person I knew who had full-on ink like that. It was badass. We started hanging out, partying a lot and getting into a shitload of trouble together. He was an individual, an angry individual, but he was who he was. Shit, I was angry, too. Over the next few years we became close friends—for better or worse. Like me, Harley was a skinhead, and while he was an angry, violent dude, he wasn't the stereotypical skinhead that the media were talking about. But he definitely had his demons, and sometimes they surfaced in dangerous, unpredictable ways.

Over the years we had a lot of crazy times and got in some bad fights, usually for no reason. It didn't take much for us to fly off the handle. We'd go around and mug yuppies that wandered too far into the East Village hunting for weed. We'd take their money and use it to buy booze. Once, we rolled a dude for his Rolex. We flipped the watch for about $150 and used the money to get tattoos in Coney Island at Mikey's Tattoos. Our attitude was: *We don't have any money. We need money to get tattoos. Let's fuckin' go rob somebody.*

We were ruthless, and we lived without fear. If we were walking down the street, people crossed to the other side. They could smell the danger and we reveled in the power. We became degenerate brothers—partners in crime. We'd go looking for fights, and we'd protect each other just like my stepdad had taught me.

Life was divided between the shit we did to survive, the crap we did for fun and the music we played because we loved it. All three worlds collided like pool balls during a break. We'd get in fights in the middle of each other's shows. We played drunk. We even did shows on angel dust. We didn't care. The shows rarely suffered.

Before the Cro-Mags formed, I jumped on bass and Harley played drums in the Cro-Mag Skins (a nickname for our inner-circle crew). From what I remember, he wrote the songs with his aunt Denise Mercedes, who was the main songwriter and guitarist for The Stimulators. I've also heard that Kevin "Parris" Mayhew banged out some of the riffs. Harley was excited to teach these songs to me. The next thing I knew, we were in the AF van, with Kevin showing me how to play the songs while Harley slapped out drumbeats on his legs. We took the stage on June 2, 1984, at V.I.P. in Brooklyn, which was the only Cro-Mag Skins show. It was the first time the Cro-Mags songs "World Peace" and "Life of My Own" were performed live. Agnostic Front headlined, and the opening bands were Death Before Dishonor, Crumbsuckers and Bedlam. Harley drummed, Kevin played guitar and little Eric Casanova was the singer. It was fun, but it was just a one-time thing.

Then Eric knocked up Lucy and they joined the Hare Krishna temple, so Harley asked me to audition to be their singer. I had already learned a few songs on bass and had heard the demo he made with his aunt countless times so I knew the material well, but I was unsure about joining the band. I already had AF. More importantly, Harley and I both liked to be leaders, not followers, and if we were in the same band we would butt heads. The songs he had were really good, and who knows how it would have gone? John Joseph was their clear choice anyway. He was eager and I was unsure. Another reason I showed up for the audition was because I wanted to chat with Kevin about starting a side project, which never took off.

There are a lot of stories I could tell about Harley and me, and they aren't all flattering. We ruled the streets, but we also did some shitty things that were worse than rolling yuppies. He was a talented kid and he had written songs for a long time. He was gifted but at the same time ruthless, angry and brutal—more brutal than I was and way more hateful. He was a loose cannon but a genuine friend. Together we could be poisonous to be around, and after a while the environment we were in became too toxic, so I had to distance myself.

Becoming a Hare Krishna saved Harley's life. I've openly confronted him about that, and he agreed with me. It may not work for everybody, but for a lot of people who are on merciless, violent paths, spirituality—be it Christianity, Krishna conscious-ness or whatever—can motivate them to change their ways, even if that path never worked for me.

Being a bassist meant I performed for a bunch of New York hardcore bands. Any time a group had a problem with their bassist they'd call me, so I filled in for Rat Poison Band, Warzone, Psychos, Sheer Terror and a few others. I tried to join Sheer Terror in the very beginning because Paul Bearer was a good friend. I'd forgotten that being in two bands didn't work out for me when I was in the Psychos. Eventually both of us had shows and we had to be in two different places at the same. That's when I realized I couldn't commit myself to Sheer Terror anymore.

One night in 1983, I played in three of the bands on a five-band bill—the Psychos, Verbal Assault (what Rat Poison Band was originally called) and Agnostic Front. Even on speed, it was exhausting.

I wasn't the only one band-hopping. Adam Mucci had played for Agnostic Front and Murphy's Law, and Harley played for M.O.I., Murphy's Law and Frontline. He even filled in for us once at A7, if my memory serves me right. None of us felt like we were competing against other bands in the scene. We were all part of one big movement and if someone couldn't make it to a show, someone gladly filled in.

I got to know Jimmy Gestapo because he was a big Psychos fan and we were both at A7 a lot. Once I was in Agnostic Front we started hanging out more and we really connected. Jimmy was a nutjob who was famous for his head stomp. Out of nowhere, he'd jump offstage while wearing boots that seemed to be made out of iron. He wouldn't dive into the pit like most people. He'd walk across people or, rather, stomp them into submission. God help whoever was standing below where he was stomping.

We always had a fun time playing with Murphy's Law, so we booked plenty of shows together. It was a good combination because we sounded quite different. A lot of times you got two bands that did the same thing and you could hardly tell one from the other. Murphy's Law did this reggae/punk thing, too, and we were straight-up New York hardcore. We were tight with a lot of New York City bands, some of which most people have never heard of: Urban Waste, Major Conflict, Killer Instinct, XKI, Savage Circle, Antidote, The Mob, The Undead, Rapid Deployment, Death Before Dishonor,

Scab, Blood, Cause For Alarm, Final Confrontation, Anti-Warfare, Counterforce, No Thanks, Whorelords, Crucial Truth, Reagan Youth, Kraut, Ultra Violence, High and Mighty, No Control, Gilligan's Revenge, Bad Posture, Mark Truthe and the Liars! And lots more. We always welcomed Jersey bands, including Mental Abuse, Fatal Rage, Child Abuse, Genocide, The Worst, NJF, Pleased Youth, Public Disturbance AOD and Bedlam. My attitude was: *Bring it on. The more, the merrier. Just don't sabotage our shows or we'll knock your fuckin' teeth out.*

About four months after I moved into Apartment X, I met Amy, who would become the first girl I truly loved. I met her at a show just after I'd broken up with Kym. She was on tour with Whipping Boy, a hardcore band from California, and had just left them in Chicago and hitchhiked to NYC.

I was psyched they were in New York, and we were hanging out with them before their show when Amy popped out of their van. She struck me right away with her black and blonde mohawk, blue jean miniskirt, fishnet tights, black wife beater, studded denim vest with a Discharge patch on the back and a loop bondage belt. She seemed different than the New York girls I had been with, who all had tattoos and a harder edge. They were tough LES Girls. Amy was not that. She could be stubborn and rigid, but she was a California punk. She abhorred violence.

Amy went back home to California for a few weeks after that and then returned to New York to start going to school at New York University. On her first day back, she was walking down St. Marks and I was hanging out on the street. I called out "Hey, you're back!" She didn't recognize me. She said she was looking for work and I told her I could probably get her a job at Free Being Records. It was just a line to get her to talk to me, but I thought they might be hiring. Later that day, we went to Free Being and I introduced her to Antoinette, who was running the store. There were no job openings, but Amy stuck around for a while and that night we got drunk in Tompkins Square Park. Nothing happened and I didn't get her number, but I knew I'd see her again.

# PART III

## Fronting an Empire: Constructing an Underground Nation from the Ground Up

# CHAPTER 12

Agnostic Front used to practice in a weird space in SoHo we called AIDS Studio. It was a big boiler room that looked like something out of *Nightmare on Elm Street* between the Bowery and Christie on Grand. Raybeez nicknamed the place AIDS Studio because he thought the guy who owned it was dying from AIDS.

The studio was in the owner's house. You had to climb down ladders to get to the basement. It was like descending into the bowels of hell. It was dark, smelled like mold and vomit and was the hottest place I've ever practiced in. After we went in there he closed the place up. There was no ventilation, which made it hard to breathe, and we were locked down there until we were done practicing.

Raybeez was never politically correct and he didn't have the best judgment. He made me break up with Chessie and got me in lots of situations that could have gotten me killed—robbing armed drug dealers for angel dust is just one example—but I loved the guy! Everything he did cracked me up, even if he wasn't trying to make me laugh. When we rehearsed at AIDS Studio it was so hot that we took our clothes off and practiced in our underwear. It would take Ray 20 minutes to get all his layers removed. Three or four songs into practice, and we'd be dripping with sweat.

Nobody knew much about AIDS back then, so everyone was freaked out that they might catch the disease if they touched anything in the place. The disease hadn't really spread outside the gay community yet, but there was still a big public hysteria about it. We didn't know it was a blood-transmitted virus that you could only get by sharing needles or having sex with someone who was infected. It was a big mystery. Even so, we didn't leave AIDS Studio because we were scared of getting AIDS. We left because it was hot, disgusting and super-uncomfortable.

In the middle of 1983, we upped our game and started rehearsing at Don Fury's place at 18 Spring Street, which was totally pro. When we practiced I had to be careful that I didn't bang into an expensive piece of gear and break it. The band had used the place before I joined them, but they stopped because AIDS Studio was much cheaper. Then we sucked it up and went back. At the time, Don was learning about producing and engineering and practiced by recording bands. Any time we went into his studio we got a tape out of it.

Vinnie still has a live CBGB's board tape of the band from when John Watson was singing with them. I believe it's the only recording of the original lineup that exists. He played it for me once and it sounded incredibly raw and primitive. It was so hard I got chills down my spine. I guess I knew from the start that I was made for Agnostic Front. Sink or swim, this was going to be the band I would be known for.

When we went to Don's we'd bring over a Maxell 60-minute cassette tape. We couldn't afford the high bias XLII, so we'd only use them if someone stole some before practice. More often, we'd use the normal bias UR60s, and those were good enough. Even though they were pretty low quality, the playing was, too, so it balanced out. When we got back home we'd listen to the tape and decide if something wasn't working—even though we were such a mess back then that if something *did* work it was usually a total coincidence. We practiced at the place where Don had his two- and four-track recorders, but he owned another practice space on 17th Street. He got it in the late '70s and artists like The Voidoids, Glenn Branca, the Bush Tetras and The Stimulators practiced there. Even so, we were the first hardcore punk band Don produced.

Vinnie wrote a lot of the lyrics for our first EP, *United Blood*, which would have been fine if they had made any sense. I sang them because it was all I had. Now, the songs are classic and iconic so nobody cares about the words. Check out the title track: "I'm a skin, you're a skin / Who's gonna suffer / Live in sin, where you been?" I still don't know what the fuck that means. One day I brought two songs to a session—"Fight," which was a Psychos song, and a new one I wrote called "Discriminate Me"—and we added them to our playlist. I don't know what Don thought about the music, but I could tell he was fascinated with us as individuals and blown away that an entire scene had grown around this music. He wanted to get in on the ground floor and he started with us, partially because we were already there.

We didn't put much thought into *United Blood*. We approached it as if it was just another rehearsal session, which it pretty much was. We had practiced the songs a lot so we knew how to make them sound powerful. We played everything live as if we were doing a show. Don hit record, Raybeez did a four-count with his sticks and we had an instant two-track cassette. We listened to it and made copies of it to pass off to friends to get everyone's opinion. Then on June 3, 1983, we went back for the final recording, which was on a four-track; that was the only difference. We did the same songs. Everything was live again, and despite the improvement in recording equipment, it sounded pretty much the same.

The EP came out in November 1983 and people immediately loved it. But I never thought of it as a true Agnostic Front release. I had joined the band in April 1983 and hadn't really found my place or my vocal style. We didn't overdub anything on the album or even remix it, so it was raw and primitive-sounding. We were like a guinea pig experiment for Don. I guess it worked because after he produced us, he went on to do records with a whole lot of bands, including Youth of Today, Gorilla Biscuits, Sick of It All, Judge and Warzone.

When I say *United Blood* wasn't a "real" AF release I'm only talking about the sound of the EP and the fact that I wasn't the main lyricist/songwriter back then. It was definitely a fierce-sounding record—not that we knew it right away. Even after it was recorded, we didn't have any idea how good *United Blood* sounded until we got the acetate (the vinyl template companies used to mass-produce records). We took the acetate to the local record stores like Rat Cage Records, Venus and Freebeing Records, another favorite hang-out shop on Second Avenue that used to screen punk rock movies like *The Great Rock and Roll Swindle*—all to hear how it sounded on their stereo system.

Then I made a dumb mistake. I thought Bleecker Bob's Records was a credible place. I dropped off my acetate for *United Blood* and a week later I went back to the store to pick it up and ask the owner, Bob, what he thought. He said he hadn't listened to it yet. I told him I'd come back in a week and he'd better have listened to it by then. I told him he'd love it. When I came back, he said he still hadn't heard it.

I was suspicious so I jumped over the counter and started throwing records aside and looking for my acetate. I didn't find it, so I got mad and started smashing seven-inch records. I accused him of stealing my acetate and waved each single in front of his face before I broke it. He ran to the back and called the police, and they filed a restraining order against me.

For many years, I never knew what happened to that *United Blood* acetate. I wondered if I had unjustly accused the guy. Then in 2012, a friend of mine emailed me and told me he had an original acetate of *United Blood*. Since I knew there were no other copies, I knew it must be the one I had given to Bob. My friend said he had gotten the acetate from a friend in Virginia who had bought it from Bleecker Bob's. I can only guess what they got for it.

**Vinnie and Ethan assembling United Blood 7-inches.**

# CHAPTER 13

Originally *United Blood* was going to be a Mob Style Records release, but we decided to do it ourselves under the guidance of Mob Style label-owner and The Mob guitarist Jack Flanagan. We called our label Last Warning, and for the logo we had a political artist named Stencil Invader make a drawing of a skinhead covering one eye with his hand, symbolizing skepticism about what others perceive as absolute truth. Aside from having a good idea for the logo and some ripping tunes, we didn't know what the hell we were doing since we had no experience making records. Fortunately, Jack was happy to show us the ropes. Our friend Ran-D Underwood, who was pretty much the first dedicated NYHC photographer, shot the cover art of the band onstage. We gave Randy's photo and the rest of the artwork to a print shop where our friend, Glen Schuler, manufactured three long rolls of the *United Blood* sleeve images. They looked like giant rolls of wallpaper printed with the images from the record.

Vinnie, Raybeez and I, along with my new girlfriend, Fee, and our friend, Lea, cut all the covers off and taped them together by hand. We then inserted 500 seven-inch vinyl discs and the photo collage inserts into plastic sleeves. We gave 300 copies of the EP to Jack, and Mob Style Records acted as the distributor, sending the seven-inch all over America. A hundred copies went to Rat Cage Records for New York City sales, and we kept the other 100 records to sell on the street. We practically forced people to buy them. We'd go up to total strangers who looked like they might be into punk rock and said, "Hey, we have this record for sale. It's two dollars." They either bought it because they wanted it or to shut us up. Or they were scared of us and figured handing over two bucks was better than getting mugged or taking a beating.

The people who bought *United Blood* on the street got a great deal, not only because they got the first copies of what turned out to be an influential record but also because there was a misprint on the 100 copies we sold. The A-side said "Agnostic Front" while the B-side, which was supposed to have the skinhead logo, had a blank white label. We were pretty pissed off about that. As it turned out, the skinhead label went on some disco record by mistake. I like to imagine some disco chick in a tight, fashionable miniskirt, carefully painted nails and fuck-me pumps scrunching up her face and trying to figure out why this skinhead logo was on the label of the dance single she had just bought.

We thought we were the shit because we finally had a record out, but to most people we were still just street punks and scumbags. They were kind of right. These tough guys we'd run into in the Village would be walking with their girls and they'd get all macho and challenge us. We usually took them up on their offer and kicked their asses. Then a new group of shitheads would walk by and make fun of what we looked like. We beat them up, too. But they had a point. In truth, we looked like Smurfs with Mohawks and shaved heads. We wore baggy, patched-up pants, sweaters and military boots with big knit hats. The funny thing is that our basic look became trendy a decade later when hip-hop became big.

What no one understood was that those were our layers. That's how we stayed warm and that's all we had. Most of us went into these squats without full wardrobes and wore those layers of clothes for a month or two without changing them. When you do that, your clothes get baggy. I had a Sham 69 shirt, and I wore that for four or five months straight.

We played shows to support *United Blood* and a lot of people who bought the EP in the streets and at Rat Cage Records started showing up. Jack Flanagan did a great job with U.S. distribution, and next thing we knew, we were getting some good underground press and fan mail. We were excited to see anything anyone wrote about us. We didn't care if they loved us or hated us.

Then a writer for this crappy but influential fanzine, *Maximumrocknroll,* started talking shit about us and calling us a bunch of fascist skinheads. That was total bullshit. We were united street punks from harsh upbringings, not university-educated punks with privileged backgrounds who liked writing about hardcore—like the guys at the magazine. We were living the turmoil of the music, mired in the filth, muck and blood of the street, not sitting in a vacuumed office thinking we were hard because we turned up the volume on records we got for free.

*Maximumrocknroll* and their ilk associated the name Agnostic Front with some sort of organized hate group, like the National Front, a movement in the U.K. that caused havoc in the punk/skinhead scene. If you listen to any of the lyrics on *United Blood*—as little sense as they make—they're still clearly about unity and self-empowerment. We've always been anti-war, anti-religion and anti-society, but pro-individual. We've never put down any other races or ethnicities. From the start, we welcomed anyone who wanted to be a part of what we were doing. I was Cuban for Christ's sake—far from the image of the blond-haired, blue-eyed Aryan *Übermensch*.

As angry as we were about the way we were being portrayed, there's a saying that any publicity is good publicity, and for us that proved to be true. We went to places like Cincinnati and people who had only heard of us because of those *Maximumrocknroll* articles came to the shows. We did our normal, energetic show and blew them the fuck away. A lot of them vibed with our anti-establishment message and came back for more.

Eventually, Apartment X got too crowded and I didn't like some of the people who were moving in. It wasn't like they were hardcore fuck-ups who needed a place to live. A lot of them wanted to be where they thought the cool people were or wanted to be around musicians who could help their band. I signed over the lease to Tony "T-Shirt," who printed up all the shirts for the NYHC bands and sang in Ultra Violence. I moved to a place on Second Street between avenues A and B that had belonged to Robbie and Michelle CryptCrash. It wasn't a mansion, but it wasn't as decrepit as Apartment X.

That's where I was living when I started writing our debut album, *Victim In Pain*. While we were working on the record, Todd Youth replaced Adam Mucci, who quit to stay in Murphy's Law. Todd was 13 years old when he joined Agnostic Front and he was a wild kid. He constantly ran away from home. His parents hired private investigators that would hunt him down. It wasn't that hard to find him. There were only so many places we hung out. Usually, the investigators would show up with his parents at CBGB or another bar and take him home—until he ran away again. Detectives were always knocking on the door looking for Todd. It was annoying, but worth it because he was a good bass player and fit right in with our crazy environment.

When Todd and I started working on new songs we were practically the only people living around Second Street. It was cool because there weren't any neighbors bothering us, but it was kind of dangerous. The streets were inhabited by junkies, drunks and criminals, and when one of them annoyed me I'd usually wind up storming out into the street to beat some heads. To be honest, I didn't think anything of it. If I had stopped to rationalize the situation I would have felt like I was in the right since they were the ones that were making noise or disturbing my concentration. That's how selfish and fucked up I was.

While there wasn't anything going on where we lived, down the avenues to the right were a few poor families and squatters. The landlord of the place where we lived never confronted us, so we never saw him. But we sure heard him. He used to blast Louis Farrakhan speeches all the time, almost louder than the hardcore tapes we would crank on a boombox. The grit, decay and danger of the city motivated me to write some pretty pointed lyrics, and Todd and I jammed out the music. We came up with some storming shit.

Gradually, a bunch of creative people moved into the neighborhood and a few restaurants opened, which was good for us—not because we had a place to spend money on food. It was even easier than that. We'd wait on the sidewalk and watch until someone who had eaten a big meal was almost done. We'd pretend we were just hanging out, then when the customer got up we'd charge in and steal the tip money. Suddenly, we had money for food, booze, drugs—whatever we wanted.

Being a Hispanic dude in New York, I surrounded myself with all kinds of people from all kinds of backgrounds and ethnicities. New York was built as a haven for immigrants and refugees, and most of us learned how to live with one other. Anyone within the community knew how open-minded we all were and took it for granted that this was the way it was everywhere. We soon learned that wasn't the case. Not long after ignorant and prejudiced people from other cities started labeling us as right-wing fascists, people who had been hiding in the scene—but who actually held those bigoted views—started to surface and latch onto us. They thought we were cut from the same cloth as they were and wanted us to be a part of their movement. That wouldn't happen because we wouldn't tolerate it. But some of these individuals tried anyway. They saw we were skinheads and that was enough for them. They didn't bother to look at our lyrics and see that our philosophies were completely different.

Neither did the privileged, politically correct hardcore fans in other cities, which judged us, labeled us and wrote us off because they wanted someone in the scene to talk shit about. None of them ever did any research into what we were all about. They just had these knee-jerk reactions. We hated that and we hated them. They were just plain ignorant. At the same time, I was ignorant, too, and unaware about how the way I looked gave people the wrong idea about who I really was.

I was looking to get a new tattoo. Being high on Quaaludes, I temporarily forgot about the episode with the Jewish woman at the airport and considered getting the Sex Pistols' "Destroy" image on my chest. But something about doing that felt wrong in my gut. Then I fell in love with a piece I saw in a fanzine called *Trans Am Digest* by Mike Spats, whose illustrations were often politically motivated. It was a drawing of Christ on a cross, wearing a gas mask and with the American flag draped around his waist. It said everything I was feeling socially and politically and symbolized every-thing the band stood for. It was anti-war, anti-religion, anti-authority.

For a while, our landlord was pretty lax about collecting rent, which was good because we didn't have any money to pay him. Maybe he was afraid of us. If so, he figured out a way so that he didn't have to look us in the eye and possibly walk away with a bloody lip or worse. He started to send pretty big people around to remind us that we owed him months of back rent. That's when a bunch of us realized we couldn't muscle our way out of the situation. It was time to move out.

Raybeez, Jenny and I got Keith Burkhardt and Angelica's old place on 6th Street between avenues B and C. A short while later, Harley and Little Chris moved in and Todd Youth and Steve Poss crashed there a lot. That was an interesting place to live because there was a decent rehearsal studio on the corner of B and 6th called Tucasa, so there were always musicians hanging around. Most of them weren't punks, but that was cool. I've always gotten along with all kinds of musicians. It doesn't matter what they played—rock, jazz, Latino—we had the same artistic drive and need to create so we saw eye to eye.

Unlike the places I had lived where I was surrounded by abandoned buildings, there were lots of tenement apartments around 6th Street and they were all inhabited by Puerto Ricans. Any time the LES girls wanted to do something, like go to the store, we had to go with them because we never knew what was gonna happen. They didn't even know I spoke Spanish until I had to. By then it was sometimes too late to avoid a confrontation. But we didn't stay there long.

We all bounced from place to place a lot. Usually, we'd move for one of two reasons. We found a better place to live or we were pressured to vacate. Jenny and I squatted with Little Chris, Raybeez, John Joseph, Harley Flanagan, Tommy Rat, Richie Stiggs, Todd Youth, Frenchie and Bobby Snotz from one burned-out, abandoned building to another up and down Ninth Street, between avenues C and D. Since the places didn't have any heating, we'd stick together and huddle around a fire for warmth.

Life in the squats wasn't easy. Finally, we found a place we called the Eastern Front, where we thought we could stay for a while even though there was no running water or electricity. There weren't even windows. There was basically just a door. We figured out how to barricade it so no one could get in. Everything was unsafe and dilapidated. I had my own little spot on the third floor with a kid named Mike from Long Island. One night, he fell through the stairs and ripped his ball sack open. We didn't have a phone so someone ran down the street to hail the police and an ambulance came. He's still alive and to this day he only has one nut.

We lit the Eastern Front with candles, which was stupid, considering how often we accidentally knocked over the candles or fell asleep over an open flame. Sure enough, one night the place went up in flames. But it wasn't from the candles. The scumbag slumlord apparently paid a few junkies to burn it down. All my friends got out okay, but a few people died. We could have all been killed in the blaze. For the landlord, we were just vermin that needed to be exterminated. If he could torch his building and collect the insurance, all the better.

After the Eastern Front burned down, we kept on squat-bouncing. Sometimes there would be junkies or homeless people sprawled out in one of the places we wanted to move into and we'd have to chase them out. We went in with pit bulls and the dogs usually scared them away. Anyone that was too wasted or stupid to leave on their own got beaten up and dragged out into the street. Getting them out was one thing. Getting rid of the stink was another.

# CHAPTER 14

**A** my was living in the NYU dorm while I was moving between squats, but she came to our shows, which convinced me that I could win her over. After one concert we hung out and she looked even better than she did the first time I saw her. She had dyed her hair purple, there was a glint for adventure in her eye and she wore a smile that could calm a charging bull.

A couple days later I stopped by her dorm and dropped off a copy of *United Blood* as a gift. Maybe I should have brought her flowers instead, but she appreciated the gesture and she loved the music. We started dating. I started staying overnight at her dorm, which was against school policy. They didn't allow overnight guests, but I would go there for days and never leave. It didn't take long for us to fall in love. She wasn't the kind of girl I usually went for, but love is strange. Attraction and lust are much more predictable, but you don't know when love is gonna hit you and how it's going to alter your life.

I stopped by her dorm a bunch of times, sometimes with my crew, and I'd leave little gifts or notes with specific hang-out details, local shows, little jokes and ramblings of how I liked her and thought she was really cool.

The first time I stayed over at her dorm, we stayed up the entire night talking. I felt comfortable with her, so I spilled my guts and explained what had happened in my childhood and how I ran away and moved to the Lower East Side. I think she was taken aback by how honest I was. She later told me I was nothing like what she thought I would be. She said we were polar opposites in a lot of ways, but she felt like I balanced her world. I think that's when she fell for me. In the days that followed, I'd go over and help her with her school film projects. Sometimes my friends and I acted in them.

After frequently going to her dorm and staying the night, she moved in with me at a place I found on Avenue C. We stayed there for a little while and did all the things young couples in love do that used to make me sick. We spent so much time together that I ruined her academic career. She was doing well at NYU and then she moved in with me and didn't go back to school for years. During that time, we were inseparable.

She wasn't covered in tattoos like a lot of the girls I used to fall for. She was a peace punk, so she got grief from her friends for being with me since there was a stupid rivalry between educated punks and hardcore kids. For a little while we were the Sid and Nancy of the New York hardcore scene. When I was single I fucked around a lot, but everything with Amy was deeper and more intense. It was like we were meant to be together. I thought we would be together forever. I thought when I died I'd still be with Amy. My family upbringing made me cynical about marriage and family, and for years I shut down my heart to protect myself. Amy opened my emotions back up, at least a little, and made me a tiny bit of a romantic.

Even though Amy gave me hope for a future, I was still a hooligan at heart. And nothing fuels a misfit's appetite better than a rivalry with out-of-towners. Like I said, I felt a kinship with most of the New York bands, but groups from Boston were another story. I have to admit that Boston had some pretty great hardcore bands that I respected, including SS Decontrol, Jerry's Kids, Gang Green, The Freeze, DYS and Negative FX.

Today I look at those bands, nod my head and think, "Respect." Back in the '80s the bands didn't want our respect. They thought they were better than us and came to New York to prove it. What a dumb idea that was. You're a band with a chip on your shoulder and you're coming to a city where everyone in the audience is proud to be from the place you're shitting on? It doesn't take much thinking to realize that's gonna blow up in your face.

Many Boston punks assumed New York City hadn't changed much since the infamous art-punk scene that was led by bands like The Velvet Underground, Richard Hell & the Voidoids and Television. True, NYHC may have evolved more slowly than scenes in Boston or D.C., but once the Bad Brains hit the New York scene it was game over. We caught up fast. We identified with this new, young scene of raging vocals, furious riffs and speed-of-sound tempos.

A lot of Boston hardcore bands were militant straight edge. They claimed to adhere to a code of celibacy and sobriety. To me that just meant they were too uptight to have fun. SS Decontrol—one of my all-time favorite bands and one of the Boston bands that regularly played New York—was the spark that unintentionally ignited the rivalry with NYHC. Even NYC straight edge band The Abused weren't as militant, and the New York scene focused on bringing people together with what the Bad Brains called PMA—rather than dividing people because they were straight edge or they partied. We were a community of misfits who lived on the street and knew how to handle ourselves. For the most part, the dudes from Boston didn't expect us to come on as strong as we did. There were some ugly confrontations when we played Boston and when they played New York. There were always fights and we usually won.

At one point, we put up a big sign at the A7 club right in front of where a big Joe Strummer mural now stands, and it said, "Out of town bands remember where you are." It was a declaration that it they were gonna talk shit, they were going to be speaking to a hostile audience and it would probably end badly for them.

A lot of skins from Boston thought they were tough, and some of them were, but the decks were stacked against them. Even if they could fight, they hadn't fought for their very survival. Even if they were tough, they hadn't been schooled by the challenges of squatting on the Lower East Side.

Basically, the scenes in Boston and D.C. were made up of kids growing up in suburban areas. Some of these kids went to private schools and took their allowance money and bought hardcore records. While they were sitting in their bedrooms losing their shit to hardcore or practicing in their parents' basements, we were outside, writhing with rage, just waiting for an excuse to kick somebody's ass. Of course, not all kids from rival cities had it made. Some came from similar upbringings and held their own in fights. There were tough, respectable figures in every scene.

I started hating bands that I loved so much because they were dissing me and my scene. I didn't hate them because they were straight edge or had a different lifestyle than I did. Their private lives were their own business. I loved the music of Minor

Threat and SS Decontrol. I was a huge fan of SSD vocalist Springa. Stigma loved Al Barile's guitar style. Al was the primary force behind that band, and following his lead, they took extremism one step further than Minor Threat.

Minor Threat was always a punk band in my eyes, and even though Ian MacKaye sang what he sang, he didn't look down on people that didn't follow his beliefs. That's how Springa was, too. Al was another story. He was more into the militant straight edge scene and some of those guys looked down on us because we liked to party and get laid. At least we were honest about it.

Some of the Boston bands, or at least the people that traveled with them, were confrontational when they came to New York. There was a guy named Punky Paul who had the balls to wear a "Kill New York" T-shirt at a show in New York! Obviously, the dudes I hung with were not having it and he was outnumbered and in rival territory. The first time we went to play Boston was in 1984 and we figured some shit was gonna go down. It was Agnostic Front, Murphy's Law and Void at a VFW Hall. Dicky Barrett from the Mighty Mighty Bosstones was at the show. "I wish those New York guys would go back home with that wall of death," he said.

Before we even got in a van to head to Boston, we heard a rumor that the Boston bands wanted to get back at New York that night. We figured that might happen so we went up fully loaded. Everyone from our scene was there. It was basically a New York show in Boston. During our set all hell broke loose. Our drummer, Dave Jones, stopped playing because everyone jumped onstage and messed with our equipment to instigate a fight. He walked out from behind his set, went up to the mic and said, "Would you stop fighting? We're trying to play our songs!"

We knew shit was about to go down and we were ready. All the LES girls were there, and the New York girls were the hardest. It was packed and everyone was ready to brawl. The girls jumped on people and attacked them. These guys in Boston who were ready to take on the New York dudes didn't want to punch the girls, who scratched their faces and necks and kicked them in the balls. We just swung at anyone that got too close. That was the point when the Boston crew realized they'd made a serious tactical error. We wiped the floor with them. The next time we played Boston we were welcomed. People realized that they couldn't continue to have beef with New York because we were pissed off, street-smart and tougher than they thought we were.

SSD played the Rock Hotel for the last time in late 1984 after they released *How We Rock*. The first thing Springa said was, "We're here to play for you, not against you." He wanted to end the bad blood. That marked the beginning of the end of whatever feud still existed between the two scenes.

Of course, there was always a rivalry between Boston and New York, but throughout the years the stories got blown out of proportion. As time passed and we toured more through each other's turf, we became friends, which is the way it should have been in the first place. Being rivals doesn't necessarily make you enemies.

Eventually, Amy and I had to leave the place on Avenue C, but winter was over so it wasn't a problem. Sometimes we slept in my van, which I had bought for touring, and on warm nights we stayed in Tompkins Square Park with the bums. We didn't care. We were so into each other that as long as we were together, wherever we were felt like home. The van wasn't as low rent as it sounds. I built a loft, and when we were on tour, I stored my equipment under it. Sometimes we'd park illegally and wake up just as a tow truck was lifting the van to drag it away. Sometimes people tried to break in and jolted us out of bed.

We bathed in the fire hydrants, which sounds more romantic than it is, especially in winter! Our living situation was okay when we were in New York. But when we toured, Amy had to find a place to sleep every night. After each show we'd drive to the next gig and do the whole thing again. That got to be a drag, and we didn't have any money. I came up with a plan to score some cash, which would allow us to get a cheap place together.

*The New York Times* was 25 cents every day except Sunday, when it cost a dollar and everyone bought it. I followed a *New York Times* truck and stole as many papers as I could fit underneath a compartment in my van, so that I could go somewhere else and sell them. I planned to sell them all for a buck apiece. In my head, I was already counting the money. Then I got caught.

Some other idiot had pulled the same stunt weeks before, so a private investigator was following trucks around. I was getting ready to close the door of my van when I heard police sirens. Five or six cars pulled up. Amy was still sleeping. They woke her up by handcuffing her wrists and dragging her out of the van in her underwear. I thought, *Oh, shit! I'm really in trouble.*

As usual, I was a smart-ass to the cops.

"What are you going to do with all these newspapers?" asked one tall cop with a strong New York accent.

"Oh, I got a pet horse and need to put paper under him so he can shit and piss," I replied.

The police arrested me, and I spent a day in the city jail with petty criminals. It was my first taste of life behind bars. They fined me $250 and gave me seven days of community service. I never showed up for the community service.

Amy and I moved into a place above Robbie and Michelle CryptCrash's apartment on 2nd Street between avenues A and B. It was a small, ramshackle building amongst empty, trashed-out vacant lots, flipped-over burnt-out cars and shooting galleries. Our space was fairly big and clean, and the junkies in the neighborhood were on the verge of getting swept away by Operation Pressure Point. Freddy stayed there with us, as did a bunch of other crazies from the scene.

The landlord hated white people and would say abusive shit to us from his little porch. His boyfriend lived across the hall from us and we were civil until my pit bull, Warrior, ate his kitten. He came out in a kimono and was calling for his "kitty" and we had to tell him what happened. The poor guy was screaming and crying. He was beside himself.

Even though Amy was with me, she was going to the School of Visual Arts during that time. All things considered, we were pretty happy. Then I got a call telling me to come to Florida right away. Freddy had shot his best friend, Michael, with my step-dad's gun.

Freddy was eight years old, and he and Michael were hanging out in the house. My sister was watching them, but she stepped out to go to the corner store for milk. Freddy found my stepdad's gun on top of the refrigerator and started playing with it. He pointed it at Michael and pulled the trigger.

Someone heard the shot and called the police, and when my sister came back to the house, there were cop cars everywhere and Michael was covered in blood. No one knew how bad it was. As it turned out, the bullet went clean through his shoulder. Thank God it didn't hit any organs or major arteries. Everyone was shaken up, but the shooting was ruled an accident, so Freddy didn't have to go to juvie. Once I realized everything was okay, I went back to New York and we focused on writing our first full-length album, *Victim In Pain*.

We lived lifetimes between *United Blood* and *Victim In Pain,* but it was actually less than a year. I had accumulated enough life experience to write a box set. Vinnie was happy to let me write most of the songs on *Victim In Pain*, which was exciting because I was assuming a more prominent role in the band. I wasn't just screaming someone else's stuff that I didn't really feel. There was one song that was a carryover from *United Blood*, "Last Warning," and "Power" was a song Vinnie had from his previous band, The Eliminators. I had an entry point to start writing from and I jumped in.

There was a challenge and opportunity for me to express myself, and I had a lot to say because I was changing as a person and going through growing pains. *Victim In Pain* had songs that were angry but somewhat positive, like "United and Strong" and "Remind Them." It was music about the strength that existed within the hardcore community and how a lot of us had developed the ability to overcome rough upbringings by sticking together and being a part of a movement. I wanted to speak out against oppression. We had learned not to trust cops or any other authority figures. We believed that you didn't have to follow other people's orders to succeed. You could be successful on your own terms. There was an anti-establishment message in songs like "Blind Justice." One of the lines I love is "There's no justice / There's just us!" I'd love to say that was mine, but it wasn't. When I joined Agnostic Front they already had a song called "No Justice." It had a different structure. There are rare recordings of it from early demos. I took bits from those and restructured them musically and lyrically. I was determined to help bring the scene together and let people know that there is no justice. It's just us out there and we had to rely on each other because nobody else would stick up for us or watch our backs.

Amy hated my form of street justice. The more she got to know me, the more she saw the side of me she didn't like—the drugs, the anger, the violence. I said some pretty stupid shit in front of her when I was wasted—crazy, retarded thug shit. I acted tough and punched people out because I was high and mad. It was never people in our scene because I had a lot of respect for them. It was mostly people who talked shit about us. But Amy didn't approve. She was a peace punk, and after she joined

Nausea in 1986 and saw a lot more of the shit that went down in the NYC music scene, she was even more convinced that violence didn't solve anything.

To me, violence was often the only answer to a dangerous situation. I reacted with fierce intensity depending on how high I was—especially when a friend of mine was in trouble. I ran to rescue dudes who got in bad situations, and in the process, smashed a few people and did some stupid, illegal shit. In the end, we left a lot of people on the ground. I don't think we killed anyone, but we came close.

On more than several occasions, a friend of mine from a respected band, who had a reputation for starting shit, got into a fight with a bunch of people. He was a pretty scrappy dude, but when he was outnumbered there was no way he could take on all those thugs alone. I'd see him swinging away and realized he was in trouble, so I came running out, frequently high on angel dust. I'd pull out whatever weapon I had on me and started attacking arms, legs, shoulders. I avoided faces, necks and chests since I didn't want to take someone out and get arrested for second degree murder or manslaughter.

I don't know if my friend picked the fights or if these guys started up with him. All I knew was that he was in trouble and someone was going to get hurt, maybe lots of people. Amy was right about me. I was out of control and didn't deserve her. I was a fuckin' chaotic, hopped-up nutjob. After I hooked up with Amy, I genuinely got more into uniting the skins and the punks and became less angry at the world. But I was still too aggressive and fought too often. I'd come home with blood on my shirt and face. Sometimes it was my own, but usually it was someone else's.

"Hey, baby," I'd slur. "How's it going?"

She'd glare at me and walk away. It wasn't long before she dumped me.

"Roger, I love you, but I hate being around you when you're like this." That was it. Straight and simple.

After Amy left me I was devastated. I was depressed and angry. The more I thought about it the madder I got, until one day I just went crazy. I destroyed everything in the apartment and started doing lots of Quaaludes and drinking. That made me even more aggressive. To an extent, I was living up to the image of the wild, self-destructive adolescent. Every era has them. There were the greasers and the James Dean bad-boys in America in the '50s and the mods and rockers in England in the '60s, like in *Quadrophenia* by The Who. The Stones revealed the ugly side of the hippie generation and set shit off at the Altamont Speedway, and guys like Iggy Pop and Rob Tyner of the MC5 were scrapping in the streets and tearing themselves up onstage. Then punk rock guys like Sid Vicious and Darby Crash (of the Germs) set a whole new standard and died in the process.

Being a singer for one of New York's biggest hardcore bands gave me this arrogance to act like an East Coast hooligan even though I was deeply insecure because of my abusive background and my lack of education. No matter what I did, I never felt like it was good enough. I can thank my dad and stepdad for that. Since I wasn't comfortable in my own skin, I acted overconfident and destructive. Plus, I had people around to support me, so no matter what I did there were guys that had my back.

One day, out of jealousy, I beat the shit out of one of Amy's friends. He wasn't sleeping with her or anything; he was one of her intellectual peers and didn't deserve to be punched out. I was angry that she didn't want to be with me and I wasn't going to take it out physically on her, so I acted totally out of line and fucked up this poor guy. In my altered state of consciousness, I thought beating him up would prove something to her.

It totally turned her off. She was furious. At first I didn't understand why she was mad. I felt like being "the man" made me a superhero. There's a power that comes with being feared and a strength in knowing you can hurt people. At the same time, I was still in love and wanted her back. So I started looking inward and realized I was trying to be someone that I wasn't. I tried to get that across in my lyrics on *Victim In Pain*.

I wasn't a superhero. I was more like a super villain. I was a Neanderthal trying to show the tribe who had the deadliest club. *Victim In Pain* songs like "Hiding Inside" came out of the realization that I wasn't acting like a man. I was acting like a bully. And that wasn't the real me. The same experiences fueled "Fascist Attitudes." I felt like I was becoming the character that *Maximumrocknroll* made me out to be and that made me sick. I took long walks around the park to try to clear my head and started doing less angel dust and Quaaludes.

The fresh air and reduction of psychoactive chemicals in my brain made me see that real power comes from being able to hurt people but holding back from doing so. I wrote about that, but some of the lyrics were convoluted because I didn't understand what I was feeling and I didn't know where those ideas were coming from. I was in turmoil because I was conflicted. I still had all this hatred and I was a total non-conformist, but I was becoming a non-conformist in a less destructive way.

The last song I wrote for *Victim In Pain* was "With Time (For Amy)." It had a different vibe than the other music. It was my version of a love song. When I wasn't with Amy I thought a lot about what I had done and how I had chased her away. Even though I wasn't with Amy, I wanted to be, and to win her back I had to change. I wanted to prove to her that I could be the man she wanted me to be. I wanted to walk a different path that would make her proud. And that started coming out in the songs. Once I could identify lyrically what my issues were and how I wasn't happy with what I had become, I started going back to where I came from. I changed my look; I grew out my hair again, spiked it with egg whites and dyed it Manic Panic green with black tips.

"With Time" and "Hiding Inside" expressed my transformation the best, and they came from being in love and trying to understand the world from Amy's perspective. I poured my heart out and revealed my vulnerability and imperfections. It was almost like emo before its time: "I'm the one who's lost inside but you're the one I can't find / Feel confused and lonely at this moment but maybe with some time, everything will pile off my mind." I had hoped the song would get to her and persuade her to give me another chance, and eventually it did. I was pretty good at getting my way.

# CHAPTER 15

As much as we acted like we didn't give a fuck, we cared about our music and still do. I can honestly say we weren't influenced by anybody. We liked quick, raw aggressive music, but we couldn't play anyone else's stuff because we weren't technically good enough. We couldn't even play Sex Pistols or The Clash songs at that time, so we didn't try. If Agnostic Front had been from Kansas, we never would have sounded the way we did. New York City was edgy and dangerous, and is one of the ingredients in our music that you could clearly hear—that crazy, violent element that we loved and couldn't find anywhere else.

My vocal and performance style came from all over the place. My favorite early hardcore band was SS Decontrol. David "Spring" Springa was one of the best front men anywhere. He knew how to control an audience and came across as intimidating without appearing unhinged. Throw that in with the wild ranting of Minor Threat's Ian MacKaye and my innate desire to purge the torment from the pit of my soul—the ultimate primal scream therapy onstage.

My stage look was a different matter—a combination of NYC and England. When I say England, I'm talking about The Who. On the surface it doesn't seem like Agnostic Front has anything in common with The Who. I was fascinated by their vocalist, Roger Daltrey, especially the way he swung his mic high above his head like a lasso. I stole that move and it worked for me for years. Sure I sometimes clocked myself or someone else with the mic, but it was worth it—until I almost broke Kabula's jaw.

We were playing in Muskegon, Michigan, and I swung the mic at an angle that was a little too steep. It swooped down and pegged Kabula in the mouth. He stopped playing for a second and reached down to pick up his tooth. As if it were the most normal thing in the world, he put his tooth in his pocket, to be reinserted later. Blood streaming from his mouth, he started playing again. After that, I never swung the mic onstage again. But I accidentally passed the torch. As soon as I stopped doing the Roger Daltrey, Freddy began swinging the mic.

I got my stage energy from the earlier vocalists in Agnostic Front, including John Watson. He was a phenomenal screamer. He just spent too much of the band's short sets in the crowd slamming. I wanted to perform with Watson's primitive crazed energy and also jump in the pit, but I timed it so that I could get back onstage to sing. I even borrowed a little bit from Keith Burkhardt, who used to hold the mic to his bare chest while he was screaming at the top of his lungs. I sometimes pressed the mic against my chest and thrust my chest forward while I shouted. I might have looked like I was suffering seizures onstage, but the crowd loved it.

We practiced a lot of the songs I wrote for *Victim In Pain*, but Raybeez wasn't getting it. He was barely a drummer to begin with. At first, that didn't matter because he was our friend, but when the songs demanded more difficult drum parts, it affected the music. I couldn't get it moving the way I wanted to because he couldn't click with the rest of us. That wasn't even the biggest problem. He was so hooked on angel dust that he didn't care about anything else. He didn't want to play better. When he sat behind the drums he was so dusted that he couldn't keep time. There was no way we were going to move forward like that so I decided to speak with him about it.

"Hey, man. You're fucking up," I said. "You're fucking wasted all the time, and you're not even trying anymore. Don't you want to do this?"

He didn't say anything. He sniffed, stared at me and walked away. I didn't need to say anything else. He knew he couldn't do what he needed to do to stay in the band. He took it hard. I could tell he was depressed, but he didn't stop getting high. He was more dusted than ever. A few days after we let him go, I saw him pick up a gun and head towards the East River. I followed him because I knew he was out of his mind, and he was either going to try to kill himself or someone else. I didn't think he'd try to do something to me.

I caught up with him standing by the river and he told me he was going to kill himself. He pointed the gun at me, then brought it up to his head. He was shaking, sweating and crying. I was probably on speed or dust. I didn't like where things were going. They could get tragic with a twitch of his trigger finger. "You know we're still brothers," I said. "You know that."

"Yeah, so what? I don't care."

"But I do care. A lot of people care about you. You crack us up, man. We love you."

"I'm not so funny now, am I?" he slurred.

"C'mon, man," I implored. "You don't want to do this. So what if you're not in the band? There are so many other things you can do."

"Like what?"

"You're alive, man. You're a character. You've got more personality that most singers. I know you're hurting, but we can't talk or work anything out if you pull the trigger."

He didn't say anything, so I continued. "Put down the gun and we can figure something out."

"What do you mean about me being a singer?"

"Put the gun down and we can talk about it."

To my surprise, he dropped the gun and I picked it up.

Then Raybeez pulled out a box cutter. At first, I was worried he was going to slit his wrists.

"Nooooo!" I screamed.

"Blood brothers!" he shouted, and I understood.

He cut his palm, handed me the blade and I cut my hand. Then we shook. We were blood brothers for life.

At first, Ray was laughing, then he started sobbing and wouldn't stop. It was a total release of desperation, depression and drugs. You could almost see angel dust leaving his body through his tears.

I got him back home and he was quiet. He seemed okay for the time being. I told him we had to move forward without him, but I promised I would help him form another band. He always had a tinge of resentment about being kicked out of Agnostic Front, but our friendship was stronger than his hurt feelings. And I was honest. I told him straight-up that he had great charisma and would be a better front man than a drummer, which was the truth. I proved it when we formed the band that became Warzone.

I got my cousin Sebastian "Tito" Perez to play guitar, I played bass and our friend Tommy Rat was the first singer. Raybeez started out as the drummer because that's all he felt comfortable doing. It was cool because even if he couldn't drum for shit, he could do what made him happy at the start of Warzone. No matter how bad he played he wouldn't be fucking up Agnostic Front.

We wanted to call the group the Rat Poison Band, but Tommy was gunning for Warzone. As a compromise we switched to Verbal Assault. We did a show with that name, but Tommy was so persistent that they eventually called themselves Warzone. It was a good name for a hardcore group. By then I was out of the band. For a minute, I was playing in Agnostic Front, the Psychos and Verbal Assault, so I got to see a lot of Ray. He seemed less depressed and enjoyed working on the new music. I had fun, but I left Verbal Assault before they got off the ground because I was stretching myself too thin again. Then Tommy Rat decided he didn't want to be in the band, so Raybeez started singing, which was the best thing that could have happened. He was a great front man, just like I told him he would be, and he kept the band going. They did six albums and a few EPs before he died on September 11, 1997.

At the same time Warzone was starting up, Agnostic Front moved forward with Dave Jones on drums. He was a kid from New Jersey who had been with the well-respected Mental Abuse. People gave us shit because everyone loved Raybeez. We loved him, too, but we would have broken up if we had tried to make *Victim In Pain* with him on drums *and* drugs. There was enough insanity between the four of us who weren't constantly dusted.

Anything could happen at a show. When we were on a bill, we owned the dance-floor before we played and then we owned the stage. No one dared infiltrate our space. We had fun stomping around, wherever we were. Just because we controlled the place didn't mean we didn't accidentally hurt each other. One of the last shows we played with Todd Youth was at CBGB on October 29, 1983. Death Before Dishonor was opening for us, and during their set Vinnie wanted to jump up on the stage. Big Robb, the singer from Bitter Uproar, gave him a push to help him get up there, and Vinnie flew over the crowd and smacked his head on the side stage monitor. He was bleeding so badly that we couldn't see the wound. He was covered in blood. He went backstage. His skull was exposed. Doug Holland from Kraut saw him and threw up. We took Vinnie out, threw him in the van and drove him to the hospital. Vinnie was telling jokes the whole time.

"Hang in there, man. You're gonna be all right. It's not too bad," I said, trying to convince myself as much as him.

Vinnie went straight into the emergency room. Doctors cauterized the wound and used four staples and 86 stitches to close the gash. After they finished, I was sitting with him, and when he opened his eyes he was still dazed. He looked at me for a second like he was having trouble focusing.

"What are you doing?" he said as clearly and quickly as he spoke after he finished a cup of hot black coffee. "We've got to do a show."

"No, we're canceling. We're not gonna play."

"What do you mean? You go back and do the show. I'll be all right."

I went back and we played. It was the only time we played as a three-piece with no guitar. It was Todd Youth, Dave Jones and me. The show was sold out. The house was packed and it was crazy. "The show must go on."

We could have done *Victim In Pain* with Todd Youth on bass. But right before we recorded it he was invited to join another band, which didn't work out, but then he ended up in Murphy's Law and Warzone. We replaced Todd with Rob Kabula, who had been in Cause For Alarm. Rob only wrote one song for *Victim In Pain*, "Remind Them," but he quickly became an important member of the band. He was great to hang out with because he was as out of his mind as Raybeez was.

With *Victim In Pain*, Don Fury started experimenting more with the recording. He had a lot more gear and had learned some production tricks. And he did it for free. It wasn't exactly a charitable move. He had a band called Balls and he wanted to make a high-quality recording. On March 3, 1984, we did a show at CBGB with Skinhead Youth, Death Before Dishonor and Balls, and all the money raised was used to record *Victim In Pain*. The following week we rented a 16-track recorder for one week. Don started recording, and three days later, when we were done, he used the machine to record his own band for the rest of the week. We didn't know from 8 tracks or 16 tracks. We wanted to do another record and this seemed like the best way.

Since we were used to recording live, we mic'd up the amps and plowed through the songs just like we had done for *United Blood*. Vinnie was mic'd in three different places. One was on the speaker cabinet, another was five feet away and the third was ten feet away, to capture the full range of his sound.

Two songs, "Fascist Attitudes" and "With Time (For Amy)," were recorded differently. We tracked the guitar separately and I sang in the engineering room, where the 16-track machine was. Don mic'd and recorded Dave's drums separately in his own little room. The bass cabinet was mic'd, and Rob played through a distortion box. There were no overdubs except for the lead in "Power" and the infamous "Stigma!" yell that became a staple of every show and album afterwards.

The album wasn't slick. Everything but those two tracks was live and raw, and there was no opportunity to do overdubs. We did a few takes of the songs. Some stuff is a little out of tune, but that gives the album character. A lot of critics have said that the record marked a revolutionary point for New York hardcore. On the 25th anniversary of the record, *The Village Voice* did a cover story about the making of the album. When we recorded it, we never could have imagined we'd still be around 25 years later. We released *Victim In Pain* through Rat Cage Records, which also released music by the Beastie Boys (their debut punk EP and their reggae dub record), The Young and the Useless, Neos, Virus, Heart Attack and Rattus. Rat Cage was the information hub for hardcore. Musicians were always there flipping through the vinyl. That's where you found out about new bands and shows.

The label was run by Dave Parsons. He was a cross-dresser, which we thought was funny. When we mastered *Victim In Pain* at Frankford Wayne, Dave showed up wearing a dress and freaked the shit out of the engineer. We didn't have any problem with that. Anything goes in New York. Plus, Dave was cool. He designed the Bad Brains logo with lightning on Capitol Hill. So what if he liked to wear silky panties and a bra? To each his own.

For *Victim In Pain*, there was a shady distribution deal with a record company owner named John Loder in England. He was fascinated by our popularity across the ocean and in the U.S. without any support from radio or a record label. He was wary of putting out our record through one of the more prestigious labels he worked with because people didn't know a lot about us. He wanted to hedge his bets in case we turned out to be the fascist band *Maximumrocknroll* accused us of being. John financed the record through Rat Cage and put it out—and we never saw a penny. We just got a bunch of records, which eventually got warped in our van while we were touring. But people started catching on to us and Combat Core offered us a deal for our next album.

Maybe John was right to look for alternate distribution for *Victim In Pain*. There was a lot of controversy surrounding that album. We had a well-earned reputation for getting into fights and not taking any shit. We liked to push buttons a little bit, too. We knew damn well that people were calling us bullshit names like AgNazi Front, and we flipped the middle finger at anyone who criticized us for using a 1941 photo from the Holocaust for the cover art of the album. We didn't just use the shot for the sake of rebellion. We had political and artistic reasons.

The picture was called "The Last Jew in Vinnitsa." It depicted a member of the Einsatzgruppe D, a Nazi SS death squad, about to shoot a Jew who was kneeling on the ground next to a pit full of dead bodies. Originally, it was in the personal photo album of an Einsatzgruppen soldier. I saw it in a book about World War II. To use that picture for album art was very fucking controversial, but at the same time it was exactly what we wanted.

Throughout history, mankind has been brutal and acted without remorse in the most hideous situations imaginable. People need to remember how horrific the Holocaust was. When I first saw the photo, I was mesmerized. It made me feel queasy, but the image was so strong I couldn't look away—kind of like that shot from the Vietnam War of General Nguyen Ngoc Loan holding a gun to the head of a Viet Cong prisoner. When I spotted "The Last Jew in Vinnitsa," I looked at the guy's face and saw his eyes. I thought, *Man, this needs to be publicized in order to prevent history from repeating itself*.

We were always interested in political commentary that went beyond *Fuck Society*, *Fuck Authority*, *Fuck Reagan*. This was a super-intense image that needed to be seen. Of course, people who hated us said we were skinhead Nazis, but they were going to find a way to do that anyway. Nobody outside of our friends understood us, and maybe that's why we stuck together and had such a big chip on our collective shoulder.

I hung out at Rat Cage a lot, and was there when *Victim In Pain* came out. I always buy my records on the day they're released for good luck. A few weeks later, a Hasidic Jew saw our album sitting in the window and came into the store. He was with his son, and he picked up the record. Dave and I were sitting behind the counter wondering what was going to happen next.

"You know what this is?" he asked.

We both nodded.

"This is very important for everyone to see," he continued. "There are people that want to erase this from history and pretend it didn't happen. I'm glad this is here to show people what happened."

Rock Hotel, 1984. Alternate Victim In Pain insert.

# CHAPTER 16

I thought Dave Jones was great on *Victim In Pain*. He loved playing the songs and liked being onstage, but our lifestyle was too wild and he wasn't digging the violence at the shows, so he bailed. If I were him I would have left as well. For a short while, we replaced him with Petey Hines, who later played in Cro-Mags, Murphy's Law and Handsome. Petey was a nice guy and was fun to hang around with, but I was a maniac. One night we were all drinking and getting high, and I was blasted out of my head on angel dust. (Old habits die hard.) I convinced Petey to let me give him some ink with a shitty, homemade mini–tattoo gun I had bought from some junkie. Petey wanted me to write "Fuck You" on his middle finger. I left the "c" out, and we were all so wasted that we didn't notice until the next day.

Petey was pissed, but he forgave me and played some killer shows with us. He was like a fully charged weed whacker. Once you pulled the trigger, he'd tear up everything in sight. And he was fast as fuck. I would have loved to keep him, but I blew the chances of that happening since I couldn't stop playing practical jokes on him.

We got to record two songs with Petey Hines that appeared on the Urinal Records compilation *Message from America: Hardcore Has Come of Age*, but that was it. It was our loss. At least we hadn't started touring yet. Since we had set up gigs for our first proper American tour, we had to find someone right away. We were able to get Jimmy "The Kid" Colletti, thanks to our friend Johnny Stiff. Jimmy was a good hardcore drummer and fit right in for a while. It would be another year before he and Kabula butted heads over the more metallic direction we were heading in. Just because Petey had put me in my place didn't mean I had learned my lesson. I was far too into chaos and childish fun to stop acting like an idiot.

I started working for the Rock Hotel around Christmas in 1983. The club owner, the notorious Chris Williamson, hired people from the scene, including Raybeez and Jimmy G. We policed the club like we had at A7. While I was there, I realized that the people I was hanging around were bad influences and I probably encouraged them to be destructive as well. It was a good chemistry for chaos and violence, but there wasn't a recipe there to be a productive member of society. As much of a clown as I still was, I was serious about wanting to be more positive. The people I thought were my friends were exploiting my sincerity and viewing my kindness as weakness. These people were just hateful, and they started attracting a negative and prejudiced element.

For example, a new wave of gay-bashing started up, which sickened me and had no place in the scene. One time, I was driving my van and some of my friends were in there with me when we saw a guy wearing an Agnostic Front skinhead shirt. He looked frail and homeless, and he had a knitted quilt with a floral pattern draped around his shoulders. One of the guys I was with said, "Stop the car." He jumped out and started beating on the guy in the quilt.

I ran up to him, grabbed him and shouted, "Hey, what the fuck are you doing?"

"This fucker's wearing a dress."

"Fuck you, man! He's wearing my shirt. Give him some respect!"

I was pissed. We weren't that far from being homeless ourselves. Gay, straight, transvestite, whatever that guy was—he hated the same things about mainstream society that I did. I was glad he was supporting the cause even though he didn't buy the shirt. When we came back from tour, I used to give leftover shirts to bums in the park. There were homeless people all over the Lower East Side wearing Agnostic Front shirts—especially one that showed a drawing of Ronald Reagan with his thumbs in his ears and his tongue sticking out. The bums needed clothes, and we needed promotion. We used to make the shirts ourselves, so it didn't cost much and it was cool to see homeless people wearing them with pride. They were representing for AF and had a weird admiration for us.

We played a bunch of shows to support *Victim In Pain* before we launched an official tour. One day we were returning from a gig in Connecticut, and we had a show that night at CBGB. We were on the Merritt Parkway and I was asleep in the back when we passed a dead deer in the middle of the road. Kabula got excited.

"Pull over, pull over!" he told Dave "Da Skin," who was driving. Nobody had any idea what he was going to do. "Back the fuck up!"

Dave gunned the car into reverse and stopped when we were next to the roadkill.

Kabula had Vinnie get out of the car with him, which was weird enough since Vinnie didn't like to do anything except play guitar. Frenchie and Dave, our roadies, picked up the deer and threw it in the van. The thud of animal flesh hitting the vehicle's metal floor woke me up.

"What the fuck?" I shouted. "Why is there a dead fuckin' deer in the van?"

"I'm bringing it to the show," Kabula replied. "We're going to take it onstage with us!"

I didn't think that was a great idea since we didn't know what kind of disease the animal might have or whether CBGB would let us take it in. It was a trophy 8-point buck. It had a huge rack of antlers. Hilly Kristal and his wife would notice. But I was too tired to argue.

Vinnie and Frenchie sat on the dead deer all the way back to New York City. When we pulled up to the club, Kabula said he wanted to hang the animal onstage while we played.

Sure enough, they pulled the deer out of the van and started dragging it into CGBG. Hilly Kristal stopped them.

"What do you think you're doing?" he said. "You're not bringing that thing in here. Don't even try!"

Kabula got mad and kicked the side of the deer. He threw the deer onto the sidewalk, but refused to leave it there because his best friend, Blu, wanted the antlers. Kabula grabbed a machete, which we kept in the van for just such emergencies, and Blu chopped the deer's head off. This was in plain sight at 1:30 p.m.!

Blu swung the machete down on the deer's head several times. *Thwack! Thwack! Thwack!* Police officers drove by and couldn't see the deer, and they probably thought Blu was attacking someone. He's lucky he didn't get shot. Cops sometimes shot first and asked questions later. The cops stormed out of the car, guns drawn. Blu smiled at them, but he kept chopping at the scalp of the deer. The antlers dangled at a 45 degree angle.

The police roped off the area, took the deer and threw it in a Dumpster in front of CBGB. The legs were poking out of the top of the trash bin. I didn't want to get in trouble, so I started walking away.

Right in front of the cop, Vinnie said, "Hey, hold on a minute." Vinnie went up to the deer. He took one of the rigor mortis–stiffened legs and propped it in front of the other so they formed an X. "Now he's straight edge!" he said.

The cop looked at Vinnie like he was crazy, which he was, and walked away.

Indeed, not all the insanity in our hardcore circle happened at clubs or shows. One time we were outside of A7 at 4 a.m. smoking angel dust, and Kabula got in his car and invited me in. Kabula hit the gas and started accelerating. The pitch of the car engine revving got higher and higher, and we were exceeding 45 miles per hour, which is fast on a New York City street.

"I wanna see how many lights I can go through before I hit a car," he said, as the car started blasting uptown on 6$^{th}$ Avenue.

I figured he was joking. We went through one light, then another. We went through a few more and he was still laughing. I was freaked out, but I was laughing my head off. Drugs will do that to you. Fortunately, there wasn't much traffic at that hour. When we approached other cars Kabula swerved around them. He wanted to hit a car at a red light, not in the middle of the road. It's like we were in a scene from the J.G. Ballard book *Crash*.

The car passed through two more red lights. When Kabula was a block away from the next light, I noticed it had turned from yellow to red and there was a car in the only lane. I braced myself for impact. When we got close enough to see the car, we realized it was a police car and Kabula slammed on the breaks. As much as I have mixed feelings about police, that cop probably saved our lives. Kabula was out of his mind, and angel dust didn't make him more sensible.

Vinnie didn't cause as much bedlam as Kabula or I did, but he had his moments. One day he nearly scalped our roadie Frenchie "Da Skin." Frenchie was Canadian. He was one of the nicest guys in the scene and had a forehead tattoo that read, "Made in Canada." He was funny and entertaining, and he could party. Everybody loved Frenchie. Vinnie didn't mean any harm on that scorching summer day when he was tripping on acid. Vinnie decided Frenchie's hair wasn't short enough and he needed to have his head shaven. But all he had on him was a broken piece of glass he found in the street.

Police had opened up a fire hydrant so that homeless people and junkies could drink some water. Vinnie didn't know what the fuck he was doing. He washed the piece of glass in the streaming hydrant water and scraped the edge of one side across Frenchie's scalp, slicing through the skin. Frenchie didn't even scream as blood ran down his face and trickled into his ears. Vinnie looked scared for a second, so he pushed Frenchie back under the water from the hydrant and the blood washed away.

Vinnie sighed with relief. I guess he figured the water had healed Frenchie's head because he kept cutting him with the glass. After inflicting 10 or 12 long gashes, Vinnie stopped and someone gave Frenchie a towel to hold to his head. Eventually it stopped bleeding, and Frenchie was sitting there smiling the whole time. I'm sure he was in pain. He was a mess when Vinnie was done. But Frenchie felt like a part of the family when he hung around us, and he always went along with whatever we threw his way.

# PART IV

## Riding the Wave: Living Faster Than Fast and Heading Towards Critical Mass

# CHAPTER 17

The bigger Agnostic Front got, the more of a target we became. To a great extent, we painted the bullseyes on our backs. We didn't back away from anyone and there were a lot of violent confrontations. At the same time, I had a blast on our first American *Victim In Pain* tour. It was a unique experience that people can appreciate and marvel about but no one can relate to. Back then, everything was different. You could beat the shit out of a heckler or a racist and not worry about getting sued or banned from a club. Even traveling was bizarre.

During the first part of the tour, I went onstage with Simon, my pet rat. When we were in the van he'd eat pizza scraps, potato chips and anything else that was scattered across the floor. Sometimes I'd feed him little pieces of food by hand. Then one day he disappeared.

"Fuck, we've lost Simon! Kabula, look in the back of the van," I said.

"I don't see him anywhere, man," he replied after searching behind the gear.

I figured Simon died or ran away to be somewhere that had less drugs and more food. A month and a half later we were somewhere in the middle of Pennsylvania and Simon popped back up. He had been living in the duct work of the van. We were so excited; it was like we had tracked down a long lost relative. "Hey, Simon! Guys, it's Simon. He's back!" We bought him his own piece of cheese to celebrate, and that was back when we couldn't afford cheese.

I don't know how happy Simon was to see us. I figured out later on that he was hiding because we had found a dog and it scared the shit out of him. Having a dog on tour was nothing new for us. Usually, I'd bring one of my dogs or someone else would bring theirs. But this time we didn't bring one; we found one. We were at a gas station in Ohio one day and we saw a skinny pit bull sitting there looking sad and hungry, so we picked him up and put him in the van. We named the dog Janutte, after a friend of ours who got shot up in World War II. We fed him and played ball with him. About 30 days later, we somehow wound up at the same gas station and we dropped the dog off. He looked healthier than when we picked him up. We couldn't afford to keep him, and I had my dogs at home to worry about.

We played Florida on that tour, around the same time that some kid had been abducted causing a wide-scale police hunt. We picked up Freddy and put him in the back of the van with us. He was like our mascot. We had a big cow skull tied to the front of the van with barbed wire, and we were speeding to the gig when I saw red and blue flashing lights behind us. Since we didn't have any drugs in the car and I wasn't drunk, I pulled over right away. Since the cops were looking for the kid they were pretty aggressive.

"Stay right where you are!" a voice shouted over a megaphone. Then a policeman walked up to the van. He had one hand on the gun in his unbuckled holster.

"Open the van door slowly," he commanded.

The door slid open, and he saw little Freddy sitting there with us. He called his partner over to back him up. The first cop asked if we were Satan worshippers and wanted to know who Freddy was.

"We're musicians, officer. This is my little brother. We're just going to a show that we're playing."

The cops didn't believe me. They thought we had kidnapped Freddy and were going to sell him into slavery or kill him in a ritual sacrifice.

"It's okay. You can tell us what really happened," the officer told Freddy. "Nothing's going to happen to you. We'll protect you."

They were trying to get him to say we kidnapped him. He was crying, "No, no. Roger's my brother. Don't take me away!" When they finally realized I was telling the truth they let us go. Of course they didn't apologize.

On that 1985 tour, we joined every branch of the military. Any time we'd see a recruiting center in whatever city we were in, we'd pull over and sign up. Most of the time we were high on mescaline, and when we walked in recruiters rolled their eyes.

We were five crazy-looking bald guys (including Frenchie "Da Skin"), and we resembled the Fordham Baldies from the Philip Kaufman movie *The Wanderers*. We filled out hundreds of pages of paperwork combined and never once got called to serve. Since there were no cell phones back then we filled in Vinnie's home number, but the recruiters knew we were just fucking around. We provided them with a little comic relief. Standing there representing for the military and waiting for people to come sign up has got to be incredibly boring. How many people drop by to join the service on any given day? We were doing them a favor.

When we got back to Florida, we went to buy guns. When I gave a salesman my New York license he told me I needed a Florida driver's license to buy a gun. I wasn't about to be dismissed so easily. I went to the Florida DMV that day and got a driver's license. I wrote down my dad's address on the form; back then no one asked for any type of proof. I waited in line like everyone else, and when they called my name, the person with the camera took my picture without saying anything. Bam, I was a Florida resident—at least on paper. I kept auto-renewing that license until 2006. Any time I got pulled over outside of New York I gave the police my Florida license. No one sent any tickets to my dad, so I never had to pay. When I got pulled over in Florida I used my New York license. It wasn't until I got married in 2006 and became a U.S. citizen that I surrendered the Florida license because I didn't want take a chance that the authorities would find it and take away my passport.

As soon as I got the Florida license, I went straight to the gun store and bought a .38 and ammunition. Whenever we were in Florida I'd buy more guns. During long van rides between cities, I'd  shoot road signs or mailboxes. When we were in the country, I pulled out a gun and shot over the heads of cows or horses to see if I could scare them and get them to run. Horses get frightened pretty easily, but cows are really dumb. You could shoot a gun right next to a cow and she won't even moo.

One time, we played a gig in Atlanta at the Metro with the Anti Heroes. Before the show we hung out and watched freight trains go by. I shot at them just to hear the bullet ricochet off the side. Sometimes the bullet would bounce from one part of the train to another like a pinball and I'd hear a rapid series of clanging sounds. That was always a rush. But it was pretty fucking stupid. A .38 doesn't have a lot of power and it's unlikely that a bullet would penetrate the side of a metal train. But some of those wooden freights are pretty rickety. I could have accidentally shot a hobo riding the rails.

In Lawrence, Kansas, we played a place called The Outhouse, which was surrounded by cornfields. I went out there with a machine gun and blew away hundreds of stalks. I'd watch them tumble and create patterns. They were like my own personal crop circles. I never stopped to think there might be a farmer out there. God, I hope there never was! Clearly I was stupid, but I wasn't stupid as fuck. I'd play around with guns for fun, but I'd never think of taking a gun to a street fight. I always left my guns at home because if you're gonna pull a gun on someone you better use it. If you don't, either they, their friends or members of their family will come looking for payback. Then you're caught in a no-win situation. You'll both have guns, and even if you use your gun, you're probably gonna get killed because chances are there'll be more than one of them. I've gotten myself into lots of fucked up situations, but that's the kind of scene I always managed to avoid.

One of the strangest shows we played on that tour was a bar mitzvah somewhere in the suburbs of Texas. This lady booked us because we were her son's favorite band and she paid us $500, which was the most we'd ever gotten for a show. It was more than five times what we were used to making! She gave us the address and we showed up at a fancy ballroom. We were unshaven, dirty and not at all dressed for the occasion. Since our songs were all so short and all we had was an album and a seven-inch, we played *Victim In Pain* and *United Blood* twice. We treated the gig like any other show, and the kid and two of his friends went nuts. A bunch of old people just sat there looking puzzled. Some of them held their ears because they weren't used to that kind of volume. They were used to classical orchestras and crooners like Frank Sinatra and Tony Bennett.

The situation went from weird to weirder. After we played, the kid's mom took us back to her house and invited us to shower and clean up. Then she brought us out for ice cream like little kids. We were cool with that. Fuck it, let's get some ice cream, a nice evening dessert after a great meal at the bar mitzvah. After we finished, she invited us to spend the night back at her house. She gave us all rooms, but in the middle of the night she tried to climb in bed with me. The dude's mom wanted to get busy with me the night of her son's bar mitzvah. I had no idea where her husband was, and I didn't want to find out.

I ran over to the room Rob was in and banged on the door. "Hey, man! We gotta get the fuck out of here!"

I didn't explain what had happened until we were all in the van.

As we were leaving Texas, we saw a real live Ku Klux Klan ceremony. We couldn't believe it. We were just driving on a secluded highway towards the interstate and there was a giant cross burning by the side of the road. It was dark, so we shut our lights off and pulled over. The flames were 15 feet high and guys in hoods were silhouetted against the blaze. It looked like we were in hell. It was so fucking surreal and terrifying. They didn't notice us and we were afraid of what would happen if they did, so we jumped back in the van and took off. It was a haunting end to a crazy night.

That tour was one big freakish carnival ride until we got to the West Coast and saw a lot of vicious violence and hate. People think hardcore was always about that, but we didn't see much of that on the East Coast. It didn't exist until much later. On the East Coast, whenever anyone gave us shit, we stood our ground and told people what we were about. We always said, "We're the working people's band. We fight against oppression to overcome oppression."

Then *Maximumrocknroll* started talking shit about us and we were on the defensive. The fuckers who aligned themselves with that mentality caused a lot of trouble. Some of them wanted to shut down our shows because they thought we were fascists, so they called in bomb threats. Next thing we knew, there were cops everywhere. That was always bad news because the cops couldn't tell one kind of hardcore kid from another and they didn't care. It wasn't like in New York where a lot of the cops seemed to understand we were musicians and that, if they let us play our shows, there wouldn't be any trouble. These cops were more like goons. If someone mouthed off or if they saw kids fighting they took out their night sticks and went to town. They seemed to enjoy cracking skinheads across the skull. Maybe it was because they could see the damage they inflicted more easily than they could when they hit a dude with hair. Sometimes the cops pulled the plug on a show, but usually they beat up whoever they wanted to and then left. They wouldn't have given two shits if a bomb exploded and killed everyone inside. To them, we were all low-lifes and scumbags. It's a good thing we didn't have the Internet back then. If people knew how many shows had bomb threats, no one would have come!

As we neared California, hate groups gathered at the clubs and shifty people started making noise. There were do-gooders who showed up to stop the shit-talkers. The talking never lasted long before someone got their head stomped. Gradually, the environment became gang-oriented. Even hooligans that weren't in gangs ran with them because it gave them an excuse to bust some heads. That made some people scared to go to shows.

The first time we went to California was in April 1985. Youth Brigade invited us to see their show at the Hanger on April 27, the day before our first official California show, so we went to check out the vibe. I had been drinking a lot so I went straight from the van to the bathroom to take a piss. About ten seconds after I walked up to the urinal, I was grabbed from behind and these two Cholo guys put a knife to my throat. I was still peeing! One of these guys said, "We don't like your kind around here. We don't like skinheads."

*Fuck, I don't know how I'm gonna get out of this one*, I thought. I started planning what I was going to say, picking my words carefully, and then Louiche Mayorga, who was playing bass for Suicidal Tendencies, walked in.

"Hey Roger, Vinnie, what's going on?"

The guys who grabbed us immediately let us go. It turned out they were part of the Suicidals gang. Louiche got them to chill out. We figured everything was good for us to watch the show. Then Louiche told us otherwise.

"Guys, get out of here. Something big's gonna pop."

He didn't have to tell us twice. We found out the next day that there was a humongous fight. The Suicidal gang fought the LADS or one of the other rival gangs over there. There were lots of them.

I never understood how anyone could call Agnostic Front part of a gang until I got to California. Over there, a lot of the hardcore punk bands were associated with gangs and there was a ton of violence. It was different than in New York, where we were fighting to protect ourselves and just trying to survive. These guys in California had other agendas that sometimes revolved around organized crime and usually involved fists, chains, knives and even guns. It was structured chaos and there were targets. It was the kind of scene we never wanted to be a part of but were accused of belonging to, and at last we understood why. The people in California who wrote about us thought that we were like the hardcore bands in their own scene. They didn't bother to investigate the scene to find out the truth.

Our first show in California was on April 28 at a hole in the wall in Pomona called 12XU. It was the old Toxic Shock Records location. The store had moved down the street, so they had shows in the old location until the lease was up. The shop held less than 100 people. Among the packed room were the guys from *Flipside* magazine, which filmed the show and used a couple songs for a video compilation that documented the hardcore scene, *Flipside Video Fanzine No. 8*. Those guys had our backs and understood where we were coming from—which didn't stop the violence. Nothing could have done that.

On May 10, we played in Los Angeles at the Olympic Auditorium as part of what was supposed to be a real triumph for hardcore and a major showcase for us. It was Agnostic Front, Exploited, UK Subs, Dr. Know and Don't No. I later heard from the people directing the *Flipside* video that there were kids *sieg heil*ing during the show. When I reviewed the footage, I saw that happened a couple times when I turned around and my back was to the audience. Every time I'm onstage, the loud music, blinding spotlights and mesmerizing energy put me in my own world. There's no way to see everything going on around me, especially when there are 3,500 people going apeshit.

As soon as we started playing our set, everyone bum-rushed the stage and the barricades collapsed. Before we were halfway through our first song we could see rival gangs squaring off and fighting. They didn't come to the show to mosh or see music. They just used the music as a backdrop for the chaos.

It didn't take long for a giant riot to erupt. Kids broke windows, flipped cars and set them on fire. There were helicopters circling overhead and cops in the street beating up all the punks. I peeked outside a side entrance and saw three or four fires burning in the parking lot. Kids were lying on the cement moaning and holding their stomachs, faces or whatever had been hit, either by a gang member or cops. All the unity suddenly crumbled and dudes were scrambling away from the carnage, flames and smoke.

There's a saying in war that you never leave a fellow soldier on the battle field.

Some hardcore kids held the same belief, but for others, life was more about a complete disregard for rules—total anarchy. They didn't try to stop their best friends from getting coldcocked or arrested. It was every punk for himself.

For a bunch of guys from the East Coast—even a tough fuckin' place like New York—it was some scary shit. NYHC was violent and turbulent, but New York City is such a small community compared to L.A. People learn how to live with each other in New York. They're in buildings, one on top of the other. They're surrounded by different races and ethnicities, and for the most part everyone learns to get along. In California everything was way more segregated, even within the suburbs: Here are the Mexicans, here are the white kids and here are the black people. They don't like each other and they clash at the shows based on territory and start kicking ass. The Southern California hardcore scene was a war, and every concert was a battle filled with gangs that would converge and raise hell. Some of the more notable gangs there were The LADS, Suicidals, United Crew Skinheads and Circle One. There were also splinter groups from the main crews and they would fight within their own subcategories. It was chaos.

At a few of our West Coast shows, white power skinheads *sieg heil*ed us. We stopped playing and made it clear that we didn't believe in separatism. We told them we were all about unity and warned them that if they kept up their ignorance and bullshit, we would end our set and leave, which we did a few times. In California, that's just the way it was.

I still loved playing those shows. We were tight, loud and explosive. It became a drag to tour for these people whose views we couldn't even begin to understand. The fascists in the crowd seemed to follow us back from the West Coast, partially because *Maximumrocknroll* and the like kept spreading lies about us. I had to ask myself: What side were they really on? It's easy for some fanzine on the West Coast to stir shit up and sit back and watch. We had to deal with the situation! Even local shows became battles between the racist movement and the anti-racist movement. I already knew most of these people were ignorant, but I learned they were also blind and dumb. They beat on skinheads and punks who didn't have any political views or whose views they didn't know. Sometimes they got caught up in the moment and swung at anyone within range.

# CHAPTER 18

For a while, we got so much shit and people scrutinized our lyrics so closely that it was hard to convince anyone we fuckin' hated Nazis and racists. *Maximumrocknroll* had writers all across the country, and some of their New York reporters tried to convince the editor Timmy Yohannan that we weren't a gang or a hate group. But he turned his back on them.

Maybe it was because they represented well-situated, American, white middle-class students who read novels about oppression and followed class struggles from a safe distance. These were guys who thought they were fighting against the system but were living in fancy houses in upscale suburban neighborhoods. We were poor-ass kids living on the streets or squats of NYC and most of us never had the money or upbringing to climb the social ladder.

They represented the ultra-elite hardcore antagonists. "You guys are always talking about uniting, yet you're always beating people up," one of their reporters said the first time the magazine interviewed me. That was a lie. We never beat up people in our scene. We took care of our own. We didn't take any shit from anyone that verbally abused us or attacked us. We stood our ground, and yes, we busted heads when we were provoked. It was survival of the streets, something *Maximumrocknroll* was too politically correct to understand. There was an us-versus-them mentality that we totally didn't ask for and didn't deserve. Our lyrics were angry but totally positive. There was nothing in there that anyone could have criticized us for.

That didn't stop *Maximumrocknroll* from making sure their readers saw the situation from their point of view, and they set us up in different ways. They'd send their writers to review our shows and then they'd be confrontational, so either we or one of our supporters in the crowd would try to knock some sense into them. Then they'd write in the magazine how we were all thugs and Nazis. They created fictitious right-wing IDs for us, calling us Agnazi Front. I was Roger Agnazi. They even created flyers for shows that didn't exist, linking hateful bands to NYHC bands. They were the ones who stirred shit up. They were supposed to be the voice of punk and they created controversy because they were trolls. Plain and simple.

After putting up with their shit for a while, I made a deal with them via Dave Scott from Adrenalin OD. I said I would do an interview if they sent me the questions and I replied to them, and that was the end of it. There would be no face-to-face discussion and no room for misinterpretation. It would be their questions and my answers, and my words would stand on their own. They agreed and mailed Dave a long list of questions. I replied to each of them as thoroughly and thoughtfully as I could. When I finished, Dave mailed it back.

I couldn't wait to see the published article. I figured it might put to bed the beef between us. But when I read the issue (#21, released January 1985), it was clear that Timmy Yohannan broke the fucking rules.

He wanted to get his two cents in, which wasn't part of the deal. Everything I said cleared up a lot of misconceptions, but then he went back and got his jabs in. He commented on everything I wrote and tried to make me look like an ass. He cheated because my answers weren't what he wanted to hear. Anyone who read that article could tell from my answers what my position was, but Timmy's comments might have left them feeling skeptical, which was mean-spirited. I don't know why he was out to get me, but clearly he viewed me as the enemy and himself as some sort of freedom fighter.

I wouldn't have cared so much, except back then the hardcore community communicated through that fucking rag. *Rolling Stone* and *Creem* wouldn't give us a second glance and metal fanzines like *Kick Ass Monthly* and *Metal Forces* hadn't discovered us yet. At least we had *Flipside* and *Thrasher* on our side, but they didn't have the readership of *Maximumrocknroll*. The crazy thing about Timmy calling me a fascist is that I was an immigrant Latino kid dating a Jewish girl, and she never accused me of being a Nazi sympathizer.

"Fuck *Maximumrocknroll!*"

I can't count the number of times I said that in disgust. When it came to opposing separatism and white power, we were on the same side. I couldn't stand the hardcore bands that held those beliefs. I couldn't even listen to their music. The ultimate hypocrisy is that the magazine had a huge collection of right-wing hardcore in its basement record collection. I've heard this from too many people who saw it for it not to be true.

To make a statement about the magazine's bias against us, we played the Rock Against *Maximumrocknroll* show at the Tenderloin in San Francisco on May 3, 1985. The show featured AF, a reunion of the Fuck Ups, Verbal Abuse and Special Forces. No one from *Maximumrocknroll* was anywhere in sight. They were intimidated that we had organized this show on their home turf and terrified about what might happen to them if they showed up. These guys were only crusaders of hardcore when they were protected from the people they were talking shit about. It's easy to be a champion of justice and hardcore purity when you're hiding behind the safety of a computer screen.

The first Rock Against *Maximumrocknroll* concert was in a shitty club in a bad neighborhood. The show was great. The place was packed, kids were dancing and stagediving and the bands were all hanging out and having a good time. After it was over, we went outside to the parking lot to drink beer and chill. But there was no time to relax. One of the local gangs had gathered and organized in anticipation of our arrival. Before we knew what was going on, a San Francisco gang member ran up to one guy who was at the show, pulled out a razor and sliced his throat open. Then the assailant took off running. It was like the opening strike of an organized attack. Before we had a chance to react, bottles started raining down on us from the surrounding rooftops. They exploded on the ground and shards of glass sprayed like nails from a pipe bomb.

We jumped in our van and stopped in front of the guy whose throat was slashed. We opened the door and pulled him into our van. He was holding his neck and gurgling blood, which ran down his shirt and stained the inside of the van. Our friend Terry Psycho, who attended the show with her boyfriend, Billy Psycho, was a nurse, and she held his neck tight to minimize the blood loss. We rushed him to a local hospital. She definitely saved his life that night. If she didn't have medical training, he would have bled out.

A second Rock Against *Maximumrocknroll* show was booked at CBGB on December 2, a few months after we returned home from the *Victim In Pain* tour.

After all the friction and bad blood, we needed some comic relief. Dave "Da Skin" was constantly falling in love with different girls. He met one named Brigitte in California and decided to bring her all the way to New York so he could be with her. He thought she could be our merch girl. Then she hooked up with a guy in Denver, Colorado. Dave caught her with the dude in the back of a club. He confronted her and she left him to hook up with the other guy. We still had her luggage, and she didn't come back for it. It was typical for Dave, and since he always fell for girls that didn't care about him, we teased him without mercy.

"Brii-gettte, Briiii-gette. She wants you, Dave! She's coming back to be with you."

Dave got pissed off, which made the routine more fun. We stopped somewhere along I-80 near Chicago. Dave was asleep in the back of the van. Vinnie and I went into Brigitte's bag and took out her lingerie. I put on matching, lacy red bra and panties, which I was practically falling out of, and Vinnie wore a black bra and white underwear, which looked like a Speedo on him. Then we stopped on the highway and pretended to hitchhike. Dave woke up and heard us calling his name in high-pitched voices. We walked out in the middle of I-80 and danced around. Dave jumped into the driver's seat, slammed the door and took off. He left us there for 30 minutes, and during that time truck drivers drove by and tried to run us over.

We'd hear a truck come, and I could only imagine what the drivers were thinking. They probably saw sexy lingerie before they could tell who was wearing it, so they slowed down. Then they got closer and saw ugly, tattooed dudes in drag. They honked their horns and some swerved towards us, and we had to jump off the road. It's a good thing we weren't wearing high heels or we might have tripped and broken our ankles. Finally, Dave came back for us and we changed. For a while we were the ugliest fuckin' whores on the road and our lives hung in the balance.

I don't know if being duped by *Maximumrocknroll* or nearly getting killed by angry truck drivers had anything to do with it, but suddenly I felt unsure of my place in the world. Everything I had taken great pleasure in and felt was important didn't seem to matter as much. I started to back away from the NYHC scene, and my friendships with the main figures in the movement became a little weird. I stopped drinking and taking as many drugs as I had been taking, and I restrained from a lot of the fighting that had been a regular part of my week. I didn't hang with my friends who were still stirring up shit and sometimes getting into unprovoked fights. I started spending a lot of time by myself. At the same time, I was afraid to hide inside myself because I didn't want anyone to think I was betraying the scene I was supposed to be a part of. In other words, I was deeply fucking conflicted.

Everything had happened too fast. There had been too much chaos and it was taking its toll. I went from being an unpopular guy in a regular hardcore band to being in this super tough-guy hardcore band, putting out a record and playing the role of the violent thug. During the *United Blood* era I talked about uniting people, but I had a short fuse and I took out all the anger from my youth and my feelings that I had been dealt an unfair hand in life on people who played no part in giving me those cards. They weren't even part of the game.

I started spending more time with hardcore bands that came through town. We had a common bond, so they were like friends from other states. The first time NOFX came to New York was in 1984, and we hit it off right away. They were playing at CBGB, and at the end of the show I was talking to Fat Mike who told me they didn't have any place to stay.

"Well, you can stay with me," I said. I've always believed it's good karma to help out other bands when you're in a position to do so.

They jumped in their van and followed me as I drove to Tompkins Square Park. I told them to park right behind me. After I jumped out of the van, NOFX took their bags out of their van and started coming towards me. They figured I was heading to a house or apartment. I stopped in front of their van, opened the door and put one of my pit bulls in there.

"Here you go. Do you want a pillow or something?"

Mike started laughing. He was sure I was joking. I wasn't. When I didn't laugh back at him or change my expression, he figured I was serious. He was gonna spend the night in the van, I would be in another van in front of his and the dog would be his protection.

I didn't figure anything was wrong and Mike didn't say anything. "Do you wanna get some 40s and hang out?" I asked.

Before we started trying to figure out what to do for the follow-up to *Victim In Pain*, we went back out on the road. The band was in a parallel state of flux. I don't even know how we recorded *Cause For Alarm*. We were trying to bring in friends who played in other bands that we liked, but Kabula was really into the new sounds that were happening in hardcore and Vinnie and I were unsure where we wanted to go. We knew we wanted the band to evolve. We just weren't sure in which direction to take it. By that point, the metal scene had infiltrated hardcore and vice versa. Bands like Anthrax, Metallica, Exodus and Slayer were hanging out with hardcore groups like us, Murphy's Law, Crumbsuckers and Cro-Mags. More than anything, they felt welcome around us because they were protected. Sometimes people got stupid and tried to fuck with them, and I stopped the troublemakers in their tracks. Usually, all I had to do was grab them or tackle them to put them in their place.

Metallica guitarist Kirk Hammett liked the vibe at CBGB, and one night he went to a show when Crumbsuckers were on the bill. Crumbsuckers were big Metallica fans, and I was doing security. The Crumbsuckers invited Kirk to come up and do a song with them. Metallica had just released *Master of Puppets* and were starting to become popular. As Kirk went onstage, Tommy Carroll, who played in NYC Mayhem and Straight Ahead, yelled, "Rock star asshole," spat on him and tried to start a fight. Kirk was a little guy and all he wanted to do was have a good time and enjoy the show. I intervened and stopped the situation from getting out of hand, but I think it freaked Kirk out. That was the last CBGB show I saw him at.

Aside from the occasional incident, pretty much everyone got along. The bands checked one another out and experimented with each other's styles. Carnivore was a great Brooklyn band led by the late Pete Steele. He loved the New York scene and was a regular at CBGB. One day Kabula convinced us to check out one of their shows. He loved anything that was visual and fucked up, but he usually had good taste in music and in this case he was spot on. Carnivore had great songs. Way before Pete Steele started Type-O Negative, he had a strong grasp on how to combine hardcore and metal in a way that would appeal to fans of both. They dressed up like characters from *The Road Warrior*, which complemented their raw, primitive music. Onstage they had the energy of pure hardcore.

We had the same manager, Connie Barrett, and she arranged for us to meet up with Pete. Kabula was so stoked he was tripping over his words, and Pete was excited because he loved *United Blood* and *Victim In Pain*. We hooked up with him backstage and he was polite and friendly, which is funny since he was seven feet tall and had a low voice and a heavy Brooklyn accent. The guy was whip-smart and sarcastic, and his dark humor always had us in stitches. He could make people laugh by making certain facial expressions. He didn't have to say a word. Over time I learned that, more than anything, he was an incredibly nice guy. Pete was cool to everybody—record label people, managers, journalists, fans and especially other musicians. He just loved aggressive music.

We hung out sometimes and got drunk. Maybe we'd sniff glue. He was a regular at the CBGB hardcore matinees, and even though he had long hair no one ever fucked with him. If I talked to him during the week he'd always mention that weekend's show and even though he was usually even-keeled, that low, gentle voice got a little excited whenever we'd discuss who was playing. Those matinees were like his Sunday afternoon church.

One of the first benefit shows for CBGB was Agnostic Front, Carnivore and Whiplash. The show was on a weeknight so we weren't expecting much, but the place was packed and all the bands killed it. Everyone was embracing each other's roots. It wasn't just happening in New York. North Carolina band Corrosion of Conformity (C.O.C.). covered Judas Priest's version of Fleetwood Mac's "Green Manalishi" on their 1984 hardcore album *Eye for an Eye*, and a lot of their other songs had some mean-ass guitar. In Texas, D.R.I. ramped up the speed and the noise with *Dealing With It!*, which came out on Death Records, an offshoot of Metal Blade. And Suicidal Tendencies were breaking nationally.

Writing-wise, it was an interesting time. Shards of thrash metal were sticking into the flesh of hardcore and freaking everybody out, including myself. To satisfy Kabula, we wrote some metallic riffs in dressing rooms when we were on tour for *Victim In Pain*. When we got back home from the tour in 1985, the band consisted of Vinnie, Kabula, Colletti and me. We messed around with something that started out called "Eat the Steak," evolved into "The Bulldog Song" and eventually became "Out for Blood." We were just jerking around, making up lyrics right on the spot. We played the song at shows, and people sang along like they knew it. I was trying to figure out what the hell they were saying because I didn't have any lyrics and I could have used some help.

When we got back home and started rehearsing and fine-tuning our new songs, we found out that a big, early NYHC band, Cause For Alarm, had broken up. On paper, they began in 1983 and were one of the pioneers of the scene. What a lot of people don't know is that Cause For Alarm started out in New Jersey as the Hinkley Fan Club with Billy Milano on vocals. Kabula was in Cause For Alarm before he joined AF. Keith sang in AF before he was asked to join Cause For Alarm. Keith was into Krishna consciousness and that didn't sit well with some of the other members. Around 1985 he got deeper into his faith and the band became really unstable. At one of their most volatile points they moved to California to try to keep themselves together. By then we had gained some credibility. We got stronger and they became more fragmented until they started bleeding band members.

When we found out Alex Kinon wasn't in Cause For Alarm anymore, we thought it would be a good idea to invite him to join Agnostic Front. We figured having a second guitar player would make our wall of sound even more powerful. Vinnie wasn't thrilled about that at first, but when we told him it was Alex—whom he knew from the scene—he was okay with it. Alex was one of us. At the time, I thought having members from Agnostic Front and Cause For Alarm playing together would create a new hardcore super-band. I figured that if we could tap into the anger of Agnostic Front and the musicality of Cause For Alarm, we'd be unstoppable. I was right . . . kind of.

There were some intense and frustrating times in the rehearsal studio during that era. *Cause For Alarm* didn't create itself. We bled for that album. When we weren't cleaning and dressing our wounds, we were still cracking one another up. One time, right after Alex had joined the band, Kabula got a live chicken and brought it to one of our shows at CBGB.

"I'm going to throw it in the pit!" he said with a wide grin.

"You can't do that, man," Alex said. "People have seen you with the chicken. They'll know it was us and we'll get banned."

Alex's girlfriend was even more opposed to making the chicken a part of the show. She started yelling at Rob and tried to pry the chicken out of his hands. The bird was flapping, feathers were flying through the air and then the chicken jumped in her face. It's hard to hold back a chicken from scratching someone. Rob held it by the legs so the chicken didn't scratch her, but it pecked at her and cut up the side of her head and one of her arms. She was furious. At first I was laughing at how ridiculous the situation was. Then I intervened and helped wrestle the chicken away from Kabula.

I took the bird to Tompkins Square Park to set it free so it could join the wild roosters on the Lower East Side. It was snowing that day, so I placed it in the snow and walked back to the club. Then we played the show. I went back the next day to see if I could find out what happened to the chicken. There was a little trail of chicken footprints that suddenly ended. I guess somebody took it home and ate it.

Original Cause for Alarm line-up.

# CHAPTER 19

O riginally we had no intention of calling our second record *Cause For Alarm*. That was a move to placate Alex. The rest of us were bouncing all over the place, stoked by every new idea and song. Alex seemed less excited. He looked like he was going with the flow, as if he didn't care much about what he was doing. Today, I realize that's his personality and he probably was into the music we were making. It didn't feel like it at the time, though, and that bummed me out. I did everything I could to make him feel welcome and happy to be in Agnostic Front. He perked up when I told him I wanted to call the album *Cause For Alarm*.

I always felt like he was resentful of something. It seemed like he was mad that we had stolen Cause For Alarm's thunder. Cause For Alarm was the big NYHC band and they released a record and went on a national tour way before we did. They were always praised and admired, and we were the laughing stock of New York because we didn't know how to play our instruments and were like a train wreck to watch. When Cause For Alarm were on the road, or weren't performing because of their internal struggles, we became a stronger band. Still, I don't know why Alex agreed to join AF, but he did. He and Kabula wrote all this crazy metal stuff that had a lot more riffs than anything off *Victim In Pain* and was influenced by Slayer, Exodus and Venom. Jimmy Colletti hated it and didn't like the direction we were headed in, so he left. The way he quit was really strange.

He came to practice with us one day in 1985, and then disappeared. He didn't come to our next practice. He never tried to contact me. I didn't hear from him again until 1997. For a while I didn't know if he was alive or dead. I found out later that for ten years after he quit, he was in and out of jail for various crimes. Whenever he got bored he'd call Vinnie, who was the only one that had an apartment with a phone. If we were on the road, Jimmy would leave a message for him with someone, and when we were at home Vinnie talked to him. For more than a decade Vinnie never told us that he was in somewhat regular contact with the guy. We weren't always the most communicative people when it came to our personal lives.

I talked to Connie about our dilemma. She was older than us and more into old-school metal than hardcore, but she liked us. She was always good to talk to—friendly, efficient and never condescending. She suggested we recruit Louie Beateaux from Carnivore.

I wasn't gung-ho about bringing more metal into the equation, but I liked the idea of going with someone we already knew. We went to Carnivore's rehearsal space in Brooklyn and took turns rehearsing. Louie would play with them, drink a tall glass of water, wipe off his mouth and practice with us. I didn't know how Pete Steele would feel about that, but he fuckin' loved it. He watched us rehearse and went out of his mind, bouncing around the room as if he were at a show.

Louie was a different kind of drummer compared to Jimmy Colletti, Raybeez, Dave Jones or Petey Hines. He was precise and flashy, and he was inspired by a lot of metal, from Black Sabbath to Motörhead. Jimmy would have hated the way our music sounded, and I had mixed feelings about it. At that point, the metal dudes in the band outnumbered the hardcore guys three to two, so Alex and Rob went to town. While I had taken the lead for songwriting on *Victim In Pain*, I stepped into the background for *Cause For Alarm*. I brought in a few hardcore-based songs and that made me more comfortable. But between the drugs, relationship problems and the musical shift, there was a time when I wasn't all there.

I was having trouble writing lyrics, and I needed help. I was so desperate I started the song "The Eliminator" with slogans from a bunch of T-shirts I saw at an Army/ Navy store: "Killing's my business and business is fine / Firing squad, electrocute, we'll execute / More than one face of death / Kill 'em all, let God sort 'em out / A soldier of fortune, I'll wipe 'em all out."

It's not like I didn't have any ideas. I wanted to do a song about Bernard Goetz, the subway vigilante who shot four guys that tried to mug him in 1984. He fired five times and seriously injured all the dudes. Then he surrendered and was charged with attempted murder, assault, reckless endangerment and carrying a concealed handgun. A jury found him innocent of everything except one charge of carrying an unlicensed firearm. People freaked out. One of the people he shot suffered brain damage and lost the use of his limbs. He sued Goetz and won $43 million. It was a huge issue that sparked debate about race, crime and gun possession. I also wanted to have a song about all the waste in Staten Island, but I didn't know what to say for either song.

To give credit where credit is due, I asked Pete Steele if he could help me out and he was happy to lend a hand. I told him about the ideas I was having trouble putting into words and Pete decided what to write. Honestly, I was looking for inspiration to stay in the band, and before I knew it we had "Bernie Gets His Man," "Toxic Shock" and "Public Assistance," which ultimately became the most controversial track that we've ever done.

Critics gave Pete, a Brooklyn white guy, a lot of grief for allegedly being racist because of the lyrics: "How come it's minorities who cry things are too tough / On TV with their gold chains, claim they don't have enough / I say make them clean the sewers, Don't take no resistance / If they don't like it go to hell and cut their public assistance."

Those were actually my thoughts based on things I witnessed and experienced, and he expressed them perfectly. I was a minority kid whose mom was on welfare and I saw all the time how other people in our neighborhood abused the system. Public assistance was designed to help people better their lives and move on, not to enable the families that used it. Those are the people the song was aimed at.

That's not how some people saw it, and the controversy quickly spread to the mainstream media. When Phil Donohue did a show about what he perceived to be the negative effects of hardcore on teenagers, he broadcast lyrics from the song on the screen.

"This has got a kind of reactionary look to it, doesn't it? Have we got racism here?" Donohue asked the crowd. No. I called it as I saw it. What does Phil Donohue know about poverty?

Fortunately, Vinnie was in the crowd and he defended the song and the band: "We just speak of social unrest," he told Donohue. "Conflict of interests and turmoil bring controversy and it speaks for itself."

Even with all the negative press, I was glad Pete Steele worked on the lyrics and relieved I didn't have to come up with vocal rhythms or be in the practice room with the guys. I didn't have any idea how the songs for the album were going, and I didn't care. When I realized I didn't care I got worried. Then I quit.

"I can't do this. It's not me," I told Kabula.

"What do you mean it's not you?" he said.

"I don't know," I said. "It's not hardcore. It's something else and I don't know how I feel about it. I need to step away for a minute."

"Well, how long is a minute?"

"I can't say. I need a break. Do what you gotta do."

I left Agnostic Front for about four months. Vinnie was cool with whatever I wanted to do. I was a big mess, and he supported me during my existential crisis. It wasn't just the music that was weighing heavily on my mind.

I was hanging with the NYHC crew one night outside A7, and some bad shit went down. I was flying high on mescaline and Quaaludes. I went to support some friends who were fighting with dudes who looked like they were from a Latin gang.

I squared off with one guy who was wielding a knife. He lunged towards me and I dodged the blade. He swung around with his free hand to punch me and got me in the chest, but it didn't knock me back. Then he hit me again with the same hand. Just as he pulled back his knife and prepared to thrust, I jabbed him a couple times in the arm and shoulder with a sharpened, rusty, old screwdriver and he dropped the knife. I pushed him aside. He held his wounded arm and looked at me in disbelief. Then we heard police sirens and took off.

Witnesses at the scene told the cops I was the aggressor and gave them my description. A sketch artist drew a picture of me. Suddenly police were looking for a guy with a spider tattooed on his neck. I was a marked man.

It's a good thing I had connections and was able to deal with the situation. During the day I had been doing construction for a plastic surgeon who lived on the Upper East Side. In exchange for some free work, he offered to do laser surgery on my neck to get rid of the spider. The first treatment was rushed, and each time he zapped away at the ink under my skin, it felt like I was being cut with a bent steak knife. It was a thousand times more painful than a tattoo gun. I was supposed to have two more treatments, but I blew them off and grew my hair to cover what was left of the spider on my neck. I faded into the background where policemen and gang members couldn't find me. That meant staying off stage.

I wasn't the only guy doing construction for the good doctor. I don't know if the other dudes got paid in surgical procedures as well. While Dr. Facelift was striking deals with these guys who did manual labor, they were making their own deals right under the doctor's nose. During the day, there was a little school bus that stopped in front of the site. Inside the bus was a guy selling coke. In the morning one of the workers would go in and buy a bag, then we would split it up, get coked out and work like crazy. It kept our energy levels up and allowed us to work much faster and longer than usual.

I felt like I was in the right place. I had always been a hard worker, and maybe what I needed to do to get my shit together was adopt a more normal lifestyle. I thought about giving up music and working in a club or going back to the hardware store. I needed to get a place of my own to think about these things, so Paul Bearer from Sheer Terror and I moved into my close friend Paula Reinhardt's barn in Staten Island with about eight pit bulls. We called it The Pit Farm. It was in Stapleton near the projects, and the place was bare-bones—just a roof and four walls. There was no hot water and no shower. Some people get grossed out by conditions like that. It wasn't a big deal for me. I had been living in vans and abandoned buildings. I liked being away from the City, and I loved the dogs.

There's a cultural bias against pit bulls. It's a stigma that has turned into a mass hysteria. The media run stories about how pits have turned on their owners or attacked children. That only happens when the dogs aren't taken care of or if they come from abusive upbringings. They're like people in that way. They get scared and paranoid, and they need to be in a loving environment to be reprogrammed. If they're around kids who pull their ears or tails or poke them, of course they'll lash out because they have a history of being abused. Any abused or cornered animal will strike out in defense. That goes for humans, too.

One day I got bit by one of the dogs, Oscar. It was an accident. He was blind and he didn't even know he bit me. As soon as he heard my voice, he let go, but he chewed me up pretty good. The doctor couldn't do anything about it. I probably could have used stitches, but I just let it heal.

During the time I was out of Agnostic Front they had a temporary singer named Carl "The Mosher" Demola, who had been in the Psychos and The Icemen. Carl was a good friend and was infamous for going crazy at shows. When he went into the pit, he had his own style and everyone gave him his space when he danced. He never played a show with Agnostic Front. He rehearsed with them a bunch, but right after my dog bit me, Vinnie stopped by the Pit Farm before a CBGB show that Agnostic Front were booked to play.

"We've got a show coming up at CBGB. Can you play it? We really miss you."

"What about Carl?" I asked.

"He's cool, but it's not the same without you up there."

Vinnie was really persuasive. He could talk bears out of the caves they were hibernating in. I did the CBGB gig with my arm in a sling (because of the dog bite) and a bandage over the third degree burn on my neck (where the tattoo was removed). The crowd went crazy, like normal. Nobody in the public knew I had left the band. They just wondered what the fuck happened to my arm and neck.

"All right, I guess I'm back in," I said after the gig.


We tracked the *Cause For Alarm* record at Systems II in Brooklyn, which was basically a warehouse, and Norman Dunn produced it. I was sick with the flu and didn't feel well enough to enter the studio, but we were on a deadline.

"I don't feel good. I don't want to do this now," I said.

"Dude, you can do it! We gotta get this thing done and release it!" Kabula said.

It's one of those records I wish I could have redone because I was sick. I didn't have a lot of time to learn the songs and rehearse them with the band, so I wasn't vocally or mentally prepared. The other guys have said in interviews that I was missing from the sessions and didn't work that much with the songs. That's true, but honestly, I didn't want to be on *Cause For Alarm*. Vinnie dragged me back into the band. Even though I was working with them again, it wasn't like everything had suddenly changed. I still wasn't comfortable with the metal material.

Everything about *Cause For Alarm* was a challenge—even the artwork. We hired Sean Taggart, an amazing cartoon artist, to make the cover. He used to sing in the early hardcore band Shök, but he was best known for the flyers he did for hardcore shows. Mostly, he did work for Cro-Mags and was their in-house flyer guy. After we decided to work with him for *Cause For Alarm* art, Sean wanted me to check in with the Cro-Mags. That was a fair request, and they were cool with it.

The images he came up with for that album were classic, and lots of our fans have gotten them tattooed on their bodies. The background featured an American flag, but you could hardly see it because there were demented figures in front of it. On the top left was a winged demon with a nose ring. There was a bald guy in a suit eating from a spoon that was full of screaming people. On the bottom were three punks. The one on the left had green hair and his mouth was wide open, exposing rows of crooked teeth. Next to him was a skinhead holding a gun to the head of dude with a Mohawk.

At first, Steve Sinclair, who ran Combat Records, rejected the artwork because he thought it was too cartoony and didn't think it was shocking enough. Sean was pissed as hell, so he drafted up a second cover, the "Eliminator," that was more controversial than the first. A military leader was holding a chain attached to a growling pit bull. Behind him were five fully exposed nude bodies hanging on meat hooks and a wall splattered with blood. On the bottom left, one naked guy was curled up in a ball and covering his head with his hands. The guy from the military was looking right at him, like he was going to be the next victim. When Sinclair saw the new art, he freaked out and said it was too shocking! How crazy is that? Here's a label that eventually put out records by Carcass, Napalm Death, Morbid Angel, Bolt Thrower and all these extreme metal bands with graphically violent or Satanic covers. Steve agreed to use Sean's original image. We loved both images, so we decided to use the more grisly "Eliminator" drawing on our tour shirts and merchandise mail order. He also designed the promo poster art for the label, which was killer, and we used it for T-shirts, too. Sean Taggart later drew the amazing cover art for the Crumbsuckers' *Life of Dreams* and got a job as an illustrator for DC Comics.

With *Cause For Alarm*, from the music to the artwork, we came to the table and smashed it to pieces. Over time it became one of our best-received records, and it's widely regarded as the ultimate crossover record for its time. Some people didn't get it right away. Other fans never got it. I'm still not sure which of those two categories I fit into.

# CHAPTER 20

The first show we did for *Cause For Alarm* was with Lou at CBGB. Youth of Today opened for us. We took the stage and did a song from *Victim In Pain* before announcing that we were playing some of the new material. There was a mixed reaction. Fans were psyched to see us perform our new songs with Alex, but they didn't know how to take the music, especially the hardcore kids. They were confused. They were used to *United Blood* and *Victim In Pain*, and suddenly we were playing these crazy metallic songs full of guitar solos. We only did two more shows with that lineup since Lou had commitments to Carnivore. It was time to find another drummer.

Alex still seemed troubled and unhappy, even after we named the album after his old band and even after he and Rob had free reign to add all this metal to our sound. We played a show in Montreal, which was cool, but Alex wasn't feeling it. He was bummed that Louie was leaving. He wasn't happy with the record. I felt like he wanted it to be more metal and wanted us to evolve into a straight-up metal band like Metallica. At least that's what I thought until I found out 25 years later that he never felt like a full band member. We didn't do anything to make him feel more comfortable when we did that show with him in Montreal. When we finished our set, people wanted to hear more, so we played songs from *United Blood* that Alex didn't know. He just stood there on the side of the stage and felt awkward. He was pretty upset about that, but we had no idea since he never told us. After the show, Alex quit.

To this day, I feel badly about it, and looking back, I wish we could have felt more comfortable playing together. We wanted to please our fans, but we ended up distancing a good friend. That was never our intention. Alex is a good guy and a bro. He went through a lot with us and helped us make a legendary record.

Kabula was bummed because he lost his songwriting partner. It was time to rebuild. We auditioned drummers first, and that's how Joe "Fish" Montanaro came into the picture. He had no idea how we rolled. He showed up for the audition and was really good. He nailed all the beats and tempo shifts and injected some stylistic fills into the songs. It was clear he could play, but he had no idea about how we toured or what our lifestyles were like.

Joe wasn't hardcore. He was a big guido from Howard Beach. Long before he joined the band, his dad worked for the Mafia as a bookie and numbers guy. But he did something that upset his boss, who took him "for a ride." Police found him cut up in pieces inside a metal drum. It was a typical Mafia hit. I don't know how close Joe was to his father, but he was really shaken by that.

With Joe onboard we started looking for a new guitarist, and hooked up with Gordon Ancis, who had played with an early crossover band called NYC Mayhem. He didn't quite fit with our image because he had wild hair that made him look like Howard Stern. But he knew our songs, and was young, hungry, super-excited and part of our scene. He had never been on tour, and we were psyched to show him the ropes. First we needed to help him straighten out an ugly situation at home.

Gordon's mom was a sweet Jewish lady, but her boyfriend was abusive and knocked around Gordon, his sister and his mom. One day after rehearsal we went back to his house and found his mom crying. She had just been beaten up. It reminded me too much of my own upbringing, and I wanted Gordon to stand up for himself and protect the women in his family.

"Gordon, man. You can't let this guy hit your mom," I said in a calm, serious voice.

"You don't know him. He's got a bad temper."

I knew all about bad tempers, and I decided that if Gordon wasn't going to do something I would. Montanaro backed me up. We sat with Gordon and waited for his mom's boyfriend to get home. We were in his high-rise apartment on York Avenue in a ritzy part of town. When we heard the knob on the front door turn, Joe and I got ready. I grabbed a chair and swung it down on the guy. I hit him in the back. He didn't know what the fuck was going on. Joe hit him with a left-right combination and he went down. I kept hitting him with the chair, pounding and pounding him. He turned to look up at me and put a hand up—maybe to ask for mercy, maybe to block the chair. I swung down even harder and his nose exploded. Blood splashed over his collared shirt and tie. He rolled over and scrambled into the kitchen. I kept hitting him with the chair. Finally, he stopped moving, but he was still conscious. His face was swelling up like a water balloon. I kneeled down and put my mouth right up to his battered ear and told him if he ever beat Gordon's mom or anyone else in the family, we would kill him.

That gave his mom some hope and courage. She kicked her boyfriend out and he never came back. Gordon's mom was nice to us before, but she had a new respect for us and was astonished that we stepped into a situation that didn't directly concern us. I didn't think what we had done was heroic. It was simply the right thing to do.

Gordon's birth parents were divorced, but Gordon stayed in contact with his dad, who was a professional joke writer. One of his main clients was his roommate, Rodney Dangerfield, a funny-looking dude whose comedy routine revolved about how he didn't get any respect and was always treated like shit. When we opened for Slayer in New York at The Ritz on December 7, 1986, Rodney Dangerfield introduced us. It was great that Gordon's dad made that happen, but I don't think Rodney felt too comfortable in a rock club with skinheads and headbangers. He spoke so fast we couldn't understand a thing he said. All I could make out was "I don't get no respect" and then, "Ladies and gentlemen, Agnostic Front!"

Gordon had never been in such a reckless band and didn't really party, but he handled himself by staying away from us when we were on a tear. I respected that, though I wished he had a bigger set of balls. I never got into a physical fight with him, but I messed with his head a lot. Gordon was a virgin when he joined the band. I told him that before he went on tour with us, he had to have an orgy. I said that I'd set it up and that he should take a shower and come to Dave Da Skin's house at 3 p.m. He was really nervous, but I told him that if he was going on the road he had to be able to deal with weird situations. I told we got drunk and had gangbangs all the time, which wasn't true, but he believed me. He came over to Dave's and took off all his clothes. I stripped naked, and so did our friend Alexa.

"C'mon, Gordon, dude. You gotta get into it," I said. "Make a move!"

He just stood there with his shirt off for a minute. When he was about to drop his pants we all started laughing.

"Dude, we're fucking with you," I said "Put your shirt back on."

He was totally embarrassed and turned red. He scrambled for his clothes and ran out as fast as he could. Eventually, Gordon did get laid on the tour.

Joe wasn't a virgin, but he had never been in a band, so he didn't know what the fuck he was doing and he bugged the shit out of us all the time. He went from practicing drums at home along with records to being on the road as a piece of this crazy hardcore machine. He was so not hardcore. He was corny and rude, and he used to embarrass us. He had a Mohawk, but it was a bullshit Mohawk because he kept his mullet. He just looked like an idiot with a confused hairstyle. Once, before a show, he was sitting in the club ripping his pants.

"What the fuck are you doing?" I said.

"What does it look like I'm doing? I'm tearing my jeans before I go onstage."

"You dick. You've gotta earn those rips," I said. "Go put on another pair of pants."

The first tour with Joe was a nightmare. We came to blows because he didn't understand that we had to live on $3 a day when we were on tour. When you got your $3, you would get two hot dogs and a drink at a Super-K. That was our life for months. On his first day, this idiot bought marinated olives. He blew his $3 in one fell swoop. Then he tried bumming off us. We wound up swinging at one another and then rolling around on the ground screaming. That was nothing unusual. The trailer behind the van that held our gear became like our steel cage for combat. When there was some sort of conflict, we went in there and duked it out, blow for blow. I threw down with everybody in my band except Vinnie.

There were several times when Joe and I would be locked in the trailer high as fuck, throwing coffee mugs and glasses and trying to kill each other. But I gotta give Joe credit. He hung in there. He'd scream like a combat soldier and whip glasses back at me, and they'd smash against the wall. Eventually we made peace, but he was never one of us.

Joe's commitment to metal was emblematic of a growing schism in the scene. Some hardcore kids had a problem with bands tapping more into a metal sound, so there was a real division between the crossover metal kids who loved *Cause For*

*Alarm* and the old-school hardcore fans that hated it.

We played a show at Rock Hotel with Murphy's Law. They all wore wigs onstage to make fun of metal kids, because they hated that crossover was getting popular. We loved Murphy's Law, but we didn't think that was cool since I had grown my hair and *Cause For Alarm* appealed to thrash metal kids. A lot of them saw us as a gateway band and they came to our shows. Murphy's Law were being elitist and territorial, trying to claim some sort of purity for the New York hardcore scene. A lot of the time it came down to how a band presented itself. If they looked hardcore but sounded metal, they were often given some slack. But when you had a guy like Joe Montanaro in the band trying to high-five guys in the front row, that was a serious blow to your hardcore cred.

Between tours I was living in a really nice warehouse apartment that I had fixed up to suit my taste. While life was improving for me on the Lower East Side, things were going to shit for my little brother Freddy back in Florida. Eventually the situation got so bad that my mom called and asked if my brother could stay with me for a while. I was happy to have him, and pretty soon it became clear that he was better off with us. We tried to be responsible. We enrolled him in school, which is crazy since we never had legal custody. Freddy never wanted to go to school, even as a little kid. He was impossible to wake up in the morning.

By the time we headed out on tour, Freddy was back in Florida, but he never stayed there for long.

# CHAPTER 21

The metal in our new sound may have bummed out some hardcore groups, but it didn't bother the British punk band GBH, who asked us to tour with them in 1986. We were worried about what they'd think of Joe since he didn't represent anything that was cool about punk rock. GBH liked him because he was a nut and did blow. I had always loved GBH, so I was stoked to be on the road with them. During that tour, we were crazy-high on coke all the time. It was like we had the last bags of it in the world and had to finish it before someone stole it from us. GBH had a connection in each city, and we were getting eight balls everywhere. Joe was doing lots of coke and having a blast, so he was okay with playing hardcore. The best part was that we never had to pay for any of it. Even if we wanted to, we couldn't have. We didn't have the money. But GBH did.

A lot of U.K. bands are really into speed and coke. The entire time with GBH we were out of our heads. I'd never done that much cocaine in my life. If we were tired, we'd do a line to wake up. We'd snort up so we'd enjoy our food more. And of course, before we went onstage we did a double dose so that we had the energy of a rocket leaving the launch pad. I loved Quaaludes and mescaline, but blow gave me confidence and fueled my aggression. When I was jacked up I didn't make any bad decisions (or so I thought), and I didn't feel awkward or depressed. It was like a carnival ride that only ended when we ran out of drugs.

One day during a drop in Atlanta, Vinnie, Joe, Rob, Gordon and I went to Six Flags Great Adventure with the guys in GBH. The amusement park had karaoke studios where you could make tapes of other people's songs. We did Irving Berlin's

"White Christmas," and GBH's singer Colin Abrahall sang, "We're snorting up a white Christmas." It was hysterical—even funnier since we were coked out of our minds. We gave a copy to New York concert promoter Johnny Stiff, and Fran Powers from the band Modern Clix asked us if he could use the recording on a Christmas album. It came out on *No Two Flakes the Same: Penny for the Guy Christmas Compilation.* We're on a hidden track with no artist credits; it just reads "Mystery Guest: The Final White Christmas."

The problem with coke is that it usually turns people into assholes. They're so convinced they're right about everything that they refuse to listen to anyone. That happened big time with AF, and it probably had a lot to do with the tensions that escalated during our tour with GBH. Kabula was fed up with Vinnie. He didn't like that Vinnie didn't want to become too metal, and he resented that Vinnie had an animated personality that made everyone love him. He was pissed off that Vinnie wouldn't hump gear, drive the van or help sell merch. All he wanted to do was play shows.

"You gotta fuckin' help out," Kabula yelled at him one day. "You gotta drive!"

"Okay, okay, I'll drive!" Vinnie relented.

It wasn't like he finally gave in to the voice of reason. He was sick of being hassled and wanted to make sure it never happened again, even if it killed him. Vinnie got behind the wheel and drove the van like he was in a fucking Corvette. He was swerving and accelerating, seemingly oblivious to the fact that we were pulling a trailer. And he was a shitty driver to begin with! We were on a winding road in the middle of the mountains, and he didn't look where he was going. He drove right up to the edge of a cliff, yelled "Oh, shit!" and slammed his foot on the brake.

We all froze. I thought we were dead for sure. When we leaned forward, the van started to tip. When we shifted our weight backwards, it tilted that way. We sat still for what seemed like an hour. Finally we agreed to get out the back door one at a time, as carefully as we could. When I looked down from outside, I could see half the front left wheel was on the rocks and the other half was dangling in mid-air. When we were all out, it felt like a weight had been lifted off my shoulders. Then I felt that weight go from mid-air right down into the pit of my stomach. Somebody had to back the trailer out. None of us wanted to get back in the van, so we made Dave Da Skin do it.

Dave held his breath and crawled back in. Without closing the door, he turned the key in the ignition. The engine revved to life and the vehicle wobbled as Dave put the gearshift into reverse. He barely touched the gas and the wheels began to spin, but the van didn't move. He released his foot on the gas. Beads of sweat were dribbling down his face. He hit the gas, harder this time. The treads caught on the cliff edge, and the van shot backwards six inches. That's all he needed. He backed the trailer up again, and without saying a word we got in and continued driving, like nothing had happened.

Looking back, I think Vinnie nearly drove the van off the cliff so he'd never have to drive again. We never asked him to get behind the wheel after that. That may sound flippant, but it's how Vinnie operates. If he doesn't want to do something, he'll agree to do it and then fuck it up.

When we got back from the tour, Kabula was fed up with Vinnie.

"We could be a better band if we got another guitar player."

"C'mon, it's Vinnie we're talking about," I said.

"He's holding us back, Roger. He's not even trying to do something different."

I kind of went along. I shouldn't have, but Kabula was calling a lot of the shots back then, and I had other shit to worry about. Vinnie didn't like having his balls busted by Rob and he wasn't clicking with the new songs, so he agreed to leave. There wasn't any major drama or anything.

Vinnie just said, "Roger, I gotta talk to you."

"What's going on?" I said, as if I didn't know.

"I can't do this anymore. This isn't fun," Vinnie said.

"Are you sure?" was the most supportive comment I could give him. I had already agreed with Rob that Vinnie should leave.

"Yeah. What's the point? This is supposed to be fun. That's why I started doing this. It's not worth all the headaches if it's not fun."

"Well, if that's how you feel."

That was it. Vinnie was done, and I had no reason to believe he was coming back. We contacted Jonny Sanchez, who was Pantera vocalist Phil Anselmo's roommate and was in this thrash metal/hardcore group Chaos Horde. His band opened for us at Jacy's in 1985, a few months earlier, and it seemed like his style of playing complemented ours, so we asked if he wanted to join AF. He appeared in our video for "Growing Concern," which is weird because it's our only promotional footage where everyone but Kabula had long hair. For me it was good because I looked way different than the skinhead with the neck tattoo who stabbed some guy with a rusty, old screwdriver and was wanted by police. But Rob, Jonny, Gordon and Joe were into the thrash metal look.

Montanaro always fucked around with poor Jonny Sanchez, but then again so did I. Any time a new member came into the band I put them through this hazing ritual, like they were pledging for a hardcore fraternity. We used to make sandwiches to eat on the road. We'd have bologna, ham or whatever meat was on sale when we went to the supermarket. I'd hand them out when we stopped on the road. One time I handed a sandwich to Jonny and it was warm.

"Oh, a hot meal for a change," he said. "This is great."

It was warm for a reason. I had taken a shit in a plastic bag, closed it and put it between two pieces of day-old white bread. When he smelled it, he was horrified. He figured it out pretty quickly, yelled at me and threw the sandwich away. I laughed and he stormed off. But he didn't have anything else to eat.

Joe was even more psychologically abusive. He used to bully anyone he thought was soft. He was always trying to get Gordon to man up. He'd get in his face and call him a pussy over and over. For a long time Johnny tried to avoid confrontation. That only made Joe more persistent.

"You fucking pussy," he began. "You're like a third grade wuss who needs his mommy to hold his hand. You hide behind your guitar and think you're hot shit, but you're just a worthless pussy. And you can't even fuckin' play!"

Johnny made some lame jokes and Joe backed off for a while. But soon after, he went back to busting Johnny's balls. It was scary for Johnny because Joe was an intimidating dude. A lot of people think it's better to try to humor a guy like that, because if they hit him he might kick their ass. And sometimes he would. But Johnny should have hit him.

"Ice boy." CBGB, 1984.

1985.

CBGB, 1983.

First Agnostic Front US tour, 1985.

Freddy with Blitz, 1985.

Living in the van on the LES with Blitz, 1985.

CBGB, 1986.

Lower East Side, 1987.

Sunday Matinee with Amy, 1984.

CBGB, 1988.

Backstage with Will Shepler, Matt Henderson and Craig Setari, 1991.

Quiet time with Nadia, 1987.

1987.

CBGB, 1988.

CBGB, 1986.

# CHAPTER 22

ohnny put up with Joe's shit for a while, and he and Gordon played well together onstage while Vinnie was on hiatus. We sounded great even without Vinnie. And luckily, he missed the Motörhead tour. We were supposed to play a bunch of shows, and when we were invited we thought it was the coolest thing ever.

Their singer and bassist, Lemmy Kilmister, was a legend. He was around when the Ramones were getting started and he was as much a punk rock guy as a metal guy—at least musically. Attitude-wise, he was all rock 'n' roll. He was a roadie for Jimi Hendrix and played with acid-casualties Hawkwind until he was kicked out for getting busted at the Canadian border. He looked like a biker, drank like a sailor and did more speed and coke than all the members of GBH combined. And Lemmy didn't take any shit. He was a true warrior and a role model for punks, hardcore kids and metalheads alike. But when shit wasn't going the way he wanted it to, he could be short-tempered and vicious.

The first show with Motörhead was at a huge stadium in New Orleans in 1986. Motörhead were supporting *Orgasmatron*, the album with a snarling locomotive on the cover, and before the show they were setting up a train that was going to come out during the set. The road crew spent all fucking day building the thing, so we didn't get to sound-check. Five minutes before the doors opened, they were still fucking around with the train.

Phil Anselmo was up front going crazy because Johnny was playing guitar. We were ripping it up. After 20 minutes, Motörhead cut our power. The amps and mic went dead, and we couldn't even thank the crowd properly. I got mad and threw my water bottle at the soundboard.

Maybe they cut us off because they were afraid we would upstage the headliner. It was a bad introduction to Motörhead, and it was about to get worse. We had a lot of fans in the crowd and they felt cheated that we played such a short set. Playing to an angry hardcore crowd can be an exercise in futility.

When Motörhead got onstage, Lemmy pulled all his classic moves. He had the mic up front, tilting down, and was craning his neck up to sing. Some of the kids who were pissed about our abbreviated show jumped onstage and knocked into the microphone stand. Lemmy said, "What's all this bullshit punk rock shit?"

He was being a big dick, and the kids in the place retaliated by throwing coins, lighters and beer cans at the band. Lemmy threw the mic stand into the crowd, the lights came on and Motörhead walked off. The crowd flipped out, tore the monitors off the stage and trashed some of the amps. A bunch of kids went outside and tipped Motörhead's bus over.

The next day we got a call that we were off the tour, as if it was our fault that the crowd rioted. They took the Cro-Mags instead and that's the tour that broke the Cro-Mags out of the local scene and gave them the national success they were striving for, while we returned home. It was demoralizing because we knew we deserved to be up there.

Years later, our friends Dropkick Murphys got a slot opening for Motörhead. Singer/bassist Ken Casey was excited.

"That's awesome that they asked you and all," I told him. "But just listen. If you go over too well with the crowd they're going to cut you off."

"No way! Not Motörhead. They're awesome!" Ken said.

Sure enough, Dropkick Murphys were playing at Irving Plaza in New York and 10 minutes into their set Motörhead cut them off. Ken was pissed. He ran backstage and started yelling. "Fuck you, you pieces of shit! We're off this tour right fuckin' now! This is bullshit." From that point on, Motörhead never cut Dropkick Murphys' set short because they needed them on the bill. Motörhead had dipped in popularity and Dropkick Murphys were doing great. Although I'd badmouthed the guy over the years, I was bummed when Lemmy died in 2015. The guy could be a dick, but he was still a legend. Respect.

At some point on the Cause For Alarm Tour, we played a show in San Francisco, which was *Maximumrocknroll*'s home turf.

"If Timmy Yohannan shows up, the first person to knock him out gets $50!" I said. And I meant it.

Timmy did show up, but I couldn't let anyone deck him because we had no idea what he looked like or how old he was. We met the fucking guy and saw he was an old man.

*Fuck, if we hit this guy we're going to kill him!* I thought.

He and I sat down and had a long talk. It was actually a good conversation.

"Whoa, you guys are nothing like I imagined you to be," he told me.

"You know, we can see what's going on here and it's very different than what goes on in New York," I told him again.

I thought that we were cool and that *Maximumrocknroll* was going to say something nice about us—finally. But the next time we were in the magazine they were still talking shit about us. It was frustrating because we met the guy, we were straight up with him and he seemed cool. And then he talked shit when we weren't around. Who knows what got him back on his high horse? When he went to our show maybe he saw some knuckleheads from his scene causing trouble. I was done trying to make nice with the magazine. They obviously had an agenda, and you can only bang your head against the wall so many times before you realize you're probably giving yourself brain trauma.

That San Francisco show was memorable for a couple of reasons. Amy, who had been hanging out in San Francisco, was at the concert and came backstage to say hello. I was surprised since we had been split up for a while, but I was happy to see her. We talked about the problems we had when we were together and reminisced about some of the good, funny experiences we shared. The longer we hung out, the more attraction we felt. We got back together and then Amy went to Europe for a few months. I don't remember this, but Amy said that while she was gone, Vinnie introduced me to some girl and I started dating her. She didn't find out about it until years later.

I still don't know if that's true, as I was so fucked up on drugs at the time.

I talked to Amy while she was in Europe and told her that she had to come home right away or I was going to do something stupid. That worried her so she came back, but she didn't tell me she was coming. She surprised me at one of our shows in New York. That night we went up to the roof together and talked. Then we started kissing and one thing led to another. That's the night our daughter, Nadia, was conceived. Amy went on tour with us for a little while, mostly to make sure I was okay, and then she left to do her own thing.

The last major date on the Cause For Alarm Tour was the No Speed Limit Festival with Voivod and a bunch of bands. That was the beginning of the end for Jonny Sanchez. The show was at the Spectrum in Montreal in November, 1986. We did a good show and went over well. After the concert, our roadie, Rob Romero—a Puerto Rican guy from Brooklyn—was speeding along on an icy Canadian highway. We were singing Simon & Garfunkel's "Slip Slidin' Away" like fuckin' idiots. Rob skidded and jerked the wheel hard. He tried steering the other way. Bad move. I looked out the window and saw the trailer fishtailing towards us. In these situations your mind works faster than your body. I didn't have time to move, but I thought, *Oh, shit! This isn't good.*

The trailer crashed into the side of our van. We skidded across the icy highway and shot out into a lake. The front part of the van was in the water up to the hood. I had one of my pit bulls with me, Warrior, and he flew through the window and into the lake. He was the nicest dog until he hit that freezing water, and then he wanted to kill everyone in sight. I was trying to keep him calm while I did a head count to make sure everyone was still in the van. We had all flown around a bit, but everyone was okay.

When the van went into the lake, the trailer snapped off and all of our gear fell out. We went back up to the freeway and packed all our stuff back in. While we were picking up the last pieces of gear, a car came out of nowhere and crashed into the side of the trailer, scattering our shit all over the highway again. We had to wait for a tow truck, which pulled the van out of the freezing water. We reloaded the trailer with whatever we could salvage, but most of our gear was destroyed—drums, guitars and amps all smashed to bits.

We were shivering and covered in mud when the police showed up. They towed the van and trailer and helped us get to a hotel. We tried a few places in town, but no one wanted to let us stay there because Warrior was growling and barking at everyone. Finally, one hotel agreed to take us with the dog and we had a restless couple hours.

The freakiest thing is that before we went to play the No Speed Limit Festival, Amy had a nightmare in which my van was sitting on a dock and everyone in the band fell through holes in the dock. In the dream, Amy got a talisman and ran toward me to give it to me so I wouldn't fall in. But just as she approached, a hole opened up and I tumbled through. The only thing left on the dock was my van. Amy tried to convince me not to go on the tour, but I said it was only a dream and she was probably just nervous about me leaving her. Besides, it was a great opportunity for us, being on the same bill as Voivod. Before we left to play the festival, Amy bought me a talisman. Unfortunately, it didn't work.

We went home angry and dejected. Jonny Sanchez stayed with me for a bit in a squat on Avenue C and 3rd Street. I was pissed about our bad fortune and feeling pretty fucking sorry for myself. I drank too much, took too many drugs and challenged anyone who wanted me to calm down. That scared Jonny, and he went back to Louisiana. Later, he formed the bands The Flying Saucers and Summer Wardrobe and played with Roky Erickson from the 13th Floor Elevators. So he had a pretty wild ride even after he left AF.

By the end of the Cause For Alarm Tour we were sick of being around Joe, but we couldn't think of a solid reason to fire him. He hadn't done anything wrong. We figured the best thing to do was to break up the band. That way Joe would have to leave, and then we could get back together without him. It seemed to make more sense at the time than kicking him out. Plus, I needed some time to figure out if and how AF could continue. A few years after Joe left, he resurfaced as the drummer for GBH.

They say when it rains, it pours. While I was trying to sort my head out, a strange thing happened. Amy told me she wanted to meet up at a coffee shop. When I sat down next to her, she smiled and looked down at the table. Then she looked at me and told me that she was pregnant and was going to have the baby. I remembered how happy I was at first when Elsie told me she was pregnant. I was even more ecstatic when Amy gave me the news that we were going to be parents. I gave her a tight hug and kissed her on the lips. She didn't resist.

I tried to make everything work with Amy. We were back together as a couple and had been living in abandoned buildings and squats. We eventually found an apartment building on the Lower East Side that the landlord was warehousing. That was a practice where someone who wanted to sell a building left it vacant so he could sell the entire building and make more money than he could if it were mostly occupied. If there were people already living there, whoever bought the place could only raise the rent so much, but if they bought a vacant building and fixed up the apartments, the investors could hike up the rent to obscene levels. That was the beginning of the age of gentrification. The whole thing backfired because scumbags like me started squatting in the empty buildings.

That place was seriously fucked up. The landlord was violent and crazy. One time when someone was fucking with him or they owed him rent, he smashed this dude's head into the banister and practically impaled him on a spike. Another time, Amy walked in and there was an armed robbery over drugs going on in the hallway. She had one of our dogs with her, so she just walked by and the robbers left her alone.

As happy as I was about having a baby, I was stressing out. I didn't have the money to raise a kid, and we didn't have health insurance. Although the warehoused apartment was pretty nice, we didn't know how long we'd be able to live there. Still, I had my romantic moments, like one time when I had a surprise for her. When she got home I had a frying pan on the stove with a lid on it. I wanted her to think I cooked her dinner. Then when she came in, I held the pan out and lifted the lid. There was a tiny, live bunny in the pan.

I teased her that I was cooking it for dinner, which is weird considering that my stepfather did that same thing with my rabbit years earlier. But I wasn't thinking about that at the time. As cute as it was, the bunny shit everywhere. I got her another rabbit years later. This was an adult and I had no idea that it was pregnant. Amy woke me up in the middle of the night because she saw that our black and white pit bull puppies, Cowboy and Cowgirl, were playing with the tiny, newborn bunnies. She thought they were puppies because they were the same color as the dogs and was yelling, "The puppies had puppies!"

During that period I had some time to think, and Kabula and I talked quite a bit. He wanted to continue AF as a metal group and I wanted to return to a more hardcore path. Neither of us was happy with the other's ideas, so we agreed that we'd return from the breakup with our own versions of Agnostic Front. We were both cool with it, but he didn't follow through. He disappeared for a while, then started having kids.

Vinnie agreed to come back, but he wanted to change up the band, as did I. I called up a guy named Steve Martin, who had played with the F.U.'s in Boston, which became the Straw Dogs. Our good friend Jon Wrecking Machine kept telling me that Steve was itching to be in the band. I brought in another two guys from the Pittsburgh area, bassist Alan Peters and drummer Will Shepler. Both those guys had been in a band called Circus of Death. They flew in every weekend over the summer to rehearse and eventually became members. Vinnie and I were glad not to be in a band with Montanaro! We started writing songs for *Liberty & Justice For....* Will couldn't move to New York to work on the album since he was only 15 or 16. But he and Alan were both really into hardcore. Steve was into thrash and hardcore, so it seemed like a good fit.

Around that time, Amy and I became friends with a couple, Ian and Sue, who lived behind the building where we were squatting. Since Amy was pregnant, they invited us to stay with them at their apartment on Avenue C between 2nd and 3rd. That was helpful since AF was working on new music and I wasn't in the house much. I wrote lyrics for five songs. Steve worked on music for seven tracks, including "Crucial Moment," which was all his. Alan co-wrote four cuts and we covered "Crucified" by Iron Cross.

Before Agnostic Front recorded *Liberty & Justice For...*, Nadia was born. Amy and I planned to have the baby at a birthing center, but on April 12, 1987—early morning on Easter Sunday and three weeks early—Amy went into labor. Amy felt the baby drop and called the birthing center. She was only 15 minutes into labor, so they weren't worried. But Amy was sure the baby was coming right away so she called again and they told us to come in.

I immediately yelled to my friend Jon Wrecking Machine to run downstairs and remove the club from the steering wheel of my Pontiac J2000! We were in a third floor walk-up, so Sue stood on one side, Jon stood on the other and I stood in the center, holding and balancing Amy as she slowly wobbled her way down the stairs. Downstairs from the apartment was a crack house, so we had to yell at all the crackheads in the hallway to get the fuck out of the way. The birthing center was on 73$^{rd}$ Street, so we had to drive uptown. We pulled the seat all the way back and put Amy in the front. Sue got in the back and I slammed the door, then ran around to the driver's side. I took several deep breaths to stop myself from panting like a dog, then began the white-knuckle ride.

I went as fast as I could, but I figured we had plenty of time to get to the birthing center. From what I understood, women were usually in labor for hours when they delivered their first baby.

"Breathe, baby, breathe!" I said from the front seat, mimicking what they'd told me in the birthing meetings. Amy swore at me, and when Sue tried to help, she yelled at Sue to stop touching her.

I turned the Pontiac J2000 onto FDR Drive, and as soon as I got into the tunnel under the United Nations building, Amy let out a savage howl that would have sounded great on a punk album!

"Fuck! I can see the head!" Sue shouted.

I knew Amy was a tough chick, but the strength she exhibited was superhuman. That baby wasn't going to wait any longer, so I had the gas pedal on the floor. The whole experience was like a scene from *The Exorcist*. Amy was screaming every swear word she knew and even some that didn't exist, while making demonic snarls that freaked me out. If I had looked behind me, I swear I would have seen her head spin. Then she stopped making noise and started the breathing techniques they taught her in Lamaze class. Finally, our baby popped right out and Amy yelled, "Oh, shit!"

Once the baby was out, we still had to get to the birthing center as soon as possible since the baby and Amy were still attached by the umbilical cord.

I was freaking out. I said, "Don't worry, I'm not going down the street the wrong way!" But I was. I corrected my mistake, and after I turned around to take a quick look at the baby, I kept driving.

"Isn't it beautiful?" Amy said.

That's not the first word I would have thought of. I was fucking terrified! Nadia looked like a space alien. She wasn't making any noise, but she was moving her arms and legs in an awkward way because she had just been born. It was surreal.

I told Amy to hit the baby to get her to cry.

"Drive the fucking car, Roger!" she responded as she refused.

I sped the rest of the way. The streets were empty, so we got there in about ten minutes. It turned out everything was normal. The staff came out, cut the umbilical cord and took the baby inside. We were so freaked out on that crazy ride that we never looked to see if it was a boy or a girl! Later, we got the birth certificate and under "place of birth" it didn't list the address of the birthing center. It said "Other." I was pissed it didn't say "1982 Pontiac J2000."

The whole experience was insanely emotional. When I was a punk teenager, I built a shell around me to keep myself from being vulnerable. I could see out, but no one could get in. Occasionally, I peeled back the protective layers and exposed myself a little, like when I started seeing Amy or when I was having a heart-to-heart with Rudy, who was just as fucked up as I was. But when I looked at Nadia sleeping peacefully in her crib, I went through a tornado of emotions. It hit me how beautiful this little girl was. I was an emotional mess, but I was so mesmerized by this precious little girl.

As joyful as I was about the birth of my daughter, I was going through a major transition, so I was worried and distracted. I wanted to keep doing Agnostic Front, but I had to support Amy and my daughter and I wasn't making enough money to pay rent. I didn't want Nadia to grow up squatting. I wasn't just living for myself anymore. I couldn't get by on panhandled money and makeshift living conditions. I had to be a provider, which meant growing the fuck up and figuring out how to take care of my family.

# CHAPTER 23

**C**onsidering how fragile my psyche was, *Liberty & Justice For...* came out pretty good. We hired Norman Dunn—who had worked with Carnivore, Crumbsuckers and Whiplash—to produce the album, and Alex Perialas engineered. The album came out November 5, 1987. Then we hit the road. When we got to San Francisco on January 3, 1988, we played a show with Attitude and Potential Threat. Kirk and James from Metallica came, and we hung out after the gig and had a few drinks. It was good to see them and amazing to see how huge they had become. I was happy for them and glad they still supported hardcore and punk.

"Tell me about your new record. What's it called?" Kirk asked me backstage. I gave him a sticker that said *Liberty & Justice For...*. He thought that was a cool name and said he'd pick it up the next time he was in a record store.

"How's your next album going?" I asked him.

"We're still writing it, but it's coming out well. We're really trying some different stuff. But we're not there yet."

In August 1988 I was flipping through a music magazine and saw a huge advertisement for Metallica's *...And Justice for All*.

"Those fuckers!" I thought.

I can't say for sure that we had anything to do with Metallica naming their album that, but it seems too close to be coincidence. Maybe the name of our album was buried in the back of their minds and they didn't even realize their title wasn't original. To this day I'd like to give them the benefit of the doubt.

When we got back to the East Coast on the Liberty & Justice For... Tour, we played the City Gardens in Trenton, New Jersey, with Circle Jerks and Sick of It All. It was August 7, 1988, and while we were outside in the parking lot, Nazis showed up and at least one of them was wearing a Skrewdriver shirt. Even though City Gardens was a predominantly black neighborhood, the shows still attracted boneheads from time to time. They came from Atlantic City, Allentown and wherever else. We were just shooting the shit, and these guys came up and started asking questions. Push came to shove, and I caught one of them pretty good—I dropped him. One of the other guys with me caught another one of them. *Boom!* At that point, these clowns did not want to take this further. They were in over their heads. We told them to give us their shirts and get the fuck out of there. We thought that was that. Lo and behold, as I was playing the show I saw the same guys in the back with scowls on their faces. This time they had a few more heads, but it didn't matter because they were outnumbered—not just by the AF crew but by the whole damn crowd. No one backed that mentality. Their presence was sometimes tolerated in small doses, if people minded their business and kept their mouths shut. For the most part, it wasn't ever welcomed. They postured and heckled us, which got my attention. I threw one of the shirts we'd gotten off them to my 12-year-old brother Freddy as he came out to perform the end of "Blind Justice" / "Last Warning." It was our way of adding insult to injury. We were basically saying, *We stripped you of your "uniform" and put it on a 12-year-old boy. Now what are you going to do?* They didn't do anything and eventually they got lumped up by someone in the crowd or security. They were out, and the show went on without any further nonsense.

We didn't realize that some people in the crowd might get the wrong idea when they saw a little kid singing with us and wearing a Skrewdriver shirt. Photographers were there, and one of them—I believe it was Ken Salerno—shot a picture that has made its way around. It caused people who had beef with us to say, "Oh, look. It's that Nazi band with the kid in a Skrewdriver shirt."

It's fucked up because it impacts Freddy, too. His band, Madball, has always had the same political and social views as Agnostic Front. We're anti-racist. For anyone who has seen the picture and wondered what was going on, now you know.

City Gardens Trenton, NJ, 1988.

# PART V

## The Crime and the Time: A Brutal Education in Correctional Rehabilitation

INMATE
STATE OF NEW YORK
DEPARTMENT OF
CORRECTIONAL SERVICES

NAME MIRET, ROGELIO
DIN # 89-A-0136
EYES Blue
D.O.B. 6-30-64
HT. 5'8"
HAIR Brown
WT. 165
DATE OF ISSUANCE 2-16-89

# CHAPTER 24

**M**any people think of Agnostic Front as a successful and influential band that helped pave the way for a new kind of heavy music. I guess that's true and it's amazing that we touched people's lives in such a profound way, but we were never financially rewarded for our efforts. In the '80s I never made money releasing albums or touring. Most of my income came from moving narcotics. I started as a runner. I'd carry shit between Florida and New York because, thanks to my brother, I had hook-ups in both cities. My brother Rudy was a tough motherfucker, and like me, he got involved in some bad shit at a young age. Maybe it's genetics, but I think it had more to do with our upbringing. When they talk about human behavior, psychologists use the buzz phrase "nature or nurture." There wasn't anyone nurturing us, so we had to fight to survive. We were both born into abuse and had to struggle to achieve better lives for ourselves and our loved ones. I was glad he was still alive and could help me out. Honestly, my brother should be glad he's still around, too.

Transporting in Florida was more cutthroat than in New York, and one day Rudy got involved in a deal that went bad. He was hooking up these two black dudes from Boston that he didn't know. It was one of those friends-of-a-friend's-friend situations. These guys had flown to Florida for one reason only, *un tumbe*. Back in the '80s, *un tumbe* was well known in South Florida; buyers would steal the product instead of paying for it. These guys were with my brother in a side room at my mom's house. She had no idea what was going on until guns started going off. The dudes didn't want to pay, so they shot him two times. When he saw the gun he instinctively put up his hand to block his face and a bullet went into the back of his elbow and got lodged in there. Another bullet got stuck in his arm right near the Ulna bone. After they shot Rudy, the dudes fled the house with the goods.

Both my mom and Freddy heard the shots and ran out to see what was going on. They saw the guys running from the side of the house towards the getaway car they had parked on the front lawn. As they ran they were still shooting towards the back of the house where Rudy was. One of them pointed a gun at my mom and Freddy while they were running to the car. My mom and Freddy froze. The gunmen easily could have shot them but didn't. They jumped in the car and sped away.

Minutes later, cops swarmed the place, but by then the gunmen were long gone and my brother was on his way to the hospital, bleeding profusely and in immense pain from where his arm was shattered just above the elbow. The gun was a 9MM. To this day my brother doesn't have full movement in the arm. If the assailants had used a bigger gun he might have lost his arm—or worse.

The cops searched the entire house but didn't find anything. Shortly after my brother arrived at the hospital, detectives questioned him about the shooting. He told them that he was out in the backyard and heard some gunshots, then felt something hot hit him in the arm. He said he never saw anything, so maybe it was a drive-by shooting and he was in the wrong place at the wrong time.

Rudy was street-smart and knew he had to convince the cops that he had nothing to do with the crime. He pointed out that the neighbor on the side of the house where the shooting was had recently moved into the home in the middle of the night. He thought that was strange but hadn't said anything because he wanted to mind his own business. He told the police he thought these guys were in a witness protection program because they kept to themselves and never talked with any of the neighbors. They never had any guests and he barely ever saw them. They had two small kids that never went outside, and he heard that the husband worked for the FBI. Coincidence or not, a few days later, that same neighbor moved out in the middle of the night.

To this day my brother has two gun slugs left in his body. A few years after the incident, I was making a pick up from Florida and bringing it to New York. My brother and I each had a package taped to our bodies, and we were getting ready to go through security at Miami International Airport. I was sweating it a little because getting caught in an airport with what we were carrying would have earned us some hard time. But the line was moving along and there weren't any problems. When we were near the front of the line, I realized that my brother still had two slugs in him that would set off the metal detectors.

"Hey, man. We need to get out of here," I said.

"Why? what's wrong?"

"Just go, and I'll tell you."

We left the line and headed back, which probably happens all the time when people forget something before their flights. We looked behind us to make sure no one was following us. We were clear.

"What the fuck was all that about?" my brother screamed.

"Dude, you got the slugs!"

"Oh, shit!" he said. The look in his eyes said it all.

In an airport bathroom, he removed the package from his chest and taped it to me so that I was carrying everything. We went back to security, and the bullets set off the metal detector. Three people checked to see if he had any weapons. I went through security with no problem.

A couple years before I started carrying large quantities up and down the East Coast, I had a smaller business going. During the Cause For Alarm Tour I made some good connections with the dealers that GBH bought blow from. They agreed to do business with me back in New York, and they were always well stocked. I usually bought more than I'd sell because I knew the guys in the band wanted 8-balls. As I went along I earned the trust of more dealers, and my circle got bigger and bigger. In the '80s there was no shortage of musicians in New York that wanted blow. If you're a good businessman, the drug trade is like any other industry. It's about supply and demand, and to excel you have to know and follow the rules. You work with people you trust, only take on what you can handle and keep your business discreet. Nothing's worse than some flashy dealer who loves attention.

There's a song on our 1991 album, *One Voice*, where I was trying to say why I did what I did and how it got out of hand so quickly. On "Now and Then" I pretty much poured my heart out: "Scared and afraid that my own child's future was at stake / Quickly reacting was where I made my biggest mistake / Filled with delusions, I fell / I fell deep in my grave, carried by deceit's devouring waves."

After we crashed the van and before we started writing *Liberty & Justice For...,* I was living in an abandoned warehouse apartment with Amy. I was about to have a kid, I had no stability or security in my life, I had nothing in the bank and I started bugging out. I saw reflections of my childhood cast on my unborn baby: living in poverty, having nothing and having to fend for myself. I was determined not to let that happen to my kid. We needed a decent place to live, diapers, clothes, toys and all the shit that goes with being parents. We needed money, so I started moving drugs. It seemed like the easy way to get everything we needed while carrying on my career as a musician.

I had sold on a smaller scale before, but this time I upped my game. Between my brother's connections and my own, my income started to rise. It was easy money. Somebody said, "Hey, take this package and bring it over here and you'll get this kind of money."

I did it again and again, and the quantities I carried got bigger. The bigger the quantity, the more I got paid. I didn't have to go through airport security or border crossing agents.

The people that hired me had a connection in New York and quickly learned that I was a man of honor. I was respected, and my word was good. I was hooked up through professional people and they knew I would keep my mouth shut if something went wrong. That's one of the most important rules for dealers. They have to know whom they can trust and they test the people they hire. It was made perfectly clear to me that if I snitched or went to the police, I wouldn't just be out of a job or blackballed in the business. I would end up at the bottom of a river somewhere. Trust is everything for people who run a drug business. If they can't trust someone, that person might as well be dead.

The drummer for Ultra Violence, Charlie Violence, ran astray of the cardinal rule.

"Hey, Roger, I need to get something from you," he said to me one day when we were hanging out in the Lower East Side. "I need to score big."

"Sure, you know," I replied, having no reason not to trust him. I thought Charlie was one of us. "Let's meet and talk. I don't carry that stuff with me."

That was the truth. Someone down the street was holding the stash. I went down the street a little later to get the package for him, and there was a parked vehicle that looked like an undercover police car. My gut instinct told me something was off, and

I started to feel wary. Then I saw Charlie sitting between the two big guys, and there were two other guys in suits hanging around.

"You got the stuff?" Charlie said.

"What are you talking about?" I replied, fully aware something was awry.

"The stuff, man. Do you have the stuff?"

He literally said that. It's the kind of shit you hear in bad movies right before the cops swoop in. This was no way to conduct a drug deal. I thought, *This is such an obvious setup, you retard.*

"No, I don't got anything. I don't know what the fuck you're talking about," I said and walked away. I should have gone back and beat his ass, but I didn't. I found out later that Charlie tried to set me up because he was busted the week before in a school zone with acid and mescaline, and he wanted to reduce his sentence by giving up other people. He wasn't just selling drugs. He was selling them to kids, which is where I drew the line. Years later I heard a rumor that Charlie was killed for trying to rat out the wrong guy.

Eventually, I got set up by someone I trusted. I never saw it coming. I was working with people who were heavily involved with dogfighting and drugs. We used to go to a restaurant in Brooklyn to conduct business. The grandson of the owner was a big Mafioso guy. They used to close the restaurant to set up a huge, illegal dogfighting ring in the back by the freezer. People came from all over the country to watch pit bulls tear one another to shreds. I reluctantly watched some of the fights to prove I was one of the guys, but I never placed any bets. The whole thing sickened me.

The dude that ran the ring got busted with some drugs and the cops got to him. It was one of those "Tell us where you got the drugs and we'll take it easy on you" situations. The guy ratted me out, along with a bunch of other dealers. The police set up an elaborate sting operation. It wasn't a simple process because there were a bunch of guys I was working with. The dude who framed me also set them up, and they all worked with the cops to get me busted.

A snitch is no better than a cockroach. All the people who framed me were eventually murdered, taken out one by one to punish them and protect the boss. The last guy standing had a mom who was holding drugs for him. He was busted, but she took the blame to save her son and was sentenced to 25 years behind bars. His own mother! I respectfully kept my mouth shut.

After I was busted, I was still on speaking terms with the guy that let his mom take the 25-year bid. He had ratted out the people he sold for, and one day we were sitting in my living room drinking beer.

"Hey, it's only a matter of days before they're gonna kill me," he said in the middle of a conversation that wasn't about drugs or hit men.

"C'mon, man," I said. "I'm sure you can work something out."

Knowing he was marked, I hoped he wouldn't get shot up when I was around. A week later, Joe Fish told me the guy called him from a telephone booth a few days after I saw him. He sounded all strung out, and during the call Joe heard a bunch of gunshots and crashing sounds. The guy got shot up in the booth and murdered.

Here's how my bust went down. It was August 30, 1987. I was supposed to bring a package to a guy I had worked with before, so I had no reason to suspect anything. I was driving from New York to meet with him and some of his people. I figured that before I made the delivery, I'd go to a punk rock picnic at the home of my friend Brooke Smith. She played the girl in the well in *Silence of the Lambs*. She had a nice house in upstate New York and invited everyone over for a pool party. She invited Warzone and Nausea to play. The place I was supposed to deliver the stuff to wasn't far from where she lived.

"Hey, I'll be right back," I said in the middle of the party.

A friend of mine came along for the ride to discuss the release date for a seven-inch on my label, Last Warning Records, which we had previously recorded.

On the way to the dropoff spot, I stopped to get gas. We were in Orangeburg, New York, right over the Tappan Zee Bridge, when a policeman pulled me over.

*He's never gonna see anything*, I thought. The stash was hidden inside a diaper bag and the law protects people from searches inside their cars unless there's probable cause. A second cop came over to help him out. Since they were tipped off that I might have something of interest, they just had to find it. When they questioned my passenger, they asked if he knew of anything suspicious in the car. He truthfully answered, "I don't know about anything in the car at all." That was enough for the cops to feel they had the right to question us further. The first cop told me he wanted to see my car's VIN, which was engraved in the driver's side door.

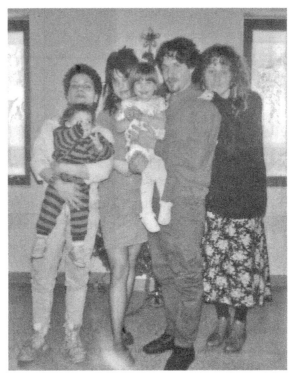

Nadia, Aviva, Alexa, Amy and Brooke visit me in prison. Christmastime, 1989.

In his police report he wrote that when I opened the door a little, he saw something suspicious. He claimed that the diaper bag was slightly unzipped and that he saw a Ziploc baggie dangling out of the corner. That was bullshit. It was just the excuse he used later to get inside my car and search it. The truth is that after I opened my door, he barged right in and started searching the car without my permission, and he soon found what he was looking for. The cop who searched my car was of medium build, and it looked like he was in good shape. He had red hair and a red beard. He wasn't rude to me or aggressive. He was just doing his job, which was to find the stuff he knew I was carrying. I couldn't stop him because he had backup and both cops had guns. I wasn't about to risk getting shot.

I took the whole rap. My passenger had no idea what was going on. The cop read both of us our rights and took us down to the police station. We went right into county jail and had to wait to be arraigned. I spent about two weeks there because

I didn't have the money for bail. My friend, who was under 18, spent five nights in county lockup until he could arrange bail. His charges were later dropped after I gave a written statement that he had no knowledge of the situation. I guess I didn't have the best judgement when it came to exposing others to the risks of my ruthless behavior. I wasn't from the area so I didn't know anybody. In a way that was good because nobody had any beef with me. I was just another criminal.

# CHAPTER 25

After I was in jail for a week, a couple of DEA officers explained how much trouble I was in. They wanted to know where I got the coke and where I was taking it. I didn't tell them what they wanted to hear. I wasn't telling them anything. They knew I was moving product for somebody else, so they tried to get me to rat out the guy I was working for. They started out by acting all nice.

"Hey, we're charging you with four ounces," one of the cops said.

*Whoa, there was a lot more than four ounces in there,* I thought.

When the cop was on the stand the next day at my pre-trial arraignment, when I was being charged with four ounces, he looked me in the eyes and winked.

I was, like, *Oh, shit! This guy's trying to give me a break.*

I didn't know what was going on, but they were pretending to be on my side to get me to talk. They figured if they did me a favor, I'd help them out. That wasn't about to happen. If they had charged me with possessing eight ounces, I would have been sentenced to eight to life.

I don't know what happened to the rest of the coke. Someone definitely took it—probably more than one person. Maybe they snorted it, or maybe they planted it on someone they busted later. Maybe they sold it. I wasn't about to say, "Hey, wait! It wasn't four ounces. It was more!"

They brought me back to my holding cell, and the cop acted like my friend.

"Hey, you know, I said you only had four ounces to help you out, right?" he started. "I know you just had a baby and I know you'd rather be home than locked up. Now maybe you can help me out and let me know who your supplier is."

I still wasn't sure what was going on, but I didn't fall for the good cop routine. "Yo, I'm telling you. It's my stuff for my personal use," I said. "It was just for me."

The cop accidentally did me a bigger favor than I realized. My lawyer told me that I could legitimately claim that I needed four ounces to sustain my habit—I'm a drug addict and that was my personal monthly stash. My lawyer used that claim in my defense so the cops dropped the intent to distribute charge. If I had been hit with that, who knows what the judge would have sentenced me to.

Once the cops figured out I wouldn't cooperate and narc on anyone, they tried to bump up my charge. They said some of the coke was used in the lab for testing so they didn't have the full amount. I was already processed and their plan backfired. Even afterward, they still tried to get me to talk. They said if I didn't cooperate I was going to do hard time. Then they softened their tone.

"Look, we know you didn't set up the deal. If you just cooperate with us, we'll help you out," said the cop who found the blow. "Let us help you."

"I want my lawyer," I said. I wasn't going to rat anyone out. Rats get their necks snapped.

Even if I had the best lawyer in the world, there was no way I'd get out of this without doing time. As it turned out, I had navigated into the perfect storm. The father of the police officer who arrested me was the sheriff of the town, and his father was a judge. I never had a prayer. The people I was moving shit for hired Charles Adler, who was a big criminal defense lawyer and I had him on retainer.

Shortly after I was arrested a cop got murdered by a skinhead. The murderer was wearing a bootleg Agnostic Front T-shirt—that we never made, printed or sold—and it had an image from an old flyer of a skinhead beating up a cop. It was designed in 1984 by CHUY, an artist from Oxnard, California. The kid with the shirt was listening to *Victim In Pain* and driving too fast, and a police car pulled him over. When the officer asked him to open up his trunk, he pulled a gun out of the glove compartment, stepped out of the car and shot the cop point-blank.

Suddenly, as far as everyone in the public was concerned, Agnostic Front were the leaders of a neo-Nazi, skinhead, cop-killing cult. The dead cop's wife sued everybody she could think of, including us, the record label, the T-shirt company and even Budweiser because they found beer in the guy's car. The multi-party, class-action lawsuit cost us about $15,000. That was money the band didn't have. Worse for me, the cop-killing dirtbag destroyed my defense and my relationship with my appointed lawyer!

My lawyer, who was Jewish, suddenly heard rumors that I was a neo-Nazi. I kind of looked the part, but if he had taken five minutes to talk to me about the accusations, he would have seen that I was the opposite of that. But he didn't discuss his thoughts with me. He sold me out and instructed me to plead guilty even though my arrest was a pretty clear case of entrapment. The people who had hired him for me said I should follow his advice.

"Don't worry about it, Roger," a high-ranking messenger said to me when I was in jail. "We're going to take care of your family. Just hang in there, and we'll get you a great appeals lawyer who will get you out."

During the time I was in county, I did a lot of thinking. I knew I was going to do time and I was okay with that, but I worried about what would happen to Amy and Nadia. We were still living in a sketchy place, and I didn't know if the guys who said they'd make sure Amy was taken care of would make good on their promise. I wasn't scared for myself, and going to prison didn't bother me because I was used to being around the same type of people on the streets. We would just be together in an enclosed space with no door to the outside. I thought I could live with that.

Before I was sentenced, it was weird not knowing what was going on with my case. I didn't like the mind games the cops were playing. They wanted me to testify and give up my suppliers, but I wouldn't do it. I didn't even take the stand. But at night I would lie in my bunk and feel I was going through the motions. It seemed like a dream. I figured after I went to jail it would just be a matter of time before I got out. But it started getting scary when the judge set the bail at $250,000. I didn't have anything to put down as collateral. I didn't have the money!

My mother came up from Florida and tried to put her house down, and they wouldn't take it because the home was out of state. Fortunately, it was 1987, and banks were still doing no income verification loans. You could buy a house and say you made as much money as you wrote down on paper. The game was rigged because the interest rates were ridiculous—like 17 percent. My mom said she made $50,000 a year and co-signed for me, and Amy and I bought a house in Staten Island that was valued by the bank at $250,000, enough to bail me out. She put down the minimum payment to secure the property, $2,500, and we used the bank value of the house to secure my bail.

I was grateful to my mother and promised I'd change my ways, but I went right back to destructive and damaging activity. I was already under enough pressure from having to support my wife and daughter and having a future prison sentence hanging over my head. Now I had a mortgage on the house to pay. It was easier to return to old habits than dig within and make an effort to change. I hung out with all the same people who were dealing drugs and partaking in dog fights. It's what I knew. It was comfortable. I was there for the ride and the money.

I got arrested twice while my case for possession was pending, which didn't help my legal situation, and both times it was because I was with two guys I should never have been involved with. I didn't know it, but those were the people that set me up in the first place. Both of them wound up doing huge prison bids, and one was murdered in the streets after I got out of prison.

I wasn't moving product with them, but I was attending illegal gambling events. Sure as hell, we all got busted. That was another strike against me—not learning my damned lesson. Eventually, my lawyer got the additional charges dropped and focused on the pending drug case, but for a while I was living like a criminal. Maybe there really is something to this idea of karma.

When you don't know your fate and you've got cops winking at you, it boosts your confidence. You think, *Oh, I'm gonna fuckin' beat this*. It's different when you've got an actual sentence. After my first lawyer sold me out, I got a second lawyer, Anthony Lombardino. He was a big, fat Italian guy who defended a bunch of mobsters in the famous Pizza Connection case. At the time that trial was the longest criminal jury case in U.S. history, lasting from September 30, 1985, to March 2, 1987. These guys were distributing massive amounts of heroin and cocaine and laundering the cash before returning it to their suppliers. It was called the Pizza Connection because the dealers sold the drugs at pizza parlors, including Original Ray's Famous Pizza on 3rd Avenue near 43rd Street, which was the headquarters for the operation. 23 dealers were on trial, and all but one was convicted.

I thought that didn't bode well for me, but theirs was an open-and-shut case. I had a much stronger defense strategy. I was set up. After my pre-trial was over, I met with Lombardino, who said he was going to get me off but it'd take time.

"We need to lose to win," he told me when I sat down with him at his fancy office in a New York City high-rise. He said if I didn't take the original deal Adler arranged, didn't plead guilty and went straight to trial, I would be facing a lot more time if I lost.

"You need to cop a plea and then we'll get you out of the Rockland County courts and into the appellate courts here in New York City, where I have solid connections. And then we'll say there was an illegal search and seizure, and whole case will get thrown out. But first you have to do your time."

I didn't know what to do or whom to trust. My first lawyer screwed me over so badly that I had no idea if this second guy was on my side or not. But I didn't really have any options. Besides, Lombardino was classy. He was well-groomed, wore fine Italian suits and was well-respected. He knew all the New York City judges on a personal level and even played golf with many of them. He wore nice jewelry, including a diamond ring. It looked like I might get a sentence of one to three years. Then something unexpected happened. Some of the litigators for the prosecution tried to tie my case to the incident in which the cop got killed by a skinhead and use my prison term to set a precedent. Lombardino argued that the two cases were totally different.

In 1988, everybody I hung out with at CBGB signed a petition in my defense—over 800 names—but the judge didn't care. As far as he was concerned, he had the leader of "a neo-Nazi drug-dealing, cop-killing organization." Those are the exact words he used, and I was shocked because the only thing I was guilty of was the drugs. I'll take the blame for that, but everything snowballed. After my hearing on December 14, the defense attorney and judge entered my plea deal. The judge let me have the holidays at home with my family because I never skipped any court dates and I was responsible.

A partner and friend, Greg "One Eye" Danelli, picked me up from the court and took me home that day. Everyone called him "One Eye" because he was a fireman and had been burned in a fire that left one of his eyes half-closed. Even though he was part of the NYFD, the guy was the furthest thing from a hero. He did all kinds of illegal shit on the side and he was heavily involved in dogfighting. I later found out he was part of the group that ratted me out. He never let on. He acted like he cared about me and was my friend. Years later, he became a social worker for the City and he made deals with young women for sexual favors. He'd say something, like, "Hey, I won't tell your parole officer your urine test is dirty if you have sex with me." He eventually got caught in an FBI sting. He was so humiliated he hung himself in prison.

On January 2, 1989, there was a huge show at CBGB—the No Justice, Just Us Benefit—with Agnostic Front, Murphy's Law, Raw Deal, Supertouch, Sick of It All, Side By Side, Straight Ahead, Gorilla Biscuits, Absolution, Wolf Pack, Vision and Nausea. It was 12 bands for $10, and the money was used to help pay my legal bills. While I was incarcerated, there were a few other No Justice, Just Us benefits that helped pay for the defense team preparing my appeal, including a show at the Anthrax club in Connecticut in March. The bands that played were Slapshot, Crossface, Insted, Vision and Blind Approach. Coincidentally Blind Approach's guitarist, Matt Henderson, would be next in line to join Agnostic Front. We re-pressed our seven-inch of *United Blood* for the first time, limited to 1,000 copies, and all proceeds went toward my defense.

Agnostic Front's first video, "Anthem," was shot at the No Justice, Just Us show two days before I went in to do my time. The atmosphere at the gig was intense. I had buzzed my hair down. I knew I was going to prison, so I was doing steroids and working out like crazy. I had to get tough and strong. That CBGB show was phenomenal. It was charged with energy. Not only was the place packed, there was a giant line of people lined up around the block waiting to get in. It felt great to play the show, but it was bittersweet.

Since they knew I was gonna be away for a while, the guys at our label decided to release a live album that was recorded on August 21, 1988. Combat Records had hired a mobile truck and taped the entire show, without any real plan to release it. The recording sat around the office for a while. Finally, they thought it was a good idea to put it out so there would still be buzz about AF while I was in prison. It wasn't anything we planned, but *Live at CBGB*, which came out in 1989, turned out to be a classic album—the *Cheap Trick at Budokan* for the hardcore generation. We had no idea how well it would go over, but that album introduced a lot of kids around the world to our music. It was the first release from the company's new hardcore imprint, In-Effect. The people at the label were serious hardcore fans, unlike the metal folks at Combat, who didn't get what we were doing. Our guitarist, Steve Martin, was their publicist, which certainly didn't hurt. On January 4, 1989, two days after the No Justice, Just Us benefit and "Anthem" video shoot, Greg Danelli took me to the court, where I surrendered. I was back in the same county prison I had been in right after I was arrested. I got sentenced to four to life. Everyone was shocked, including my lawyer. The judge gave me the maximum sentence he could give me.

*Oh, shit. This is real now*, I thought. *I'm gonna be here for at least four years.*

Four to life. The first number was the minimum. There was no possibility back then of getting time off for good behavior. I was looking at doing some solid time.

Before I was dealing with actual numbers and was behind a locked door, it was more like a game. Go, come back. Go, come back. When you're always going back and forth like that, you don't think anything's gonna happen. So much time had passed. I was arrested in 1987 and I started my sentence almost two years later. During that time, nothing seemed real. I was still young when I was busted, 22 years old, and I had never been in serious trouble for anything before. At first, it seemed like I'd luck out again.

Two years later, I was in another world. A lot of it had to do with Nadia. She was an infant when I got arrested, and I didn't have much of a connection with her other than the fact that she was my kid and she was amazingly cute. She didn't recognize her nose, let alone her dad. Now she was 18 months old and she knew who I was. We had a relationship. I thought, *Man, this is gonna be tough.*

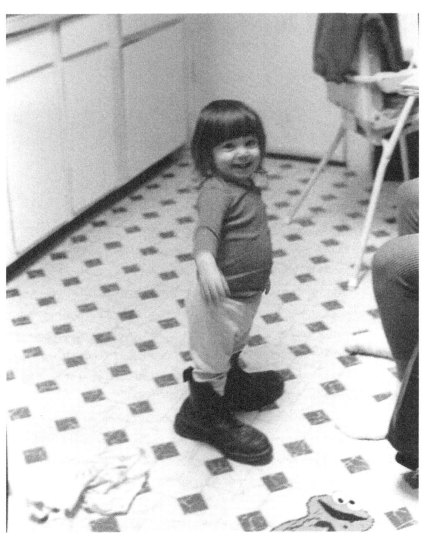

Nadia in my boots while I was in prison.

# CHAPTER 26

had done what I could to get ready—the steroids, working out. I tried to prepare myself mentally. After I was sentenced I was cuffed and led behind the courtroom, where the county jail was. I sat there in a waiting cell for two and half hours while other inmates were sentenced. Then it was my turn. Two guards led me down halls like a lab animal in a maze. They stripped me down and searched me. It was all processing stuff I had already gone through. You bend over, grab your ass and spread it while they look up your colon with a flashlight. They ask you to cough to make sure you're not hiding anything up there. After they searched me they sent me back to county jail, where I finally felt normal again.

I could barely sleep that night. I was thinking about not being with my family and my band. I got up late the next day. It was like that for two or three days. I felt like I had fucked over my daughter and negatively affected my family. I didn't see any of them for three or four days. Then they came up and visited and we talked. There's nothing much you can do in county jail but sit around, lift weights, play basketball and read books. I was in an eight-person cell. There were four bunk beds and I took a top bunk.

Jail is full of thieves, rapists, dope dealers, murderers and other people who have done unspeakable things, yet the minute you get in there, you have to be well-mannered. You have to be quick. You have to be prepared. As soon as I was incarcerated, a huge Hispanic guy who had been there a while told me how things worked in jail. He told me who to sit with and who to talk to. Every new inmate experiences that, and the shot caller who comes up to you is always of your race or ethnicity. If you don't run with your people while you're there, you'll be run out because you'll eventually face some shit and only your people will have your back.

That wasn't my thing. I'm used to being around people of all races and religions. I liked finding out how different people think and what they value. But when you get to prison, if you're not racist or religious, you will be shortly. You need to associate with your people and take sides.

I even said that on *One Voice* in "Force Feed." There's three shades of green: light (meaning Caucasian), medium (Hispanic) and dark (African American). You have to run with your own, whether or not you want to, or you're gonna get hurt.

All these people you hang with are way cleaner and more polite than anyone on the street. After you use the toilet bowl you have to clean it. You have to make your bed. The COs don't give a shit, but your people care. It's about respect. There are a new set of rules and attitudes. The day I got out, I left it all behind me. But while I was there, I didn't have a choice but to be someone I didn't want to be in a place I didn't want to be in. That's what happens when you fuck up and get locked up.

When you're in county you don't know when you're going to be moved. After being in an eight-person cell for two days I got moved into a cell with a light-skinned black kid, who seemed nice enough. We stayed up all night talking about what we were doing. It's not like the movies at all. There are all these films where one guy goes, "What you in for?" And the other dude says murder or robbery or claims he's innocent. When you're in prison, you don't tell anybody what your crime is. It's nobody's business. But I hadn't learned that yet, and I figured I had nothing to hide. I told him I was in for a possession charge. He told me he was involved in an assault, which wasn't exactly true. We were friendly for a day or two. In jail, no one has any real connection to anything outside his immediate circle. The only way to know about what's going on at the prison is from the local newspaper brought in by the guards.

The Monday after I met my cellmate, the paper got handed out to everyone. There was an article about how my cellmate had raped his three-year-old niece and given her gonorrhea. They traced the diseased sperm back to him. He was a child molester, which is probably the worst thing you can be in prison besides a snitch. As soon as some guys in my crew found out I was in the cell with him they let the leaders know and the shot callers decided that I had to get to the guy. One way you get to people inside is to burn them out.

Some of the Hispanic brothers came up to me and said, "Yo, you gotta hit him because he's a piece of shit." They gave me a large, open can of tomato sauce three-quarters filled with boiling hot baby oil and told me to throw it at him when I was out on the floor on mopping duty. The order was given, and in prison you either do unto others or others will do unto you. I knew there would be consequences either way. If I didn't do it, I might be burned out instead. If I did it I'd get caught and receive a longer prison sentence. I weighed both sides and decided I was better off being the aggressor instead of the victim. I psyched myself up and got ready. This motherfucker lied to me, then he acted all nice. More importantly, he did something really sick and needed to pay. I headed back to my cell with the hot oil.

On the way, I thought about how I was gonna do it. If I dumped a little on him he'd be able to fight back and I'd end up in a messy brawl. I considered splashing the oil on his chest. That would do enough damage to incapacitate him. Then I visualized what he did to this three-year-old girl and God knows how many other kids. I thought of Nadia and my temper started to rise. I decided to splash all the oil in his face. I raised the container and opened the top. It seemed like time had slowed and the last few steps to my cell took forever. I gritted my teeth and got ready to attack. The fucking dude wasn't there.

I looked around and didn't see him, so I went back to the guy who set up the whole thing and said, "Yo, the cho-mo is gone."

"Are you sure?" said one of the more muscular Hispanic dudes with more of a threat than a question.

"I'm telling you, man. He's gone."

"Okay. I hope you're not playing us. If you're backing out and you don't want to do it, you're gonna be dealt with."

They sent another guy to check out the cell and he saw that I was telling the truth. The pedophile wasn't there. I was relieved because as much as I wanted to hurt the guy, I knew it was a no-win situation.

If you commit murder in prison the penalty isn't as severe as if you kill someone in the street. But I wanted to get out in four years. When you hit the board with life, everything you do adds time to your sentence. If you get sentenced to two to four, you're out in four years no matter what. They can't tack on an extra year for shitty behavior. They can make you stay beyond your minimum, but they can't keep you in prison for more than your max time, unless you catch a new bid. It was definitely in my best interests not to throw hot oil in this asshole's face because I would have gotten caught. It's not like I could say anyone else did it. I was mopping the floors, so I was the only one out on that tier. Everyone else was locked up. No one could have gotten to him but me. Still, I would have taken the fall if I had to.

A few days after my near miss with the pedophile, I was processed out of county to state prison. When you leave county, you get sent to a state correctional facility. You don't know what part of the state it's going to be or how long you'll be there. That's unnerving, but prisoners are transferred all the time to every type of facility, from medium to maximum security. Sometimes officials transferred guys who had been involved in riots or fights and had become a danger to themselves or others. They shifted dudes around to keep more of an even balance between the whites, blacks and Hispanics. And they transferred prisoners to get some fresh faces in the crowd. I think they also did it so inmates never feel settled. You're not as likely to form attachments if you realize that any day you could be put on a bus and sent somewhere else.

My first stop out of county was Fishkill Correctional Facility, a maximum security prison 75 miles north of New York City. The ride was uneventful, but my head was racing. I had no idea what to expect and was determined not to be someone's bitch, even if some motherfucker tried to kill me.

When I got there, they gave me a state-issued prison outfit and inmate ID. They shaved my head and told me to close my eyes. I was no longer human, I was just a number: 89A0136. Then they put insecticide all over my head. It felt like being sprinkled with baby powder, only it didn't smell like a clean infant's diaper and it was toxic to bugs and probably humans. Nobody cares what prisoners are exposed to. Maybe they know that shit causes cancer. It wouldn't have mattered. We were just scum to them.

The whole process was humiliating, but that's what they do to prisoners. They take away your individuality and humanity and turn you into a number. Every time guys would go out for something or come back to their cells, they had to get checked. Same drill as in county. You'd strip down and raise your arms, then bend over and spread your butt cheeks. You got used to it quickly. It happened all the time—after visits, after riots, any time you went to the yard. If they had any reason to suspect you were hiding anything, they reached up there. Or they'd put you on observation until you had to take a shit and then they'd check your bowel movement. The only time someone was excused from any part of the routine was if it conflicted with their religious beliefs. Rastas were allowed to keep their dreads, and Muslims didn't have to shave their beards. The same went for meals. Jewish prisoners could get kosher meals.

Being in prison was different than being in county jail. In county they came around to everyone's jail cell with food, then they opened the doors and you went right out to the yard, where you could lift weights or play basketball. I went from having that to being in lockdown in a solo cell for 23 hours, with one hour of rec. For the hour break, they didn't even take you outside. You went to a little recreational area. This continued for a week or two until you got classified. At that point you were mixed in with different people. You didn't know your classification until you got called into the office to meet with a counselor. They wanted to know that you were in good health and weren't going to commit suicide and what skills you knew or wanted to learn. They needed to make sure they were placing you in the right prison. Different facilities specialized in particular trades. The counselor checked out your tattoos for gang affiliations to see if they might be a problem and if they needed to keep you away from rival gang members.

When the prison officials shaved my head they saw several tattoos: my "skins" tattoo, a pair of spider webs and a spider. That's how I got the nickname Araña, which is Spanish for spider. In prison, being a skinhead wasn't very popular. Everyone had seen the vicious segments about skinheads that Geraldo Rivera and Oprah did, and I got weird looks from people that didn't understand the non-racist side of skinhead culture.

Everybody tried to figure out which gang I was associated with. Right away, being that I looked white and had all these tattoos, they tried to stereotype me as something I had nothing to do with. No one could tell I was Cuban; their first impression was that I was a racist skinhead.

In county you didn't have to surrender your clothes when you went in. But when you went upstate to serve your real time, you have to give up all your clothes and put on a prison uniform. Amy had to pick up my clothes. It was just sweatpants and a T-shirt. If you had anything fancy, it'd get you in trouble. I was in Fishkill for two weeks. The rules were stricter than county. We had to dress in the same colors and walk down the halls in formation. Different groups came out at different times and followed a stringent set of guidelines. They weren't divided by race, creed or age. There were guys that had already done 20 or 25 years and were getting ready to get out. Then there were people like me who were getting ready to be processed into the prison system.

You had to be even more polite than in county. If you were sitting around the mess hall, you couldn't reach over someone's plate to get the salt or pepper. That was disrespectful. That was grounds to get shanked up. When you were ready to leave the chow hall after you ate, you knocked on the table, *bump-bump*, and excused yourself.

Being in a maximum security place like Fishkill meant being locked up 23 hours a day. That was confusing at first, but the key to survival was to keep your eyes open. You started observing stuff—who sat with whom and how people who were being accepted behaved. You always had to be prepared to move because you never knew when you'd go to a new facility. You just got a knock and someone said, "Pack up!"

You didn't even ask where you were going. They weren't gonna tell you and they wouldn't give you a warning. Amy visited me in Fishkill, and she said she was going to come back in two days. Later that day I got sent all the way upstate to the Cayuga Correctional Facility in Auburn, far from New York City. I didn't know where I was going, and there was no way to let Amy know I wouldn't be in Fishkill when she came back.

# CHAPTER 27

My little brother had been living with me in New York before I got arrested. He didn't want to go back to Florida, so he stayed with Amy, but that didn't work out. One day they had a big fight and I wasn't there to smooth out the situation.

"Fuck you, Amy!" Freddy unwisely blurted out. "I'm gonna go live with Stigma!"

"Fine. Go live with Stigma! You're just like him anyway!" Amy shouted. I don't know if she really thought it would happen.

The time that Freddy was living with Vinnie was crazy. Freddy was a wild kid and was mad that I was away. He had all this pent-up anger, so he freaked out all the time. Vinnie still has holes in his door and walls from Freddy's tantrums.

Vinnie told me that for the longest time, it was impossible to get the kid to go to sleep and even harder to get him out of bed. If Vinnie didn't wake him up gently, he'd burst out of bed like a firecracker and break apart the fucking house. After Freddy woke up, Vinnie had to take Freddy to school. Otherwise he wouldn't go.

That worked for a while. Then Freddy flat out refused to go. Vinnie couldn't force him, so Freddy stayed at Vinnie's and slept all day. During Freddy's vacation, Rudy called the house now and then to see what was going on.

"Yo, where is Freddy? Is he in school?" he'd asked Vinnie.

"Yeah, he's in school," Stigma would say. "Yeah, everything's okay, Rudy. Everything's good."

Meanwhile, Freddy would be sleeping, jumping on the bed or tearing the place apart. Eventually Freddy went to school on his own, and he went until eighth grade.

That was good because I was in no position to be anyone's big brother, especially when I was getting ready to be moved to Cayuga Correctional Facility in Auburn, where I did the majority of my time.

During the bus ride there, I was shackled by foot and arm to another prisoner, and he had to take a shit. The guards weren't allowed to unshackle us, so they took us both to the bathroom in the back of the bus. I had to stand next to this guy while he went to the toilet. He was nervous and had loud diarrhea. The sound and smell made me gag. He kept apologizing, but it was fuckin' nasty.

Every 45 minutes we'd pull over at another prison and some of the convicts got out. Sometimes we stopped at mental institutions. They picked up some people and dropped off others. I had no idea when my stop was coming, so every time we stopped I was ready to get off. When we got to Cayuga Correctional Facility they dropped me off and I realized how far away I was from home. I thought about my family even more because Amy couldn't just drive an hour to see me. It was a huge road trip. It would take eight hours for anyone to drive from New York City to see me and they'd only get to visit for a few hours.

A couple weeks after I got there, Amy came up with Nadia, who didn't understand what was happening. We got candy and chips from the vending machines, which she liked. But afterwards, she started crying. She wanted me to come back with her. Amy kissed me goodbye. She looked sad. She waved goodbye and headed out with Nadia in a stroller, still crying. I couldn't say anything. I felt helpless and my spirits dropped. It hit me hard that I couldn't go with them and wouldn't see them for a while.

I found out later that the guards messed with Amy when she came in. They told her they wouldn't let her in because of how she was dressed or that visiting hours were over or that I wasn't available. They didn't give a shit about the prisoners and they liked to exert their power and have some kicks. But saying that to a mom and her little girl was fucking heartless. Amy used to sneak me cartons of cigarettes in cereal boxes and I gave some boxes to prisoners that were artists. They drew Nadia's favorite Sesame Street characters on pieces of cloth for her. Nadia was so sweet, and even though she was young, she knew I was her dad and felt strongly that I should leave with Amy when it was time to go. Amy told me that Nadia was inconsolable when they left and that the long rides home were heartbreaking.

The Cayuga Facility had opened a few weeks earlier, so everything was new. They had metal silverware in the dining hall. Within a week after I got there, there was no more silverware. You'd expect the knives would be gone, but so were the forks and spoons. Prisoners sharpened them into homemade shanks and stashed them in case they needed them. What the fuck were the people running the prison thinking? In the days that followed, I heard inmates sharpening the utensils all night long. While I was lying there awake thinking about my family, I'd hear, *skritchhh, skriittcchh, skriiiittttch.*

I decided the only way to keep myself from getting severely depressed was to distance myself from my old life. I needed to get in a different mindset in order to do my time. It's a different world, and it's a distraction when people visit. It takes you out of the zone and sets you back. While someone's visiting you it's good, but it reminds you what it's like to be free, and when they leave it's like going through a breakup. You feel empty and incomplete.

I told Amy only to come once a month because the more contact I had with the outside world, the more I missed it.

One time Rudy came to visit. He said, "Great news!"

*I'm getting out!* I thought. Maybe my lawyer had contacted him and he had come straight to Cayuga to give me the news. My stomach fluttered, and it felt like I was starting to levitate.

"Roger, I'm gonna be a dad!" he exclaimed.

All my excitement evaporated and I crashed back to reality. I was still stuck in prison. His great news wasn't that great for me.

*Awesome, I can be an uncle in prison*, I thought.

It was selfish of me, but that's how I felt. It was a complete letdown. The next time Rudy visited me, he told me our mom found out I was in prison. I don't know how she heard. He swore he didn't tell her. That wasn't good news either. It was shitty news. From the time I got busted until two years later when I was incarcerated, I was in contact with her.

"Everything's good. It's all fine. I'm not in trouble or anything anymore. I'm touring a lot. The band's doing great."

Now she knew that I had been lying and there was nothing I could do. I didn't want to see anyone anymore.

In prison, even if you're a petty, non-violent criminal, you're in there with all the rapists and murderers who aren't ever getting out. Normally when inmates get sentences like mine, they go straight to maximum security, but I got lucky. I was classified medium right away. I came out of a maximum security prison, Fishkill, and went into a medium security facility. I figured that medium would be a cakewalk compared to maximum. Actually, max seemed easier. You get your own cell, or at worst you share it with one other person.

While I was at Cayuga I was in a room that had 50 people. There were dividers between the cells that looked like office cubicles. If shit went down, it usually happened at night because there were only two COs in the dorm. There were times when I tried to sleep and people jumped over the dividers trying to shank someone. If there was gonna be a hit, that's when it'd happen. Or it'd be in the shower. That's where a guy would get taken down if people found out he was a child molester. Some prisoners would hold him still while someone kept watch for COs. Everyone took turns beating on the cho-mo. And maybe someone would shank his ass up and leave him there to bleed to death. I can understand why people like Jeffrey Dahmer didn't last in prison and got beat to death.

I only saw that go down once; that stuff didn't happen often because there wasn't time. Child molesters are usually put into protective custody right away. That's a red flag to all the other prisoners that you're a rat, a coward or a cho-mo and it sticks with you like an infestation of ticks. Guys only sign themselves into protective custody if they know something bad is going to happen if they stay with the other inmates. It's not that easy to do, either. You can't just say you want to go to PC. You gotta tell them why and have a good reason. It never seemed honorable to me even to try; I didn't want to be with those people. I don't get them, and I don't want to get them. I'd much rather be in population and take my chances.

One of the first things you do when you get transferred to a new place is meet your counselor. He or she is the one who sets you up with your work programs, hooks you up with any schooling you want to do and gives you your daily routine. If someone needs it, they set them up with an AA or NA program. They make sure the prisoners stay busy. You're not allowed to go to prison and sleep all day. Everyone has to get up and be counted in and counted out at every chow. If you're sick you can get a pass to go to the doctor. That's the only time you're allowed to stay in bed. Other than that, you've got to be on the program. It keeps the prisoners active so that time passes faster, and it probably cuts down on the fights and riots because everyone is so tired when they get done with their work day. But sometimes a guy's job could lead to an extreme act of violence.

In prison, inmates work in all the offices, from laundry to the dentist's office. One inmate was working as a clerk in a counselor's office and learned that a guy had raped his mother. Can you fucking imagine that? The inmate reported that to the shot caller, and they ordered an attack on this guy. It wasn't anyone from the group I was hanging with, and I wasn't there to watch. But they were loud and I heard the beating and the screams, the shuffling of feet and cracking of bones. It seemed like the beatdown went on for 20 minutes, but it was probably less than five. There was some pleading and whimpering, then a pause where it seemed like everything was over. Then the commotion began again. Everyone knew what was happening. Even the COs could hear the noise, but they ignored it. They were in on it, too. Whenever there was a piece of shit on the block or in the dorm, an officer would let us know. They wanted us to get those guys. Some people deserve what they've got coming to them.

While I was in Cayuga the place got overcrowded quickly. At one point there were 110 people in a dorm that was built for 50. To accommodate all the extra people, the prison officials put in bunk beds. Think about that: 110 criminals on top of each other under the watchful eyes of two COs! The bathrooms were overcrowded and everyone was tripping over one another, and if you bumped into someone you had to apologize. Then you'd watch your back and hope that the person you bumped into didn't have a chip on his shoulder.

Being in lockdown with people doing heavy time is easier than being around criminals with short sentences. The guys who are new have something to prove. They're usually young and bubbling with testosterone. They're quick to anger and slow to forgive. The prisoners who have been there a while are usually mellower and less aggressive. They've learned the codes of conduct, and they stick to them. They don't even think about what they have to do in any given situation. I met some guys that had been locked up for 20 or more years—so long they were practically in a time warp. They even dressed like they were from the '70s. They didn't know what was happening on the outside and they didn't care. Maybe by that point, the order and structure were what gave their lives meaning.

In certain prisons, married guys could get trailer visits if they behaved. Their family would come for the weekend and stay in a special trailer with them in a separate area. They were still inside the prison so it wasn't like being on vacation. A lot of people thought Amy and I were married, but we never were.

When I first went to prison, we thought it might be a good idea to get married so that when she came to visit, we could have these conjugal visits for the sake of our young family. We got all the paperwork and we signed it. But then I found out I wasn't eligible for trailer visits since I wasn't a U.S. citizen, so we scrapped that idea.

If I had done my full sentence I probably would have been in prison for six years because while I was in Cayuga, I got in trouble for being involved in a few riots. Having that word "life" tagged to the end of my sentence felt like a trap. I knew I was doing at least four years, but it made it seem like there would never be an end point. I had no idea when I'd get out, so I needed to be in the proper headspace to deal with that. I was different than ordinary prisoners. I thought differently; I had no max date.

Your mind plays tricks on your when you're in a bad place. You start to think about worst-case scenarios and what your friends and family are doing while you're locked away—how they're going on with their normal lives and not thinking of you. Then you get paranoid. I once received a strange package from Amy's father. Inside were legal papers asking me to sign over custody of my daughter to him. I was furious. I don't remember if I confronted Amy about the papers. Amy didn't have a relationship with her father, so she was already taking on a huge commitment as a single mom. I think he was trying to get back in her life. I still believe that she *never* would have allowed him to help raise her child. I have to give her credit for supporting both herself and Nadia during that tough time and for helping to pay my legal fees.

Even when you think you've adjusted, prison can make you crazy. For whatever reason, I felt betrayed and I wondered which side they were all on. The truth is that most of them probably had my back the whole time.

# CHAPTER 28

In prison, cigarettes were like money. I'm not a smoker, but I needed packs so I could trade them for stuff I wanted. I wrote all my relatives and asked them to send me as many packs of cigarettes as they could. For my birthday and Christmas, I wanted cigarettes. Money was no good. Any cash that came in went on your books, and it's best not to have much on your books. If you have too much money, someone will try to get to it. If there's too much of anything, you become a target. The inmates run the prisons. They know how much money you have. They know what you're reading. They know who's taking prescription medication. They're like Big Brother.

I could get a loaf of raisin bread for two packs of cigarettes. When they had chicken on special holidays, you could get a half-chicken for two packs. I quickly went vegetarian, though. The meat they regularly served was turkey and it was tinted green. I wasn't gonna eat that shit. I wasn't vegan; I still ate dairy and there were people in the kitchen that would make you cheesecake for eight packs of cigarettes. I did that a couple times and each time I savored it for two days. At first I was eating a lot of fish cakes, so I got three pieces of fish for a pack.

Mostly I used cigarettes to buy food and clothes. Other people used them to buy drugs. I never went there. Doing drugs to kill the time is a losing battle because they're in short supply and if you're addicted you need more. And you'll do anything to get them. That's a surefire way to get in trouble. Prisoners hate junkies but thrive on making money off their addictions.

I tried to keep myself clean and occupied in a positive way as the time passed. But since I was busted for possession, my sentence required me to take Narcotics

Anonymous classes, which were boring.

The only trouble I got into at Cayuga was for fighting. Some things never change. The thing about hanging out with people from your group—whether you're black, white or Latino—is that when there are riots, you have to be with your people and be ready to back them up. The interracial shit got really tense, really fast.

I was sharing a cube with a black guy named Jay for about eight months and we became buddies. We worked out together and talked about all sorts of shit. We were always cool with each other, except during one riot when it was the Hispanics against the blacks. He had to take his people's side. If we had to square off against each other we would have done it. Fortunately, that didn't happen. We had one shank hidden well in our shared locker.

Those two or three nights were pretty intense. I don't know if he ever slept, but I sure didn't. I didn't know if someone was going to make this guy cut my throat, and I'm pretty sure he felt the same. Two or three days later, after the storm had passed, everyone said there was no more beef and everything went back to normal. We played spades again and worked out together like nothing had happened. We never spoke about the incident again.

There were two barbed wire fences at Cayuga, a 15-footer and a 20-footer. Guards walked around between the two fences during the day, and at night the guard dogs kept watch. There were several big riots when I was there, and they were pretty brutal. You always knew when something was going to go down. When one group was getting ready to go up against another, everybody got ready for war. People buried shanks the day before to dig up and use in the fight. The day of the riot, inmates had their hoods up so no one could see their faces. Everyone wore more clothing than usual—two pairs of pants, long sleeves and gloves—even if it was hot outside. The more covered up you were, the more protected you'd be.

The prison guards didn't break up riots, but they blew whistles and drew their guns to stop the commotion and clear the battlefield. Prisoners went out, picked up the injured guys of their color or ethnicity and put them on a stretcher.

Guys from both sides carried the wounded to ambulances lined up at the main gate. State troopers around the facility kept watch to prevent anyone from trying to jump the second fence and running away. Anyone who did that would be shot, probably more than once. Between the warring sides, there was a mutual respect. You didn't attack your enemy when they were picking up their injured. But after the wounded got taken away, it started up again.

One riot involved a Spanish guy who had converted to Islam and joined the Five Percenters, an extremist radical group of Muslims that basically hated white America. The group was founded in 1964 in Harlem by a former student of Malcolm X, who went by the name Clarence 13X. These guys thought they were the original inhabitants of the planet and the mothers and fathers of civilization. I thought they were unstable and unpredictable. When the riot started, a Hispanic guy stuck with the Five Percenters since he had just converted. At the time, the prison was again more controlled by the Spanish people. That decision didn't go well for him. As soon as the riot was over, the Spanish guys went up the leader of the Five Percenters and said all they wanted was that guy. They gave him up. The dude got wrecked by a bunch of guys with a mop-wringer and shanks. There was blood everywhere. Someone had to use a heavy-duty mop to clean up that shit.

During that riot, I got in some shit with some of the Five Percenters. I roughed up three guys. None of us had shanks and we went at it on the pavement, like kids in a street fight. I flashed back to when I was younger and Rudy and I were beating the crap out of those dudes in the neighborhood. But these weren't unskilled fighters. They were guys who knew how to put their weight into a punch and block an attack.

The Five Percenters yelled "Five Percenters unite," and they went back to back in a circle. You couldn't jump them from behind because they were back to back. One thing the Five Percenters always practiced was strategy. We attacked them from the front and we outnumbered them, so our attack crushed their circle. Once that circle was broken it was more like man-to-man combat.

I was doing a good job smacking around one guy, then his friend jumped on my back. I was able to knock him off, but I lost my balance and fell on the ground. The rest of the fight was more like a wrestling match. I'd like to think I won, but by the time it was over I had a bloody broken nose and my clothes were torn and filthy. It was clear I had been involved in the riot, so the officers put me in solitary confinement.

Being in solitary is just what it sounds like. You're in a bare, empty room without a mattress. There's a slot in the door where they slide you food and water. It's uncomfortable not to have a bed or a chair, but having to lie on the ground is hardly the worst thing. What gnaws at you is the lack of activity. It isn't just the boredom; it's the emptiness and solitude. Your start thinking about something, and then you overthink it and your mind starts to race. Before you can stop yourself, your brain is bouncing from one idea to another like a character in a video game.

After a while, I could feel my heart racing and I felt dizzy. Breathing deeply and counting to five between breaths helped, and so did sleeping. But there's only so much you can sleep when you're not tired. It's the hours I was awake that were torture. To keep myself from freaking out, I tried to spend a half-hour or more thinking about a single subject. I tried to remember the names of all the bands I had played with, then I thought about all the concerts I had been to in my life and all the records I had listened to. Whatever I did, I could only go so long before I thought about Amy and Nadia. In my most vulnerable moments I'd switch off between that and remembering parts of my childhood that I'd tried so hard to forget.

While you're lying down in solitary, you know there are prison guards going through your belongings. Just to be assholes, they throw some of your shit away and keep whatever they want to. A lot of times, they'll ship you off to another facility when they pull you out of the hole. If you've been involved in a riot and they think you're a troublemaker or a marked man, they'll send you wherever they want to—either another dorm or a different prison.

One time I got sent to solitary after a riot I wasn't involved in. After the riot, the correctional officers conducted random searches of all the cells and found a homemade tattoo machine that a friend of mine had built out of a Walkman motor I had. Owning a tattoo gun was against the rules. That and the fact that I had been in the yard during the riot earned me four days in solitary.

Nothing toughens a guy up and builds character like going to war or going to prison. There are definitely drawbacks to both. I'm not suggesting anyone join the military or get themselves arrested. But in prison and in war, you're there with dudes who are in the same situation as you are. To survive, you have to learn to trust your comrades and work as a team. There are two big differences. When you go to war you're with a group and you know who your enemy is. When you're in prison you don't know. He could be right next to you. He could be the same color but from a different set or from a different background. I worked hard not to make enemies in prison, and aside from the guys I squared off against in riots, I don't think anyone wanted to kill me.

The other difference between war and prison is that in war, if you want to run or be a deserter you can. People might look at you as a coward and you might have to go into hiding, but it's an option, if only as a last resort. There's nowhere to run in prison. You have to face your problems and resolve any conflicts quickly unless you check into protective custody. That option is worse than deserting your fellow soldiers on the battlefield because you're caught and still right there in the same facility. You're just shoved in with rats, cho-mo's, cowards and other guys with targets on their backs—just a sitting duck waiting to be attacked.

When I was at Cayuga the Latinos were running the place and doing a good job. There was friction between different street sets, but they kept the "Hispanic" community together. Every night they cooked together and hung out in the rec room. When there was beef they made sure the fights were one-on-one and didn't turn into free-for-alls. Most conflicts went right to the shower area. The stuff within the family was usually settled with a quick fight to squash it, and then everyone cleaned up and went back to business.

Whatever ethnic or color group made up the majority of the prison block or dorm population had the upper hand. That meant they were in control of the TV room and the phone, which was a big deal since those were the only daily forms of entertainment for inmates. After a big riot between the whites and the blacks, a lot more black people were transferred to the dorm and the Latin people lost the majority. It's like what happens when control changes in the House of Representatives, except there's no vote. We went from watching whatever the Latin group leaders put on TV, which was sometimes in Spanish, to watching stuff that the black leaders chose. That meant we had to sit through *The Cosby Show*, *Different Strokes*, *The Jeffersons* and *Sanford and Son*, like it or not. Two weeks later, more new people came in and the balance shifted again.

Probably the worst thing about being locked up was the constant movement, which kept my friends and family from being able to find me. They moved me at different times of the night. I went from county prison in Rockland County to Fishkill to get processed. Then I went to Cayuga for a year. I finished up with five months at Wallkill in Shawangunk, New York. Every time I switched from one facility to another I had to go back to Fishkill, which was the main hub. Prisoners also got transferred any time there was a disturbance or if they were sick.

About six months into my sentence at Cayuga I got influenza, and it got worse. The doctor said he couldn't give me antibiotics since the flu is a virus. He told me to drink a lot of water and rest when I could. That didn't help. I had bad headaches, the chills and chronic diarrhea. At night I would lie under my blanket shivering, so I'd kick off the covers. I'd feel better for a few minutes and then I'd start sweating like a construction worker digging up roads in the summer. Aspirin and Tylenol didn't help. When it was really bad, I got delirious. I don't know if I was drifting in and out of dreams or if I hallucinated, but one time I saw my stepdad sitting in a chair in the corner of the cell holding a shovel covered with dirt. If that was my subconscious trying to tell me something, I didn't know what the message was, but it scared the fuck out of me. Then I started throwing up every time I tried to eat or drink.

Since I couldn't hold anything down, the docs at Cayuga sent me to Auburn, a maximum security prison with a better hospital and medical staff. They put me on an IV drip and gave me strong antibiotics. Antibiotics don't do anything for influenza, but since I was coughing so much and had so much phlegm, I developed a bad bacterial infection and was running a fever of 104 degrees. Even after the virus went away, the bacterial infection was ravaging my system. It took three or four days for the infection to clear up and my temperature to return to normal. When the doc gave me a clean bill of health, they sent me back to Cayuga.

That was a short-term move. After a couple of the riots I was in, they sent me back to Auburn Maximum Security prison while they sorted out the prisoners and made sure guys wouldn't be a problem when they got back. When you're moving between prisons, you're in limbo. You have no contact with people on the outside. Once you got moved it could take two or three weeks before you were allowed to send a letter or get a response. It was bizarre. I couldn't get in touch with the people I wanted to contact the most and they had no idea where I was. I felt like the system was rigged against me.

Even after I had mail privileges, I couldn't just send a letter. I had to request contact permission. They let me communicate with some strange characters as long as I got approval. At one point I exchanged letters with Lynette Alice "Squeaky" Fromme from the Manson family. She was at the Federal Medical Center Carswell in Fort Worth, Texas. This chick was arrested in 1975 for pointing a loaded gun at President Gerald Ford in Sacramento, California. She was tackled by the Secret Service. There wasn't a bullet in the chamber, but there was a clip in the gun so she went down. Like the rest of Manson's followers, she was crazy. She said she brought the gun so she could talk to him, and she never thought she would get arrested. After they got her she said it was an act of fate. She supported Manson long after most of his followers abandoned him. Those were some interesting letters—some had normal shit and others rambled about crazy, political, hateful shit, but for the most part they were unstable. I have no idea why I was allowed to communicate with her.

I got a lot of mail from fans. People like Dave Brown kept me entertained with their letters. Brian Quin, a friend who worked at The Record Collection on Long Island, sent me a copy of the *Live at CBGB* record cover. I wasn't allowed to have the vinyl in prison, probably because the plastic could be broken and shaped into a shank. But he sent me the *Live at CBGB* cassette, Metallica's *...And Justice for All* and various hardcore cassettes. I asked him to include a fake invoice because I wasn't allowed to receive music as a gift.

During one visit with a friend, I told him to cut open the bottom of a cereal box, put in a packet of Anadrol 50 steroids, glue the box back up and send it to me. It worked twice, and the third time the guards found the steroids. My friend was carefully briefed to make sure each package had a completely different name and return address. When they came to me to accuse me of receiving contraband, I told them I didn't know the guy who sent them and had no idea what was going on. I told them it might have come from a crazy AF fan. They didn't believe me and they kept the steroids, but I didn't get in trouble.

Random fans visited me. It was a relief to have an hour to shoot the shit with someone who liked my band. Once Slapshot was on tour and stopped by. Unfortunately only one person was allowed in, so they sent in their roadie and my old friend Jon Wrecking Machine.

To kill time, I read a lot of books. My friend Brooke sent me *Silence of the Lambs*. *Helter Skelter* presented a thorough description of all the Manson murders, the motivations, the police investigation and the trial. I saw Adolf Hitler's *Mein Kampf* in the prison library and thought, *Let me see what this freaking maniac was thinking*. It was mind-blowing to read the thoughts of this megalomaniac psychopath and learn just how evil he was. A population of blonde-haired, blue-eyed Germans looked up to him and applauded his crazy notions of the master race when he didn't look anything like them. He was a short, angry, dark-haired guy with a fucked-up moustache.

The Bible was probably one of the worst things I've ever read. Every Christian prisoner is given a copy and a lot of them find religion. They feel lost and alone, and they're told that if they put themselves in the hands of the Lord, they will be forgiven for their sins and freed of guilt. It doesn't matter if they raped or killed someone. If they believe and repent they'll go to Heaven. That's such a fucked-up way of thinking.

Everyone wants to be forgiven for the terrible things they did. I did, and I didn't do anything that terrible. So I thought, *Well, fuck, I'll give this a shot*. I wanted to do things right, so I went to church and started reading the Bible. It was mythical and full of ridiculous metaphors. What would happen today if someone saw a man talking to a burning bush like Moses did? The guy would be committed to a mental institution.

There was walking on water and being swallowed by a whale and not dying. Reading the Bible made me more of a non-believer. I wanted to believe, but it seemed like something was twisted. It was a lie. I started questioning myself and realized that wasn't my path. The only useful thing I found in the Bible was in the part where Jesus went to a church and saw people selling everything outside. People had to pay to get in, turning something that was meant to be charitable into a profitable venture. He was, like, "This is not it. You don't get it. This is not what it's about. Worshipping isn't about making money." And I thought, *It shouldn't fuckin' be*, but that's what it has come to. Of course, you don't have to go to church to find that out. Just watch or listen to the news.

# CHAPTER 29

While I was in prison at Cayuga, I joined a Hispanic band called La Fuerza Latina, which meant The Latin Force. I was hanging out with Hispanic dudes when a guy named Oreja (which means Ears) found out I played bass. He was the leader and the singer, and his bass player had just gotten released from prison. We did covers of Santana, Top 40 and classic rock. It was a Latin band, but since we were the only band in the facility we played all the festivals. We had to be able to play Latin music, popular music, funk and even disco to appeal to all the inmates. There were four or five festivals during the year, and they were for Spanish, black and white prisoners. Usually the prisoners went to one or two festivals per year, but since we were the entertainment we went to all of them. They were like outdoor picnics and everyone's family could come. There were wives, girlfriends and kids there. Being in the band was a nice way to break up my schedule. During one of the festivals, Amy and Freddy came up with a friend of mine.

As cool as it was to hang out with my family, one reason I wanted to play with the band was so I could get guitar strings. Normal prisoners can't have strings because they can be used to cut someone's throat. I wanted to get a high E guitar string so I could use it for tattooing. But the first time I used it in my makeshift tattoo gun, I didn't know I was supposed to sharpen the tip to remove the hook. I used it to write something on my arm and the tip of the string snagged my skin. It hurt like a motherfucker.

Eventually Oreja did his time and was let out. Since he was the singer, the rest of the band didn't know what to do. We thought we were through. Two or three weeks after the band broke, Oreja was busted for a parole violation. La Fuerza Latina was back in business.

The last prison I was at was Wallkill Correctional Facility, a medium security prison in Shawangunk, New York. I got transferred there from Cayuga after I got my electrician's degree. It was like that part of *Shawshank Redemption* where the warden found out Andy Dufresne was an accounting wiz, so he singled him out to work on his personal finances. The warden needed his house wired and found out that I could do it. Technically I wasn't supposed to because I wasn't an American citizen and non-citizens need special outside clearance. Since the warden needed work done and didn't want to pay for it, he bent the rules.

Wallkill has an interesting history. The place was built in the 1930s as part of a program sponsored by Eleanor Roosevelt when her husband, Franklin D. Roosevelt, was governor of New York. It used to be a maximum security prison that housed well-behaved white-collar criminals and corrupt police officers. As the state's prison system became more crowded, they built a wall of razor wire around the place and started bringing in guys with heavier sentences. When I arrived, I saw some bad-ass motherfuckers who looked like they were born inside those walls.

The place had a creepy vibe that easily could have been a setting for *American Horror Story*. There used to be a boxing ring, and prisoners would fight one another as entertainment for the guards and other inmates. Everyone used to be in on the fights. The convicts bet packs of cigarettes, but the guards used real money. If a guard that had a bad temper lost a bet, the fighter he had his money on sometimes got a second beating. No one wore boxing gloves for that one.

Wallkill had a slaughterhouse on the grounds, and they taught prisoners how to butcher animals. That's where the meat for a lot of the prison system came from. That's another reason why it's a good idea to go vegetarian in prison. Guys that have no skills killing animals or making cuts of meat are in charge of providing food for thousands of people. The meat always comes out tough and full of gristle. I never figured out why it was always green. Maybe they treated the meat with so many chemicals to preserve it that it changed color. I never got close enough to anyone who worked in the slaughterhouse to find out.

The prison had a locksmithing program, which never made sense to me. They were teaching guys about breaking and entering! I understand that prisons need to teach inmates different skills and keep them busy. It would have made more sense to get some boxing trainers so there could have been some good fights to watch, not just glorified street brawls.

Since Wallkill was a medium security prison they put me in a two-man cell. I learned that I could sit in chow hall and eat slowly while other prisoners kept coming through for their food. If I stayed long enough I could go back for seconds. I wasn't a free man by any stretch of the imagination, but I felt like I had a little bit of slack on the rope that tied me to my cage. One night I was lying awake and heard a meowing sound. At first I thought one of the other inmates was sick, but sure enough there was a cat. I called out to it, crushed up a cracker and spread the crumbs on the ground.

"Here, kitty, kitty. Come here, kitty."

Sure enough, a grey kitten poked her nose through the bars and pawed at the crumbs. I waited for her to eat the cracker and gave her more. I stroked her furry head and scratched behind her ear. She liked that and rubbed against me. I was on the ground floor, so I figured the cat was a stray that came in through a window. Every day after that, I saved a little bit of bread from dinner to feed the kitten. It was a little reminder of the humanity I had left behind.

A couple weeks after I got to Wallkill, I was transferred from a double cell to a single cell. I think the warden was giving me a little payback for doing his electrical. The environment in Wallkill seemed more civilized than at Cayuga. Maybe that's because I had learned how to function in prison and no longer had that glaze in my eye that all the newbies have. But it's weird. There were riots, turf battles and all sorts of conflicts in every other prison I was in. The one thing I never saw was any type of homosexual relations or prisoners that had been without a girl for so long that they started to experiment.

Soon after I got to Wallkill, I was working out with some dudes and felt this vibe from one of the guys. The cells were all on tiers and they were open. One day the guy left the weight area and went back to his cell. I was, like, "Whoa, it's rec, where is this guy going?" He was an older prisoner who had been there for 20 years. I walked by and he had a curtain over his cell. I heard him and another guy grunting and moaning. I don't think they were doing yoga. Everyone figured something was going on, but no one said anything. They let him have his curtain and they left him alone because he had been there long enough to earn a little privacy.

What seemed crazier to me was when I'd bump into guys that were doing shorter bids and only had a year or less left in their sentence. They'd say they were straight and talk about girls. The next thing you knew, you'd be watching a movie and two guys would be sitting together holding hands—even though it wasn't allowed. I knew that when the film was over, they were gonna go do what most couples do after watching movies together. I thought that was weird. If they were gay to begin with, then fine, whatever. But these guys claimed to be straight and seemed to be. They just couldn't control their sexual urges. It's, like, you're getting out soon. Can't you just wait? I never understood that.

I once saw a crazy fight between two guys over another guy. A guy ran through the whole damn facility in broad daylight to try to get away while his pursuer chased him with a giant shank. The guards usually let skirmishes like that run their course, but sensing something potentially lethal, they stopped the guy with the weapon and he went to the hole.

It would have been interesting to see what else went down in Wallkill, but a couple months after I got there I heard my number called over the PA system. It was the first time I was ever called for anything, and it happened the very minute I walked out of the front gate to do some work for the warden.

"Inmate 89A0136, report to security."

*This is weird*, I thought, wondering what I had done and what kind of trouble I was in. I had never heard anyone's number called over the loudspeaker.

I went to security and they told me to go to my counselor's office. When I got there he said, "Your lawyer just called and he's going to call back."

*What the hell?* I thought. I hadn't heard from my lawyer since he convinced me to plead guilty more than a year earlier. I sat there quietly, my heart pounding like a double-bass drum. A couple minutes later the phone rang.

"Roger! We won!" Anthony Lombardino, my attorney, said from his car phone. "You're out of there!"

"For real? How?"

He explained that he convinced the judge that the police had conducted an illegal search and seizure and violated my Fourth Amendment rights. I beat the appeal and they reversed my case. I was free.

I was happy and did some stupid shit. I was especially excited since I had recently found out that I might be looking at more time behind bars. Even if my sentence had ended after four years, I could have been shifted from a state facility to a federal prison since I wasn't a U.S. citizen. Back then, when prisoners from other countries were released from prison for a felony, the government deported them back to their home country. But they couldn't do that with Cubans because the government under Castro would not accept them. Or far worse, if accepted they could be executed. Since that would have been cruel and unusual treatment, Uncle Sam felt it was much more humane to transfer Cubans from state facilities to federal prisons and give them life sentences.

When I found out I'd soon be a free man, I told everyone and gave all my shit away. I unloaded my Walkman, headphones and cassettes and got rid of the dress clothes I wore when Amy came to visit. Since I was sure I'd get out the next day, I gave away the food I had in my locker and my nice blanket. But 24 hours later, I was still there. A couple days went by, and I was fucking cold because all my shit was gone. It felt like a trick. I went to see my counselor to find out what the fuck was up.

"We don't have any paperwork about your case being dismissed, so you have to return to your cell until we get some sort of confirmation," he said without any sympathy.

I knew I was gonna get out. My attorney wasn't lying. I had beaten my case. But the people in the office that handled court documents were dragging their feet. They didn't give a shit if I got out the next day or two years down the line. They probably figured that I was a lowlife scumbag and that society was better off the longer I was behind bars. Maybe they thought they were doing the world a favor by dragging out my sentence.

I was at Wallkill for three more weeks, and it seemed like everyone wanted to fuck with me. Two nights before I left, they processed me into a four-person and then a six-person cell. It was like all the privileges I had earned were being revoked. Maybe the warden was mad because I wasn't gonna finish the electrical at his house.

The last night I was there, a beef broke out in my block and one guy got shanked up. He was practically bleeding out, so the attacker's clothes were splattered like a modern art painting. The guys in the cell had to get rid of the evidence. Then the prison loudspeaker finally called my number to check out. I grabbed my laundry and my stuff, and the prisoners threw their bloody clothes at me and told me to get rid of them. I put them in my bag, went to the laundry room and gave them to the guy there. He saw the blood, but he ignored it and threw the clothes away. That's prison code, prison life.

It was a bad idea to tell everyone I was leaving. Prisoners get jealous when they hear shit like that. It's good news for you, not them. You're gonna be free and they're still gonna be stuck there. Telling them you're almost free is like rubbing it in their faces that they're not going anywhere. I didn't mean to upset anyone and I thought I was helping them out by giving away my shit. These guys took advantage of my good news by making me dispose of those goddamn clothes. If I had gotten caught, we all could have been in serious trouble. Then they might have gotten mad and tried to take it out on me. Fortunately that didn't happen.

I contacted Greg "One Eye" Danelli, the guy who later hung himself. He drove all the way to Wallkill and gave them the paperwork from the court.

"Pack up," one of the guards said. "Hurry up! You're leaving!"

Finally, after one year and eight months, I was a free man. I threw together all the shit I had left and whatever they gave me from when I checked in. I had $17, and they gave me a one-way bus ticket back to New York City. I didn't need the ticket. Greg waited around while the prison processed me and then we drove to Staten Island. When we got there, he took me to my friend Paula Reinhardt's house, and she took me to the home that my mom bought to get me out on bail.

I knocked on the door and Alicia Morgan answered. She was a singer for one of the crustier punk bands, Insurgence, and she later joined the doom band 13.

"Can I help you?" she said, not recognizing who I was.

"I live here," I replied.

"You live here? Who are you?" she said, eying the room for a weapon in case I was a robber or a pervert.

"I'm Roger."

"Oh, my God! You're Roger! I thought you were . . . I'm so sorry."

I never knew this girl, so I hardly expected her to know who I was. I guess I forgot that Agnostic Front were influential to a lot of young hardcore musicians, so even though she didn't recognize me she knew my name. Besides, she thought I was still locked up. Everyone did. I went in the house, but no one else was there.

"Where's Nadia?" I asked Alicia.

"She's in Florida with your mom. Nausea are on tour in Europe."

I picked up the phone and called my family in Florida. My mom, my brothers and my sister were ecstatic that I was out. I couldn't really talk to my mom because she was crying so much, but I had a good conversation with Rudy. They bought me an airline ticket to go to Florida because I couldn't pay for it myself. All I had was $17.

Coincidentally, before I left for Florida, Amy called them from Europe to check on Nadia. Then she called me at the house where Alicia was staying—my house. Alicia picked up the phone and handed it to me.

Apparently, she knew there was a slight chance I'd be there. She had paid for the court appeal and knew I would be getting out, but she had no idea when. Since she was going on tour and thought I might be released while she was away, she bought me new clothes and laid them out on the bed with a welcome home letter—just in case. I hadn't seen her letter yet when she called.

"How the fuck did you get out?" Amy said.

"I got thrown out! They told me to pack up my shit because I was leaving. I won my appeal! I'm done with prison time."

Amy was ecstatic and told me to go into the bedroom to pick up my clothes and read her letter. She said she'd be with me as soon as she could, but she couldn't come home right away since Nausea was in the middle of a tour. So I went to Florida.

Mayra had just gotten married, and she was living in a nice home with her new husband. She was watching Nadia when I got there. My stepfather was at the house with my mom, but I knew better than to say anything to him. I kept my distance and he didn't pay me no mind.

My mom took Nadia and me to Disney World. It was my first time there. It may sound stupid or soft, but I always wanted to go and I had a good reason. Every time Nadia came to visit me in prison, I'd say, "When I get out I'm taking you to Disney World." I was finally able to do it, even if I wasn't footing the bill.

Nadia was four years old and I was 26. It was unreal being in such a happy place after having been locked up. Everyone was laughing. People were stuffing themselves with burgers, hot dogs, ice cream and popcorn. No one had to ration anything or trade packs of cigarettes. It was expensive, but at the same time everything seemed free.

Like a lot of people who get out of prison, I had a hard time adjusting to civilian life. I was always on edge. It felt like someone would grab me, say "Sorry, we made a mistake," and drag my ass back to prison. I stayed with my family in Florida for two weeks while Amy was on the road. We planned to go back to New York together when she got home.

While I was visiting my mom, I played basketball with my brother and some of my sister's friends. They tried to make me comfortable. I just felt weird. I kept thinking about the last time I played basketball around my stepfather and how that episode ended in some of the worse violence of my life. But it also led to my escape from the tyranny of being in his house in Jersey. If that horrible episode with the hammer had never happened, I might have never been motivated to restart my life and become a major part of this incredible subculture on the Lower East Side. I might never had met Amy or had Nadia. I also might not have wound up dealing the drugs that led to my eventual arrest. Life's a trip that way. You can always look back to a pivotal experience and say, "What if I made a different decision and took another path?" Some people spend their whole lives looking back like that, obsessing over old choices and building up mountains of regret. I'd rather leave the past behind me and focus on the here and now.

There were people at my mom's house that I didn't know, and they felt uncomfortable being there with an ex-con. I felt out of place and judged wherever I went. People I had never met eyed me with suspicion and held onto their belongings a little tighter, like I was going to steal their shit just because I started dealing to feed my family and then wrongfully got arrested. It was strange even to go into the kitchen to make a sandwich when I was hungry. No one in prison gets to do that. I kept looking over my shoulder like I was doing something wrong. I was out, but I still felt like a prisoner.

I kept getting dragged back into criminal waters. The people I had been doing business with—and who ratted me out—were charged with a murder I had nothing to do with. It was linked to my case because it involved the same gang I was in. I can't go into the details because of a gag order, but the cops tried to pin that on me, too, and get me to talk. The motherfuckers wiretapped my house right before I was arrested!

When I was back home and a free man, I still had to go back to criminal courts. The authorities had the wiretap recordings from my house of these fucking idiots talking about doing illegal shit because they figured my place was safe. Amy and Paula let them in because they were caring for my dogs and, supposedly, making sure my family was okay, but she had no idea what else they were involved with. They used my phone and talked about the crimes they had committed.

One of these guys was a maniac. He sedated a dude with heavy animal tranquilizers that left him unable to move and then slowly and systematically killed him. He cut off his fingers, slashed his wrists and broke his knee-caps and legs. All the guy could do was look at his killer while he slowly bled to death.

Thank God all these recordings were made while I was incarcerated so there was no way they could tie any of it to me. I had 18 dogs at my house and these guys, my partners, would come over, feed my dogs and talk on the phone. The police had all these recordings so I beat the rap—for the third time. It went as far as a pre-trial. I still had Anthony Lombardino as my lawyer, and he proved that not only wasn't I there but that the evidence was inadmissible because it was obtained illegally. There was an invasion of my privacy because no one had a warrant when they put the wiretaps in.

Gradually the paranoia and discomfort of being free but feeling out of place wore off, though it didn't take much to awaken those feelings. It's like when a recovering alcoholic who hasn't had a drink in years gets that craving. To this day, I can't sleep without wearing a bandana over my face. It's a habit I picked up in prison. At the very beginning of my sentence upstate, I was in the last cell in the block and there was a light over my head the whole fucking time. My bandana became like a security blanket and I still can't fall asleep without it. My wife, Emily, tried to take it away from me with my permission, but it didn't work. I still need it. It's why you rarely see me without a bandana.

# PART VI

## The Bittersweet Taste of Freedom: Rebuilding Bridges on the Path to Redemption

# CHAPTER 30

**G**uys who get out of the military or prison return as changed men. It's bad enough that people around them treat them differently, but dealing with normal social interaction is a major challenge. Anxiety, anger and depression are all on the menu, and sometimes it's a losing battle. When someone tries to sympathize with you it seems like they're being annoying or condescending, and when they're not paying close attention to you it feels like you're being ignored. I started thinking that Amy could have been with other guys while I was locked up, and I could feel my temper rise.

I tried to keep my shit together and Amy tried to help me out. But years later, she told me I was pretty far gone. I was always quiet and uncomfortable, no matter what. When we tried to watch a movie, I got fidgety. I couldn't relax. Amy later told me, "You were you, but not like you. I couldn't figure out how to help and I hated that I couldn't really reach into you and fix it. I thought we could just sort of fake normal until we became normal, but it didn't work. We never really found normal again, but not for lack of trying."

There are lots of movies in which a guy walks out of prison to be met by all of his friends and family, and everyone's happy. Roll credits. Finish your popcorn. That never happened to me.

When I got out of prison in September 1990, only the scumbag who helped set me up, Greg Danelli, knew I was out. There wasn't a welcome home party. There wasn't a show or any sort of hardcore community tribute to welcome me back—not for a while. I'd go to gigs and people were, like, "Holy shit! Is that you?

Are you out?"

Amy and I tried to act like a normal couple when she got back from tour, but our relationship was strained. The people around us didn't help. Once I went with her to a punk party in Brooklyn. We entered the house together and joined the other people in the living room who were hanging out and laughing. As soon as we sat down the laughter stopped. Then the conversation stopped. I don't remember being confrontational, but Amy told me I threatened to beat them up and they were afraid of me. So everyone stood up and went to the kitchen, including Amy. I sat there in silence for a few minutes. Then I split. I felt awkward and betrayed, dissed by my own girl. At the same time, I got it.

Nausea was a political band and her friends didn't like what they thought I had turned into. What pissed me off was that they had no idea what I represented. They knew I broke the law and did my time, but they didn't have a clue that I only did it so my family would have a better life than I had growing up.

Later that night, Amy and I got into a big fight. She told me she couldn't figure me out anymore and that I was erratic and irrational. She even said she was sometimes afraid of me, even though she knew I would never hurt her.

Amy and I grew more distant by the day. We were living together, but there wasn't much warmth. Even Nadia could tell something was up. It was a difficult situation to be in. I was trying to cope with freedom, but I felt confined. One time I got pissed off and smashed all of Amy's records and a vase her grandmother had given her, which had a lot of sentimental value to her. I was furious because she was pushing me aside and I didn't understand why. I wasn't able to articulate except by acting like the old aggressive Roger.

The irony is that I came back from prison a better person. I was healthy and in good physical shape. I was a vegetarian. I had picked up some education and some skill as an electrician. I had learned how to hold back my anger most of the time. But achieving real balance requires being centered in both mind and body, and I wasn't mentally stable. I was torn up about my relationship and just plain torn about what to do with Agnostic Front.

While I was in prison, *Live at CBGB* came out. Everyone figured that was all they would hear from us for a while. Then all of a sudden I was out and ready to play shows. It was an abrupt situation for everyone to deal with. And I wasn't just dealing with the old-guard anymore. There were a bunch of new faces in the hardcore scene, and people were trying to see if I was still a part of the scene or if my head was somewhere else. They were feeling me out and I was checking them out, too.

It made me angry, and the last thing I wanted was to get into a fight and give the state ammunition to use against me for my third appeal. That was scheduled at a later date. When it went down, I won and the case was reversed, sealed and dismissed like it had never happened. But while I was waiting for a decision, I was stressed out and frustrated. If I were somehow to lose, I could have ended up right back in prison. Being in that situation really fucks with a guy's head. Try to live normally under those conditions—not fuckin' likely.

I tried to get back to my old routine of going to shows, dancing hard and hanging out in clubs. But I could tell right away that shit had changed while I was away. When I went into prison there was a unified scene with punks, skins and metal fans. Now I saw kids who used to be headbangers but shaved their heads because they wanted to be skinheads. Okay, fine. I did it, too. But these former longhairs were beating up the metalheads. It was like they were ashamed of what they used to be, so they picked fights with kids who still had long hair.

"What's wrong with you? Why would you do that?" I'd say to them. "Back when you had long hair nobody fucked with you."

I let them know how I felt, but I didn't get into any fights because I had to maintain a low profile. Even though I wasn't part of their scene, there was a level of respect they had for me as one of the pioneers of New York hardcore. They weren't going to throw the first punch. They knew better than that. But I really didn't like what I was seeing. I couldn't understand why there was suddenly a division between hardcore kids and metal kids. I always felt we had more similarities than differences as far our backgrounds and values went. Punks, hardcore kids and metalheads were all outcasts and nonconformists. They were dysfunctional and angry, and they needed to be unified against a common enemy. Now it seemed like the enemy was within.

This new wave of hip-hop–oriented hardcore kids had no respect for one another or anyone else. They were into newer bands on the scene, none of which had much of a punk rock vibe. They were still a part of the scene, but the bad atti- tude left a bad taste in my mouth. The new hip-hop mentality brought a different violent gang mentality. It was different from our Beastie Boys or even some of the early pioneers of rap who sent mostly positive messages to the kids on the streets.

My first week out of prison, I went to a record store called 99X to buy a new pair of Dr. Martens. The guy who ran the store was named Duane and was a nice enough dude. I didn't have enough money to buy the boots, so I told him I'd go get the cash and come right back. As I was leaving, I saw twins walk in. They knew who I was. They looked at each other and looked at me again.

"Hey, yo, Roger, what's up?" one of them said. "Hey, it's good that you're out."

"Way to go, bro. The things is, you should really leave, man," his brother added, not looking me in the eye.

"What do ya mean?" I asked, not grasping what they were getting at.

"You can't be around here right now for a few minutes—not if you're just out of prison," the first kid said. "So, really, just go."

I could tell they didn't mean any disrespect. It felt more like a warning. I knew something was gonna happen. I just didn't know what. I had to leave anyway to go to the bank to get money for the shoes. While I was gone, the dudes shot Duane in the face. They held a gun in his mouth and pulled the trigger. They wanted to kill him. Luckily for Duane, the bullet exited the side of his cheek, leav- ing a gaping wound.

When I stepped back into the store to buy my shoes, the dudes were gone and there was blood everywhere. Duane was bleeding profusely. I got down on the ground and held him until the ambulance came. He didn't deserve that. He survived, but he was never the same. He was on heavy duty meds and always anxious. I knew who shot him, of course, but I never said anything. It wasn't my business. The word on the street was that Duane was shot for selling sketchy records, but I never believed that. It was clearly a robbery because there was money missing from the cash register. The assailants have been on the run for years for various other crimes. They realized that they shit in their grave too many times so they stopped coming around. If they showed up, they would have gotten their asses handed to them.

This new hardcore crew were young and impulsive. Hanging around them could get you killed. They were thuggish and they weren't there for the music, unlike the punks I grew up with. I still loved hardcore and thought I could continue to make a difference, so I kept making records. Not long after Duane was almost killed, I had a meeting with the guys in Agnostic Front at Umberto's Clam House in Little Italy. It was me, Vinnie, drummer Will Shepler, bassist Craig Setari, who later joined Sick of It All, and Steve Martin.

Everybody was happy I was out of prison, but Steve said he didn't want to be in the band anymore. He wanted to work for a publicity company and didn't want to tour. He didn't want to play with a certain member of the band, and that member had way more seniority than Steve did. There was a power struggle and Steve flat out lost. In the end he won, too. He worked as a music journalist for a while and did publicity for Relativity and Earache Records. Eventually he opened up his own company called Nasty Little Man and worked with bands like Helmet and Sugar. Over the years he became the publicist for the Beastie Boys, Smashing Pumpkins and Foo Fighters. He handled David Bowie before he died and now works with Paul McCartney. Clearly Steve made the right move.

Agnostic Front kept going. We auditioned a couple of guitar players, but none of them seemed right. Then we remembered playing with a band called Blind Approach from Minneapolis. They had played one of the No Justice, Just Us benefits. We liked their music and guitarist Matt Henderson was a solid musician and a nice guy. We called him up and he fucking dropped everything to come out from Boston, where he was attending the Berklee College of Music. He moved into my house and started playing with us. Immediately we could tell he was right for the band. He had a good attitude and was professional. Rehearsals with him were great. I just didn't know if he was road-worthy. One day he was in my house hanging out.

"What do you think?" asked Craig.

"I like him," I said. "But I gotta give him a test and see if he's gonna be able to handle being in the band."

While Matt was chilling on the couch, I got balls naked and stormed out of my kitchen screaming like a maniac. I charged at him, jumped over him and landed on the other side of the couch.

"Yo, what the fuck was that?" he asked without leaving his spot. That's all he said. He didn't freak out. He didn't ignore me. He gave me just enough attitude, and I went, "Okay, this guy's good. He can take it."

Matt adjusted to Agnostic Front better than Craig (aka Skully), who wasn't as quiet, which made him a better target. Craig was my masterpiece. I destroyed him. I always played pranks on him because I knew he'd eventually lose his temper. It was perverse, but it was entertaining for me and helped pass the time when we were in a van for weeks on end.

Craig and I fought all the time. In Denver, on my first show out of the joint, I almost broke my ankle fighting with Craig. We were arguing about something, and whatever he said pissed me off. He went to make a phone call and I yanked the phone out of his hand and hung up. We went at it like two dogs in a yard. He flipped me over his hip, and my ankle slammed down on a brick fireplace mantle.

Right away, it swelled up like a tennis ball, so I could tell it was badly sprained. Everyone tried to pull us apart and I took a hard swing at him on the way out, barely missing. Even though both of us were battered and bruised, we didn't miss the show. The next day all was forgiven, and I probably turned my ball-busting weaponry on Matty or Will. Vinnie and I squabbled like brothers, but we didn't physically fight and he usually got a pass when it came to pranks.

A little later on the tour, we drove to Pittsburgh to play a show at the Graffiti Club, where shit exploded. Usually when something went down it wasn't because of us, but this time it was my fault (with some assistance from our old roadie Squirm). I was downstairs hanging with the rest of AF while Submachine, a local punk band, was onstage. Suddenly, Squirm ran downstairs like he had a bathroom emergency.

"Roger, Roger! The singer is talking shit about you! They called you Nazis!"

I saw red. I couldn't believe a band that was opening for us was talking shit. I grabbed a beer from our cooler and whipped it against the wall. I ran upstairs while Submachine were still playing and charged the stage. Their singer, Alex

Lewinger, was excited to see me come towards him because he was a fan. Maybe he figured I wanted to do a song with them. He never could have imagined I was there to do a number on him. I started wailing on the dude. Will Shepler charged their drummer with cymbal stands and started hitting him with them. It was mayhem. It was a sold-out show, so there were 600 people in the crowd watching the opening band get tuned up. When we felt we had gotten our message across, we walked off the stage.

Alex got up off the ground, picked up his mic and wiped his bloody nose with the back of his hand. "Whoa. Fuck. Shit, man, I don't know what just happened. Did we do something wrong?"

As it turned out, the whole incident was a big misunderstanding. Alex had said, "We're not Nazis, like Agnostic Front." What he meant was that they were like Agnostic Front and that they weren't fascists. But Squirm thought the singer said Submachine weren't fascists but Agnostic Front were! I still wonder if Squirm made a mistake or was just creating a scene and paying me back for a prank I had played on him.

Alex explained to me what he meant before we went on and I felt horrible. During our set I wanted to make a formal apology.

"I want to dedicate this set to Submachine. It's called 'Your Mistake,'" I said. Just like Alex I didn't stop to think about the exact words I was using. It didn't even dawn on me that people would think I was dissing him and saying he made a mistake. Maybe I should have dedicated the second song to him instead.

Once I got my life back together with Agnostic Front, it was time to reconnect with my little brother. Amy reluctantly agreed that Freddy could move back in with us, and I enrolled him in school. It was great to have him around. He was old enough that we could have real conversations about music and life. I gotta admit it was fun to break his balls and get him riled up. We'd say the meanest things. He'd run to Vinnie breathless and pissed off, and Vinnie would act like his kind uncle.

"Yeah, Freddy. Fuck those guys. Don't worry about it," Stigma would say.

The first New York City hometown show with the new Agnostic Front lineup was a big show with Sick of It All and Gorilla Biscuits at the Ritz in January 1991.

That marked my return to the scene. In-Effect Records taped the concert, interviewed all of the bands and put it out on video as *Agnostic Front, Sick of It All, Gorilla Biscuits: Live in NYC '91*. Combat Records had done well with a tape they had put out earlier called *The Ultimate Revenge Combat Tour Live*, which featured Venom, Slayer and Exodus, and this was In-Effect's hardcore version of that.

We played a new song, "Infiltrate," that the guys had worked on, before we kicked into "Strength." We did a lot of songs from *Liberty & Justice For...*, and even though that's not my favorite album, it felt amazing to be back onstage with Agnostic Front. I didn't know what to expect, but the place was packed and the audience went nuts.

It was one of my most memorable concerts, up there with the CBGB show we did right before I went to prison. This was even better because I was free, and there were 3,500 people there to celebrate. Most of them knew I had been away, were excited I was back and were looking forward to the next phase of AF. The whole night was amazing. Sick of It All were just starting to bust out and played like they were out for blood. Gorilla Biscuits killed it, too.

If I could go back, the only thing I might have done differently was to tell the guys in the band that the taping of the show would be used for a big video release. We always played really loudly, and that night was no exception. I didn't know how important it was for the audio to be perfectly engineered. We had done *Live at CBGB* straight from the board, and it captured the energy of the band. I didn't want to make any of the guys nervous by telling them we had to be at the top of our game and that the show was going to be used for the video. Matt and I were the only ones that knew because I wanted it to be natural.

Vinnie is a real showman. He's almost as much of a band mascot as he is a rhythm guitarist. People love him because he's a character. At the same time, he's real. He's not trying to be someone he's not. The Vinnie Stigma that you see onstage lifting his guitar above his head is the same Vinnie you'll find after a show drinking black coffee with no sugar and chatting it up with everyone in the place. He's an entertainer. I didn't want to tell Vinnie that we needed to sound perfect and he needed to perform for the camera. That would have thrown him off guard.

When they recorded us, Vinnie did what he always does. He took his hands off his guitar to wave at the girls in the crowd, and he did plenty of his signature spins, which looked great but made it difficult to pull off even the easiest riff. We knew sometimes he wouldn't be playing because he'd be busy entertaining the crowd. So we made sure his guitar was lower in the mix than Matt's. And we split Matt's guitar so he would run in full stereo. For the recording, Matt's parts were over-distorted in the mix because he was playing louder. Vinnie's audio quality was better, but if you isolated his tracks there would be these long, blank spaces where nothing was happening.

After the show, our record label, Relativity, called me in for a meeting and I went with Matt. They started yelling at us right away. The label manager said that the recording was ruined and that Vinnie's track wasn't even audible. I didn't see what the big deal was. Even if they just used Matt's tracks, the music was so fast and loud that the audio quality wasn't going to make a difference.

But the dudes at the label kept bashing on Stigma and bringing up his guitar parts. They told us he was the weak link of the band and, without exactly saying so, suggested that we get rid of him. We went back and told Vinnie what they had told us and he was furious. He told his mom, Teddie, who was an incredibly nice Italian woman who knew everyone in the neighborhood.

That night we were all downstairs having pasta at his mom's house, which we used to do once a week.

"You tell the people at that record label that Vinnie started the band!" she shouted. It was unusual to hear her yell. She was like a mother bear protecting her young cub.

"This is Vinnie's band!" she continued. "You know what. You call a meeting for next week. You have another meeting with the record people and we'll have a talk with them."

Teddie had lived in the neighborhood for decades, and was well loved. All the mafiosos loved her because she always respected them and minded her own business, but she knew what was going on. She had never asked for anything. So she took the opportunity to pull her card. She called on a "favor" to get us some new managers, and she wanted them to come in and muscle the label. They appointed two mobsters from Jersey to come with us. So we told the label we wanted to meet with them.

Paulie and Sal came in wearing suits. They looked like legitimate thumb-cut-ters. I'm sure they knew how to dispose of a body, but they didn't know shit about the music industry. During the meeting they puffed up their chests and acted all macho. They called the label "Realistic" instead of "Relativity." And they told the label manager that they were doing big things for us and that they were going to get us a show at Madison Square Garden. Then the meeting was over. The new head of the label just sat there in awe. I wondered what he thought of these meatheads who couldn't even pronounce the name of the label correctly. I imag-ined him walking nervously from his subway stop back to his apartment every day, fearful of some overdressed thug who might confront him as he rounded a corner. He never bothered us again or said anything else about Stigma.

Backstage with Vinnie, 1992.

# CHAPTER 31

Even though the Ritz crowd had been huge and the offers to play other gigs were flattering, the hardcore scene was heading towards its lowest point since its inception. I couldn't believe how much everything had changed in just 18 months. Part of the reason it became smaller was because it had gotten so dangerous. The mosh pits were violent and unpredictable free-for-alls. There was no structure whatsoever. The people were different and the music was different. It was a little unnerving. At least we knew that as soon as we took the stage the crowd was gonna blow up for us, regardless of what they were previously into. We always got a good reaction when we played live.

There had always been a risk of violence at New York hardcore shows, but usually not in the pit. Before, if anyone bullied someone who was dancing or moshing they had to deal with me, Jimmy G, Raybeez or one of the other guys who kept the pits moving. We made sure everyone was having fun and no one was there just to hurt other people. Suddenly, people in the pit were acting crazy and decking guys who were smaller than they were. Kids were getting beat up over stupid things. I didn't like that and I knew it wasn't a smart place for me to be in case the cops showed up.

I focused more on my family. Amy, Nadia and I were living in our house in Staten Island, but we couldn't keep up the payments. The projects had expanded, so we couldn't sell the house for what we paid. We ended up in foreclosure, and the bank took it away.

Amy found a squat on 11th Street between B and C, and we worked on it together full-force so that we could move our family in. Back then, it wasn't hard to find a place; it was just difficult to keep it. A lot of the buildings on the Lower East Side were owned by landlords who had mortgages to pay. They couldn't charge rent because the places were in such bad shape and they were losing money. A lot of them hired arsonists to set fire to their buildings so they could collect the insurance money. It wasn't legal, but if they were careful they usually didn't get caught. A lot of the buildings that weren't torched remained empty for years as they fell apart.

A couple of the squats we moved into—besides the legendary Eastern Front— burned down. There's no way to know whether it was faulty electrical or landlords looking for a return on their failed investment. All I know is the fires caused a lot of heartache and property damage, and one of them could have killed Freddy.

Back in 1991, when Freddy was 14, he was home alone with my dog Vern, who was in a cage. Vern was a Jack Russell terrier, and he could get out of any crate. We didn't want him wandering around the house, eating whatever he could find and shitting on the floor, so we were crate-training him. He had a cone on his head from the vet. Amy, Nadia and I were out since AF were playing a show with The Bruisers in New Hampshire. While we were gone, the place went up in flames. Freddy was sleeping, but he woke up coughing from the smoke and managed to get out unharmed. Sadly, Vern was in his crate and died in the blaze. If he didn't have that damned cone on his head he may have escaped. There was another casualty of that fire: my cherished record collection. I lost some amazing gems, like first pressings of records by Misfits, Necros, Fix, Pagans and many New York hardcore bands, as well as a wall of posters and memorabilia. Three of the squats Amy and I lived in caught fire. I wasn't living there when the last one burnt down in 1995, but Nadia and Amy were there watching my two dogs while I was away. They started barking and woke up Nadia. They saved her life.

The place we picked out when we left our Staten Island house wasn't even an apartment. Talk about an open concept. When we walked in there was no floor and no roof. We took over the whole building with 10 or 12 other working-class families— not punks. We wanted to live in a place that was more family-oriented. We all worked together to build a roof and floors, make stairs and repair the walls. Each floor had two doors and a living space.

One guy was really good at mudding, which you do after you lay down drywall. So I did the drywalling and he mudded up the walls in exchange for some electrical work. I wired our whole apartment for almost no money using leftover parts from my electrical jobs. I found a barn heater for the main room, put air conditioning in my daughter's room and installed a shower. Some visitors said it was nicer than a lot of regular New York City apartments. In all honestly, it was!

When Amy and I worked together on the squat, we got along better than we had in a while. But we had been through a lot and there was too much baggage for the seams not to burst. We met when we were young and we probably would have split up way sooner, but we stayed together to try to do the right thing for our daughter. That's what I had been doing since day one. I always had good intentions. It's my actions that weren't always legit.

I worked more electrical jobs and spent time with Nadia. I avoided a lot of riff-raff because I didn't want anything else to happen, and everyone around me knew it. The episode at 99X wasn't an isolated incident. Any time something was going to happen anywhere, someone would tell me to leave. If I was at a bar and two guys were about to go at it, I'd hear, "Roger, man. Get out of here," before anyone threw a punch.

Even though I looked over my shoulder when I was at clubs and bars, I still loved being onstage. I'd been doing it since I was 16. When we played shows I felt like I was where I was supposed to be. It was good to be with the band again, and I loved seeing my hardcore family in the pit, even though that family had become a minority, I loved looking out at the people in the crowd who were psyched to see me performing again.

A lot of bands have great memories of going to England for the first time and spending a few weeks playing all the neighboring countries. Not me! The first Agnostic Front European tour was a complete disaster! We were booked by Syd and Loraligh, two pen-pal friends. Maybe we were doomed from the start, but that's the way things worked. Syd was in a hardcore band called Cheetah Chrome Motherfuckers (CCM), who were based in Pisa, Italy. I guess he didn't know I was Cuban-born. We flew into Holland on October 16, 1990, they stamped my passport and let me in.

We drove to Germany with no hassle at the border and played in a big circus tent in Oberhausen, Germany, with a psychedelic alternative group called Space Monkeys.

The members of the audience didn't know whether to come closer to check us out or cover their heads and flee for the exit, so they stood at a distance from the stage looking uncomfortable. It was a strange way to start, and it was about to get weirder. We drove to Belgium to continue the tour, and when we got to the border we handed over our passports. I wasn't an American citizen yet and still had my Cuban passport. No one told me I needed a visa to get into each country. The customs officers detained me, questioned me and deported me. I had to catch the next flight back to New York.

The rest of the guys continued with the tour and got our roadie, Mike Shost, to sing. Man, did he have a good time! And I'm not talking about the thrill you get from fronting a hardcore band. For years, Mike would go to local bars and tell girls that he was the singer of Agnostic Front to get them into bed. He had the pictures to prove it—he was onstage singing with our banner behind him and the guys playing next to him. I didn't know he exploited his brief tenure in the band like that until many years later, when my then-wife, Denise, was bartending at Wetlands and told me this crazy story.

She was pouring drinks for customers when one of her best friends from high school, whom she had lost touch with, came up to her. They were happy to see one another and started talking. The girl said, "Oh, my God! You'll never believe whom I married."

"Who?" Denise asked.

"I married the singer from Agnostic Front!"

"You're married to Roger?" said Denise. For a split-second she wondered if I was living a double life or if this girl was bat-shit crazy.

"Who's Roger?" the girl answered.

She had married Mike Shost! I didn't see him much after the European tour, but apparently a lot of Agnostic Front groupies did. And one of them ended up marrying him!

When we returned from our comeback tour, we went into recording mode. We locked ourselves up in a rehearsal space for a couple months and wrote songs. This time there was less fucking around. I wasn't partying anymore and was focused on making a great album. When we weren't writing, we'd sit at my kitchen table over homemade cockroach-spiked paella and go over lyrics with Craig and Matt line by line to make sure they had the right flow.

For the first time, I wanted to release a record that had a strong theme. It's a full-blown concept album like *The Wall* or *Tommy;* I wanted to tell my story about going to prison. "New Jack" is about walking into prison and being approached by an old-timer there who explains what life behind bars is all about: "You thought in the streets that your life was so unfair and cruel, make one careless mistake here, boy, and you'll drown in your own pool / So take this advice, stay alert and on cue / Keep only to yourself and your ears in sharp tune."

"Over the Edge" is about being betrayed by the guys I had worked with: "I thought you were a friend I'd trust 'til end /These days you learn to trust no one, you must include those closest friends."

At the last minute we needed one more song so I wrote "Bastard" about my step-father. It only took a half-hour to complete, musically and lyrically. Although it didn't quite fit in with the prison theme, my experiences with my stepdad are part of the story of how I landed behind bars. Plus, it was therapeutic to write exactly how I felt about that abusive coward: "When it came down for mental support, a blatant strike was how you would resort / Tell me what I have done wrong to deserve such pain so strong."

I liked having a record that told my story. I didn't want to glorify prison, so I told it like it was and explained how it strengthened me as a man. I wouldn't wish the experience on anyone. There were a lot of nightmares that I'd rather forget. But it lets you know who you are. It grounds you. You learn exactly how to walk the line. If you don't, you perish.

We planned to record *One Voice* at Normandy Sound in Rhode Island. Matt wanted to record it with Tom Soares, who had worked with Cro-Mags and Leeway. We booked the studio and Tom tracked with the band for two or three days. When I showed up with Don Fury, who was going to help engineer the album and work with me on my vocals, Tom took off. He appeared nervous and said he had to leave and do last-minute sound for the band Scatterbrain. Was seeing Don Fury in his studio intimidating, or did Tom's by-the-book, radio-minded, technical approach clash with Don's homegrown, hardcore way of doing things? Tom might have felt slighted, but thank God Don Fury was there.

Tom told us we'd be in good hands with his engineer, Jamie Locke, and he couldn't wait to hear the record when it was done. Jamie seemed talented, but he didn't know us and he didn't know our scene. Don Fury was a friend and we wanted to get some of that old, classic New York hardcore sound out of him. *One Voice* came out in 1992, and it was one of those pace-setting records. It was different than anything that was coming out—a mixture of old-school grit and new-school groove—and it introduced a new sound to NYHC. Again, AF were on the forefront of something unprecedented.

Having a new record out felt like a real accomplishment. I already knew I could still perform onstage after I got out of prison. The album proved to me that I hadn't lost my ability to express myself in the studio. In fact, my songwriting got better. But there was no question that the album was less popular than *Liberty & Justice For...* and *Cause For Alarm*. The scene had gotten smaller. A lot of punks, skins and hardcore kids from the '80s had moved on.

We were biggest during our *Cause For Alarm* cycle, but we didn't want to return to that sound. All our records sound different even though they're recognizable as Agnostic Front. Our attitude has always been *Let's always be on the edge of the scene, not caught up in the wave we helped invent and that everyone else was playing*. We don't like to follow anything, even ourselves. And we've always played with different members in different studios, which has contributed to our shifting sound.

In addition to being a cohesive concept album, *One Voice* introduced what would be considered new-school hardcore. If you dropped my vocals off the record and put my brother Freddy on instead, it would sound like a Madball album, but with a bunch of killer leads. You can attribute most of that to Matt Henderson's guitar style combined with the rhythm section of Will Shepler and Craig Setari. All those guys played a big role in *One Voice*. They'll always be my brothers and they'll always have my thanks.

Musically *One Voice* is a crazy train ride and a lot of people love it, but they started loving it a while after it came out. The hardcore scene didn't take to the album right away. People hated it, which was a bummer because we worked so hard on it. We went from *Liberty & Justice For...*, which was chaotic and on the verge of speedcore, to *One Voice*, which was raw but fresher and had more groove to it. The people who liked *Cause For Alarm* and *Liberty & Justice For...* were, like, "What the fuck is this? We wanted something wild and crazier."

Looking back, it was a transitional record for us, and it showed change and growth within the band. A lot of people who lived with it for a while say it's one of their favorites. As American bands often say when something didn't go exactly right, it did phenomenally well in Europe. And the shows there were huge.

But huge didn't always mean great. Some people in the German hardcore community didn't welcome us because we didn't fit in anywhere between Fugazi and Bad Religion. They bought into the hateful shit in *Maximumrocknroll*. Some haters printed up a seven-inch bootleg that featured us on one side and a band called White Pride on the other. I guess it was their idea of a sick joke; I didn't think it was funny and it caused us some grief. Some of our supporters hated that they were trying to align AF with White Pride. They were outraged and scratched up the A-side in the shape of the anarchy symbol. They put a sticker on the record depicting the German flag with a zipper on it, a swastika and the words "Bad News."

We once played an *anti*-fascist show in Berlin at So36, which led to a deep friendship between the So36 community and us. It also caused a big misunderstanding. We performed in front of a big anti-Nazi banner—a swastika smashed by a fist. So36 was packed and stage-divers swarmed the front of the stage for the whole night. Later, a picture from that show was used to depict us as fascists!

The photo was shot from the left side of the stage and the person who took it was standing at a weird angle. The shot caught a stage-diver in front of me and a big swastika flag behind me. The fist smashing the swastika wasn't visible. When you're playing a benefit show to oppose fascism, you never think that people will misinterpret—or misrepresent—your motivation. Even something as innocent as lifting a hand to show unity can be viewed in a photo as something terribly wrong, like *sieg heil*ing a crowd!

Aside from the bizarre and unexpected episodes in Germany (where we still make lots of new friends), the European tour was a lot of fun and we sold a bunch of records there—more than we did in America. There might have been a reason for that.

In Europe the record came out on Roadrunner Records. They put it out on vinyl, cassette and CD, just like all their big releases, and they gave it a lot of love. We did tons of press in every country and got great bookings for the entire tour.

I don't know if Relativity still had some sour grapes over when we brought Murder

Inc. to our meeting or if the label just didn't understand the record, but they didn't do anything to help us out. The marketing and promotions department seemingly didn't even know the record was out and *One Voice* was Relativity's first record that was only released on CD. Back then people listened to hardcore on vinyl. Maybe that's why *One Voice* was not well received in the U.S. Our U.S. concerts were still strong— maybe because, unlike the vast majority of hardcore shows, Agnostic Front shows were still unpredictable. It wasn't the '80s anymore, but you still never knew what would happen and if something crazy might go down.

If a security guard got out of hand and manhandled the kids, I'd reach out and crack him in the head with the mic. They usually figured out I wouldn't put up with their shit, so they stopped it. Sometimes they needed a little extra prodding. During a hometown *One Voice* record release show at the Palladium on June 17, 1992, the atmosphere was tense all night. The bouncers were being assholes, the crowd was getting agitated and it felt like a powder keg was ready to blow. During the show the bouncers fucked up kids who got too close to the stage. Vinnie was the first to react. He took his guitar off and started swinging it at the bouncers. Then EZEC, a singer in a bunch of NYHC bands, picked up a big stage monitor and brought it down on a security guard's head. It was on. I smacked bouncers with my mic, and the crowd flooded the stage in solidarity. It was us, the crew and the fans facing off against the meat-head security guys. Needless to say, the show abruptly ended. Ministry's "Thieves" played over the PA and a full-on brawl ensued. The club called the cops, and we got the hell out of there so we wouldn't get arrested. We still had our AF banner up, and regrettably we left it there. It was a major fuck-up. We had a rule never to leave our banner behind for someone else to steal. It's like letting the enemy capture your flag. We never saw that banner again, and we didn't get paid for the show. We heard later that the bouncers had a party and burned our banner. At least some of them went home with busted skulls, black eyes and fat lips. Motherfuckers!

Even though we were playing new music, doing some of the shows was like turning back the clock. The same old radical right-wingers we thought we'd left behind years earlier would storm in and cause shit. They could turn a great show upside-down in an instant. One time, we were booked at the Airport Music Hall in Allentown, Pennsylvania, along with Sheer Terror, Life of Agony, No One's Hero, Vision and

Wrecking Crew. The area had a strong white power movement. Hundreds of guys came to the concert with swastika flags.

I was on my way to the show, but Vinnie later told me that when Life of Agony were halfway through their set, one racist in the crowd started picking on a black guy. One of these fascists punched the poor kid in the back of the head and another kicked him in the face, knocking out one of his teeth.

Life of Agony stopped the show and said something about not tolerating racism, and the place blew up. The crowd broke all the windows. The fighting spilled onstage and backstage. Some big skinhead wanted to beat up Little Zan, who was the cousin of Life of Agony guitarist Joey Z. Vinnie broke apart the mic stands and handed out pieces of metal to everyone backstage to crack some heads. He was like a general sending his troops out to battle. All hell broke loose.

I showed up after the fact, just before we were scheduled to go onstage, and the place was completely wrecked.

"What the fuck happened?" I asked.

I got the story and went upstairs, stepping over broken tables and chairs and piles of glass. I collected our money and we left.

Shortly afterward, I suffered a hernia from jumping around so much. I wasn't doing anything different, but one day I landed wrong and it felt like I had pulled something above my right thigh. Later I noticed that the flesh between my bladder and my groin was swollen on my right side. I didn't think anything of it, but the pain got worse with every show. By the second week of July, I was in agony. Even though we weren't doing a Madball set anymore, Freddy was on the road with us and performed "Over the Edge" and "One Voice" with us.

Agnostic Front was co-headlining the Complete Control Tour with Obituary, plus special guests Cannibal Corpse and Malevolent Creation, promoting *One Voice*. We were booked to play the Milwaukee Metal Fest on a hardcore/death metal day. Before the show started, my hernia was throbbing so bad I could barely walk. I got through the show on sheer adrenaline, but afterwards I was screaming in agony. I had to fly back home and get surgery for a right inguinal hernia, which required two weeks of recovery time.

I told Freddy that he would have to fill in for me. I thought he'd be honored, but he was pissed off! He loved AF, but he had never done a full AF set.

"Fuck! I'm not gonna do it. I fuckin' can't," he said, fists in tight balls and nails cutting into his palms.

"Don't be a fuckin' prick!" I shouted, partially because of the pain I was in and partially because Freddy was being difficult. "You can do it. You have to do it and our fans love you."

"No, Roger. I'm gonna get laughed off the fucking stage!"

"You're not. You know all the songs. You're the only one who can do this."

Mind you, Freddy was only 15.

Not only did Freddy play the shows, he killed it and our fans instantly loved him. Freddy stayed on the road and filled in while I had the surgery.

I was supposed to spend three weeks recovering before I did anything physical. Two weeks after I had the procedure, I was going stir-crazy and dying to get back on the road. Agnostic Front were driving back down the East Coast so they planned to pick me up on their way to Washington. The incision from the surgery had healed and the spot below my groin didn't hurt all the time, so I made my way to a truck stop in Jersey where they were gonna pick me up. But I could tell something was wrong. By the time I got there my head was spinning and the pain was so bad I threw up in a trashcan. I tried to get into the van, but it wasn't happening. I thought Freddy was gonna be mad if I couldn't go back on the road. But he was the first one to tell me I should go home and fully heal. He was having a great time. AF continued another two weeks with Freddy before he handed the mic back to me.

Playing those dates was important for Freddy. His insecurity about taking the stage for a full show disappeared. By the time he was done, he was itching to apply what he had learned to Madball, which had only played a handful of regional shows at that point. That was the moment when he went from my little brother who sometimes took the stage with me to the commanding leader of his own band. Those shows gave Freddy the confidence and fortitude to lead Madball into the future and allowed him to shine.

# CHAPTER 32

**1**992 was a wild year. The first Gulf War had ended, George Bush was wrapping up his term in the White House and angst-filled bands like Nirvana and Nine Inch Nails were changing pop culture. There was a new level of anger and frustration in society, and the hardcore scene was always ripe for harboring contempt at the world around us. We were the epitome of "disenfranchised youth" since day one. That part of us hadn't changed much since the '80s. Only our surroundings and circumstances were different.

Violence is a part of American culture. It's all around us. Growing up in certain areas, you either assert yourself or get eaten alive. The Lower East Side was well into gentrification mode. That said, the early '90s were the last of the "wild days" in NYC.

One time our friends from Detroit came to visit. If anyone could relate to the streets of NYC, it's folks from Detroit. They came to play in their band Cold as Life at CBGB with AF. Their crew was called CTYC. We had befriended them in Detroit and were of the same ilk. Before the show, Freddy and I were hanging out in the East Village with Rawn (the original singer) and Dougie (crew). We walked into Venus Records on St Marks. When we passed the counter, Dougie noticed a copy of *Victim In Pain* displayed on the wall. He said, "Man, I want to buy that but it's kind of pricey."

"Hold on," I said. "I'll talk to the guy behind the counter and see what he can do for us."

"Excuse me. My friend wants to buy that record. Can I look at it?" I said to the guy at the register. Once I confirmed it was legit I said, "It's actually my band. I'm the singer. I was wondering if . . ."

"I don't care who you are. You're not getting a discount," he said. At first he probably didn't think I was in the band.

"Let me show you—that's me on the inside of the gatefold. That's my name there. I have ID," I said, trying to reason with him.

"I don't give a fuck if your mother was fucking the owner of this place," the guy shot back at me.

Freddy and I looked at each other. Not only was the guy disrespectful, but he brought our mother into this. I put the record back in the sleeve. Freddy calmly walked over to the door and locked it. He looked over at Rawn and Dougie, and no words were needed. Everyone knew what had to happen here.

A second dude who worked behind the counter realized we were getting ready to show his co-worker that there were consequences for his actions. He turned around to call the police. Rawn yelled in a very menacing voice, "Put the fucking phone down." I simultaneously ripped the phone off the wall, leaving a trail of severed wires. We went to work on both guys and delivered an extra beating to the guy who was stupid enough to badmouth our mom. Afterwards, as they lay there licking their wounds, I grabbed the record, threw some money down and off we went.

Did we have to take it to that extreme? The way we grew up, disrespect was not tolerated. We did not start or escalate this, but we surely asserted ourselves. I gave Dougie the record and I hope he still has it, along with the memories.

Record stores were supposed to be a haven for punks and hardcore kids. Too often in the '90s, they were elitist clubs run by dudes who had no respect for the musicians that kept them employed.

There was another record shop called Sixth Street Record Collective, which was run by hardcore fans. They had a decent collection and bought used albums. I had a few copies of a rare Agnostic Front record that was only released in Europe, so I went over there to sell it. The buyer said, "I'll give you $10 a piece." I felt that was low, but I accepted his offer. A week later I went back and looked in the AF bin. Sitting next to our other albums was the record I had sold to the store. It had sticker that read, "This record costs $20 because Roger Miret from Agnostic Front is greedy and wants to rip off his fans, blah, blah, blah." I couldn't believe it!

Our attorney and longtime friend, Dave Stein, was a part of the collective, but I didn't want to involve him. I did some sniffing around, hung out on 6th Street a little more than usual and figured out who had badmouthed me.

One day I caught the guy off guard when it was just him and another employee. I walked into the store with Freddy and two of his friends. I could see their composure change as they made their way to the counter. I picked up a Madball seven-inch and a couple other singles from NYHC bands and put them on the counter.

"How much?" I asked.

He tried to keep his cool and tell me how much, but I could hear his voice shaking a bit. He told me a price and I asked Freddy for the money. He purposely lifted his shirt as he reached for the money, slowly pulling out a 9mm pistol. They looked down and pretended not to notice, as the color drained from their faces. I crumpled up the bills, threw them down on the counter and gave them a deadpan stare. As they collected the money, Freddy said, "You should show more respect. One of the reasons this store exists is standing in front of you."

We walked out with the records, and they were so freaked out that they immediately called Dave Stein. He told them they shouldn't have antagonized me. He was not happy about the gun, though. We had no intention of shooting anyone. We wanted to scare the shit out of them and teach them some manners. A week or so later, I passed the store again and it had closed down. I don't know if I had anything to do with their decision, but I'd like to think I did. This wasn't about being a bully. It was about respect, plain and simple.

The One Voice tour was the first time we played in South America, and that was even crazier than the U.S.! In Brazil, the promoter booked one show at a local club and a second private show just for the fans, which I thought was a cool idea. But it ended up being in a weird disco full of rich people. It wasn't our crowd at all; it was a private, elite show.

I saw a bunch of real fans outside trying to get in but they were turned away. The promoter was trying to throw a party for himself and his friends, and no one else was welcome. We told him we wouldn't do it unless he let in our real fans. We opened the back doors of the club, and our fans started rushing the club. We got an icy vibe from the owners and it felt like something was going to go down.

"Fuck it, we'll find somewhere else to play," I told the promoter. Our real fans were there standing by us, so none of these rich dudes were going to try anything.

We took everybody down the street with us into a restaurant that had an open outdoor area. We played a concert just for the fans. We didn't even get paid, but we didn't care. We weren't about to play a private gig for wealthy people and exclude the kids who turned to us to hear music about overcoming oppression. That would have gone against everything we stood for.

We played a packed show in Argentina in a club outside of Buenos Aires. It got so hot that the mixing board caught fire. Our soundman, Jay, rushed over and said, "We gotta get out of here. There's a fire!" The flames had started to spread. It could have been like that Great White show in Rhode Island in 2003, when the place burned to the ground and 100 people died.

There was only one exit and we saw smoke filling up the club. People started to panic and all the power went out, so we ran out into the street. Fortunately, the place didn't burn down and none of our equipment got damaged. It just smelled like smoke for a week.

Down in South America, there are no rules. Some dodgy promoter shows you where you're going to play, and you know it's going to be a wild night. Since they don't get to see American bands often, people lose their minds. Kids do insane things, like spraying fire extinguishers at people while a band is playing.

Chile has one of the craziest and most thriving scenes in South America. Even getting into the venue was an adventure. They didn't have ushers and ticket takers, but there were riot police and tanks. Fans who didn't have tickets bum-rushed the door and stormed past the security forces that were spraying them with high-powered hoses. There's strength in numbers, so most of them got into the building. Others were pulled out and got the shit kicked out of them. Maybe they even got arrested.

When we entered the building, we had to run past these crazed people and a lot of them grabbed at us. It made me wonder what it was like for bands like The Beatles and The Rolling Stones when they first came to America. By the time we got inside, there were already about 3,000 fans and others were trying to barge in, so the police fired tear gas at them and into the venue. Everybody scrambled to get out because they couldn't breathe. I ran backstage so I didn't get tear gas in my eyes. Everyone was reaching for water and trying to get outside for fresh air. In the middle of the chaos, the promoter ran up to me.

"Please, please, you have to play for them!"

I was, like, "Dude, relax. We're going to play. We just can't play for them right now. We can't breathe and everyone's bugging out."

The last thing I ever want to do is cancel a show. About 30 minutes later, the place calmed down, people went back inside and we jumped onstage. All the energy, fear and aggression were transmitted back and forth between us and the audience, and it was a passionate, memorable and insane experience.

At another show in Chile, I walked out to get close to the crowd while I sang a song. As I leaned over, an arm reached out for me, then two, then 10, and dragged me into the audience. Before I knew what was happening, my clothes were ripped off. I swung my arms and scrambled away from the crowd and towards the band. By the time I got back to the relative safety of the stage, I was in my underwear. As much as I would have liked to keep my clothes, whoever got my shirt, pants and shoes definitely earned their souvenirs.

Our craziest experience in South America was in the late '90s in Colombia. All these men with machine guns greeted us at the airport. We'd never had that kind of welcoming party before. They took us to the house we were staying at outside of Bogota. It was a beautiful mansion with four watch towers. It was an armed house with a wall, and I had to ask them why we were staying in what looked like a prison. They told me that it was normal for bands and performers and that even with armed guards people sometimes got robbed. Thugs would break in and slap them around a little bit, scare the shit out of them and take their money.

Since I spoke Spanish and was from Cuba, I didn't want to be treated like a tourist. We got there a couple days early and I wanted to enjoy some down-time before the show. I said, "I don't want these people around me. I want to go into town."

I asked them to leave the armed guards behind and they agreed, so they just sent one guy in a pickup truck to travel around with us. I saw there was a fiesta going on in town, so I asked the driver to take us there. We danced with the girls and hung out with the guy who brought us. We looked for souvenirs and felt great. All of a sudden we noticed that there was a big arena with a bull tied up outside. It turned out there was a bullfight happening there. We had never seen a bullfight, so we went to check it out. Next thing we knew everyone was cheering, and it was fucking Vinnie there with the bull. Vinnie has a way of magically talking his way into anything. He had managed to convince someone to let him be one of the clowns who agitates the bull to get him all riled up. Without warning, the bull started charging at him and Vinnie freaked out.

Vinnie didn't know what to do. He was waving a little spear in the air, not even pointing it at the bull. Our jaws were on the floor. I was, like, "Shit, there goes our guitarist. How are we going to find someone else to play this gig?" Then the midget clowns came in and distracted the bull, and Vinnie ran off. Later Vinnie said that he told the bullfighters that he knew the bulls were drugged up and didn't have a chance and that the whole thing was rigged. So they said, "Oh, really, gringo? Well, do you want to get in the ring and see how tame they are?" Since Vinnie is crazy he said yes—and found out that the bull was pissed off and completely sober.

Later that night, it was getting dark and everyone was dancing with girls. One guy kept tapping Kabula on the shoulder asking for cigarettes, and he'd say, "Sorry, man, I don't smoke." After a few times we could tell the guy was looking for trouble. Kabula squared off against this dude.

While they were fighting, a girl jumped on Kabula's back. He didn't know it was a girl. All he knew was he was trying to fight someone in front of him and someone else was on his back choking him. So he threw an elbow backwards, hit her in the face and knocked her out. It was a total accident. All these people saw was four Americans who had just knocked out a young girl. Suddenly we were the enemy. It seemed like everyone in the town started chasing us. We had to fight our way back to the pickup truck. We were getting attacked from all sides. I don't know how we made it back. It must have been a case of a massive adrenaline high because we knew we had to get the hell out of there. I jumped in the front passenger seat. The driver was sitting there waiting. Vinnie, Colletti and Kabula jumped in the back. I yelled, "Go, go, go!" I looked to my left and saw a fist smash through the window, and someone clocked the driver in the jaw. I could actually see his jaw slip out of place and slide to the side as it broke. I hit the gas with my feet and the driver steered out of there. After we got away, the driver went to the hospital to get his jaw wired shut. We returned to the fortress and I said to the manager, "You know, that was good enough. Send back the armed guards."

# CHAPTER 33

On our final One Voice Tour in Europe, we flew into Germany. We met our booking agent, Marc, whom we named Frankenstein because he's a giant, block-headed German. We hooked up with our merch guy, whom we called the Mummy since he was pale white. Eventually we changed his name to Mosh because, at our first show, he got into the pit and danced like a nutjob NYHC skanker. Our roadie, Squirm, and my friend, Paula, were with us, too.

We were happy to be back in Europe, where we were really appreciated, and stoked to have a tour bus for the first time. It wasn't exactly a modern Provost luxury coach. It was a really old black bus with squeaky brakes, beat-up bunks that rattled when you drove and a lounge that lacked amenities. The bus had to be push-started every time we wanted to move! Have you ever tried pushing a full-size bus loaded with gear?

We called the driver the Colonel because he looked like an extra from the '70s TV series *Hogan's Heroes*. When we were ready to go, we'd beg anyone we could find to help us push-start the bus. After the thing slowly started rolling, the Colonel would do a black-cloud–polluted victory lap around the lot. The seats in the lobby were made of wood, so one day I carved "Elvis" into the side of a seat with my knife, then rubbed some dirt into the carving and pissed on it to make it look old. That evening I told Vinnie that the Colonel said this was one of the first tour buses Elvis Presley used when he came to Europe. I showed him where I had carved "Elvis" and told him to ask the Colonel, who simply replied "Ya, ist Elvis." To this day Vinnie believes we were on Elvis's bus.

The starter wasn't the only thing wrong with the old Elvis bus. The Colonel hadn't been given the right tags and paperwork to drive from one country to another. After we played a huge show in France, we successfully push-started the bus and were on our way out of Paris. As we drove through the mountains we got pulled over by French police. They asked us for our papers. I was traveling with a re-entry permit and had the right visa to get into the country, so this time it wasn't my fault. The Colonel didn't have the right sticker to be on the highway. I figured they would simply fine us and make us pay for the necessary permit sticker. Instead they removed all the lug nuts from the wheels of the bus, then left us there to fend for ourselves in the middle of a French highway in the wee hours of a Sunday morning.

While Marc was scrambling to get the bus situation sorted out, we needed to find a way to get to our next show. We hitchhiked and someone picked up Mosh, Squirm and me and drove us to an Avis van rental place. Mosh had a pouch full of merch money from the tour, but no one had a credit card. They said they'd only take credit cards, so I held the pouch of cash in front of them. There was so much in there we could have bought the fuckin' van. Money talks. Mosh talked them into it, and I'm sure they charged us more than usual, but we got a van. We drove back to the bus and took enough of our belongings for a day or two. Then we left for the next show with our equipment, and the Colonel waited for a tow truck.

The show was great. The French kids were really losing their minds. The next day Marc got a call that we weren't expecting. The Colonel had gotten a tow truck and the truck was towing the tour bus somewhere to get the forms and stickers we needed. But as they towed the bus around a big turn in the mountains, the driver miscalculated and the bus fell right off the cliff, with all our clothes and some of our personal belongings. We never saw it again. We never knew how far it fell or where it landed.

We saw the Colonel a week or so later when we were driving to make our last show of the tour in Prague. We still had the van and Marc was driving insanely on the highway to get us there in time for our set. We got to the border entry point in time and everything seemed okay. Wouldn't you know it? I didn't have the right visa for their country and they wouldn't let me in. We drove around the country trying to get to another border that would let us in. And the same thing happened. We were about to leave when the officers at the border stopped us.

"Are you that band?" one of them asked, as he shined a flashlight in our faces.

Marc explained to them we had a big show and we needed to get into the country. The guard's face lit up.

"Everyone has been waiting for you," he said. "The promoter called from the venue and said you must let this band in or there will be destruction all over Prague. Come, come!"

We got a police escort from the border all the way to Prague. Marc drove 100-plus miles per hour in fog and cars were swerving out of the way for the police. We made it just in time. We jumped onstage, and though we were frazzled and exhausted, we played like we had just gotten eight hours of sleep. All the adrenaline and frustration ignited into a beautiful, climactic and explosive cocktail.

After the show we were totally spent. We were through—and not just with touring. The events that led up to the show and the volcanic way we finished the tour left us with an empty tank. It was time to head back to the States. I had problems I needed to sort out at home.

By the time I got off tour and back to New York, Amy and I weren't acting like a couple. She had built up a lot of resentment against me. While I was bouncing from prison to prison and learning to survive, she had to go on with her life as a single mom and try to keep her band together. I sort of stranded her. Did I mean to? No, of course not. Did she stand by me? Yes, she really did. At times it was weird, but while I was away she really gave us a shot. When I got back, though, we became more like roommates than a couple with a kid. I figured that might have been how things were between couples who had been together a long time and grown comfortable with one another.

Nadia was growing up. She was no longer the little girl who had to be taken care of and told what to do. She was becoming headstrong like her parents and wanted to make some of her own decisions. I hadn't been there for her when I was in prison, and it killed me when I was on tour and away from her. Every time I got back she knew something she didn't know before or could do something new. It killed me to miss seeing her develop and mature. It wasn't like I needed to stay in the band to support the family.

The fans reacted great on tour, but there were fewer of them at our shows and playing smaller venues meant less money. We'd go out for two or three weeks at a time and come back with nothing to show for it. Between the small guarantees and the money we made selling T-shirts, we got by but it was rough. I didn't have the kind of cash I had when I was dealing, and even though we were squatting again and didn't need much to survive, I had Nadia to worry about. I needed more income and health insurance.

I still loved hardcore, but Nadia needed me more, so I stopped Agnostic Front in December 1992. It was a hard decision because I had just gone back to the band and we had done a great album that I really poured my heart into. We played what could have been our final show with Cold as Life at CBGB on December 20, and we told the crowd that Madball would take over and carry on our legacy. As much as our fans loved Madball, they were understandably upset and some of them lashed out. There were a bunch of fights in the crowd, and some people got hit on the head with bottles. But all things considered, it was a good show. We recorded it and it came out as *Last Warning*.

I had worked in construction from time to time when I was younger, so I went to work with my friend Ray Lam. I had done framing and sheet rocking for him and now I had electrical training, so Ray hired me as an electrician. It was more advanced than the work I had previously done, so I felt more accomplished. At the same time I worked on bikes with early pioneers of the New York chopper scene. I loved working on these sleek, powerful machines. I wasn't a trained Harley Davidson mechanic, so I went to the Harley Davidson School MMI (Motorcycle Mechanics Institute) in Orlando, Florida, to get more training. I figured that if I had more hands-on instruction and made more contacts, I could land a job at a dealership so that I'd have a steady paycheck for the family and health insurance for my daughter.

While I was away at Harley Davidson School, Vinnie, Will and Matt continued doing Madball with Freddy and replaced me on bass with Jorge "Hoya Roc" Guerra. He's a friend who was in a band called Dmize, and when that group broke up I suggested him to Freddy.

Those guys recorded a pair of great albums, 1994's *Set It Off* and 1996's *Demonstrating My Style* before Freddy continued the band with new members. I was stoked that Madball were doing well and have been doing well ever since.

My favorite photo with Nadia.

I still thought things were all right between Amy and me while I was at Harley Davidson School. I figured we were still together because we had a kid and that's just the way it was. But when I got back a year later, she set me straight.

"Roger, I can't keep doing this." she said.

"Doing what?"

"I can't pretend like things haven't changed. They've changed. They're totally different. They have been for a while."

She said we had outgrown one another and she wanted to be on her own. The strangest thing about our split was that even though we weren't a couple anymore, we were living across the hall from one another in the same squat for a few years. After we split up, another space opened up on the same floor so I took it. It was awkward at first, but we both had Nadia to raise and that was our priority. Neither of us wanted to be away from her.

What upset me most was that I left everything to have a family. I did everything I could do to keep the three of us together. And I got the shit end of the stick. I felt betrayed and pissed off. I gave up something I loved to be with people I loved and now I was losing one of them. Shit happens.

Of course, there are two sides to every story. When I contacted Amy for this book to address some of the ups and downs of our relationship, she had a very different perspective on how and why it fell apart. She was angry—rightfully so. The truth is that we were young and we had a difficult relationship, both after I got arrested and after I got out of prison. But there was a time when we loved each other deeply, and when things were good, they were really good. In the end, we tried to make our relationship work and we couldn't. Revisiting our past triggered some great memories as well as some bad ones. Here is the truth that we addressed and some faults that I do need to own.

I was responsible for actions that led to poor outcomes. I pushed her away, subconsciously or intentionally. I chose my band and the chaos that surrounded it at times, when I should have supported our family. I shouldn't have ignored her educational goals, but selfishly I would run off on a tour, leading to the loss of her scholarships. The list goes on and on. I put her through this wild journey because of my riot. Eventually what she wanted was to take back her life, regain her self-respect, grow and move forward as a strong woman in order to provide a secure future for our daughter. I can respect that very much. Someone had to change, and it wasn't going to be me.

As easy as it was for me to see Nadia, it became just as easy to argue with Amy. We tried not to fight and we were as civilized as we could be when Nadia was around. But I was mad a lot, and for someone like me who came from a background filled with chaos and domestic violence, the situation could have spun out of control. I worked hard to control myself. I felt bad when Nadia heard us fight. I also felt rage burning inside of me—the kind of anger that made me violent. I knew I could never lay a hand on Amy. I've never done that to Amy, Nadia or any other woman in my life. I saw it happen my whole life with my mom and it disgusted me. I needed to do something to put out the fire. It was time to give up Amy and move on.

I got a great job working at Reggie Pink Harley Davidson in White Plains, New York. I spent a lot of time riding around the City with all the early NYC chopper guys like Steg Von Heintz, Indian Larry, English Don, Paul Cox, Willie Garcia and Rick Esposito, to name a few.

One night I went with some buddies to a hotel bar for a drink, and the bartender, who was a hot brunette hardcore chick, recognized me. Her name was Denise and she was a big fan of Nausea and Agnostic Front. We flirted a little and exchanged numbers, but I had just started seeing someone else that a friend had introduced me to, so nothing came of it. But I didn't have a lot in common with the girl I was seeing. She was cute, but it was a short rebound relationship. Not long after we started seeing each other, we ran out of things to talk about and we'd sit there with long moments of silence. While I was over at her house once, I got paged on my beeper. I went to a pay phone to check the message, and it was Denise. Since things weren't going anywhere with the girl I was seeing, I left and went over to Denise's.

We connected right away and she quickly became a big part of my life. I went over to see her a lot, and if Amy was out of town or it was my night to babysit, Denise would come over to my place. She liked kids and was good with Nadia, which was important to me. Eventually, she lost her apartment and moved in with me. My daughter was thrilled. My ex, not so much. Amy was always cold to Denise, even though Amy was seeing someone else as well. Denise told Amy she was a Nausea fan and was always nice to her. They knew each other from the scene, but I later found out that the rivalry had to do with Denise and Amy's close friend crossing some boundaries. Amy said Denise was a bitch to her until she no longer saw Amy as a threat. You say *potato*; I say *potahto*.

One time, Denise went to the laundromat and some of Nadia's clothes were in there, so she folded them up. Then she knocked on Amy's door and gave her Nadia's things.

"Oh, I see you can do laundry, too. I'm impressed!" said Amy, her voice dripping with sarcasm.

Denise stormed back to our apartment and slammed the door.

"That fucking bitch! If she ever says anything else to me I'm gonna fucking lay her out." She wasn't kidding. Denise had a temper, and I knew we had to move.

# CHAPTER 34

On July 29, 1995, Madball played at Coney Island High and Freddy asked me to come onstage with him and sing "Crucified," the Iron Cross cover from *Liberty & Justice For…*. The song ripped and the crowd went nuts, since they hadn't seen me for a while. After the song ended, I wanted to make a big exit so I dove into the crowd. As I entered the sea of people, my body turned. I was on top of the crowd looking up at the ceiling and the stage, and I was smiling because I was having such a great time. Then a giant dude climbed onto the stage. He had on a black T-shirt and a big grin. He looked right at me and was excited to see me there. Then he decided to jump right on top of me. I saw him start to dive.

*Oh, no, no, no! What are you doing?* I thought.

His 300-pound body seemed weightless as he left the stage. Then, he descended in what seemed like slow-motion and landed right on top of me. The crowd couldn't take the weight of both of us. We crashed to the ground and he crushed me. I can still picture the guy's face, but I've never seen him again. I'm sure he thinks that if he comes around he's gonna get a serious beatdown. But it was an honest accident. His weight was mostly on my midsection, so my back hit the ground first and then my head smacked against the floor. A high-pitched buzz drowned out the band, which finished two more songs before they realized I hadn't gotten back up.

I was conscious, but I couldn't move. Madball stopped playing and cleared the floor, and the venue called 911. When the paramedics arrived they carefully picked me up and put me on stretcher. The ambulance driver knew who I was.

"Oh, my God, Roger! I can't believe it's you," he said. "I'm a big fan. Can I have your autograph?"

"Just get me to the hospital," I groaned. It felt like the pain was radiating from my the top of my head all the way down to my toenails.

By the time I got to Saint Joseph's Hospital in the East Village, I was delirious. Numbness had settled over much of my body and the doctors hadn't even given me any painkillers. I knew my back was broken and I should have been asking big questions like "Am I ever going to walk again?" and "Will I be able to feel my daughter in my arms the next time I hug her?" But my biggest concern was "Does *it* still work?"

"All right, close the curtain," I said to Denise as soon as she showed up at the hospital. "I gotta make sure everything still works down there."

Ten minutes later: "Okay, open the curtain! We're fine! It's all good. Everything else will take care of itself."

I probably shouldn't have done anything sexual since I had fractured my L2, L3 and L4 vertebrae. Fortunately, Denise and I didn't cause any further damage. Since the fracture was clean I didn't need surgery. I spent most of my time in the hospital in a slow traction bed. About a week later one of the nurses told me not to worry because I would learn to walk again.

"What do you mean? I know how to walk."

I got out of my wheelchair to show her. I actually could walk. I couldn't walk right or for any distance, but the doctors and nurses were amazed that I could even take a couple steps on my own.

I underwent extensive in-hospital rehab for a month to strengthen my legs. Then I was released and sent home with a hospital bed. For the next three months I had to lie in the hospital bed and undergo more physical therapy before I was able to go up and down stairs, which was pretty important since Denise and I lived in a fourth-floor walk-up.

It's a good thing I had insurance through my job. They took care of the hospital bills, and I had a nurse who came to my house and helped me work the muscles in my back and legs. Eventually I was able to navigate the stairs, but I was out of commission for the better part of a year. It could have been a lot worse, but my body's not what it used to be. When the weather gets cold my back starts to ache, and I can feel it in my bones when it's going to rain or the seasons start to change.

When my back healed and I was able to move around I started thinking about getting onstage again. I had a good job with Harley Davidson and was keeping busy, but the punk rock virus isn't something you can vaccinate against. It never goes away. I started hanging out with Vinnie on the roof of his place on Mott Street. It was like our little getaway where we'd go for some peace of mind. Then one night in 1996, Madball was playing a show at the Wetlands and they were going to do an Agnostic Front cover. While he was onstage, Freddy scanned the crowd.

"Wait a minute. What are we doing here?" he said into the mic. "We were going to do an Agnostic Front song, but that doesn't make sense. My brother Roger's here. Kabula's here. Vinnie's here. Fuck it, I'm gonna bring 'em all up onstage. You guys play your song!"

We did "Crucified," "Victim In Pain" and "Your Mistake." We got a good taste of what we had been missing. Man, it felt good. After the Madball show I was really Jonesing for more.

Benefit flyer for my medical expenses.

# PART VII

## Reconstruction in the Age of Retirement: Persevering Beyond the Lifespan of Most Hardcore Bands

# CHAPTER 35

"Vinnie! You wanna play some shows?" I said, bubbling with excitement. "Let's get the band back together."

"Whoa! You really want to do this? You're not just still buzzing from the Madball thing?" Vinnie said.

Given our history, he was understandably hesitant.

"Yeah, man. I do," I assured him.

"Well, who's gonna play with us?"

"Let's get the original band back together," I said.

I felt like the hardcore scene had become one-dimensional and sounded too new-school. I wanted to bring back that old, crazy style and no one was better at that than the guys from the original band.

Vinnie stopped and thought for a moment, which was unusual since it's nearly impossible to get him to be quiet. "You know, I just talked to Jimmy Colletti," he said.

"Really? He's around?"

"Yeah, we could probably get him over and bring back the original guys from the *Victim In Pain* tour."

"That would be awesome!" I shouted, unable to control my excitement. "Let's play a couple shows and see what happens."

We invited Kabula to meet us at Vinnie's for some spaghetti, and during dinner we told him what we were thinking. I suggested we put our past differences aside. There wasn't any real resentment. Back then we just had different ideas of where the band should go musically. Kabula's a great guy, a person I can call my brother. I see him all the time and he still plays music. He did two albums with us after we reunited. But he's got a phenomenal job. He's a union guy and he's committed to that, so these days he only comes out with us here and there.

The person I was most nervous about was Jimmy Colletti because the last time I saw him was in 1985, when we came back from tour and started recording for *Cause For Alarm*—stuff that he hated. I heard he had been in and out of jail for various offenses and was dealing with all sorts of personal shit, so I didn't know what it would be like to play with him again. But when we all got together it was great. We did a couple big reunion shows with the original Victim In Pain Tour lineup in December 1996 at Wetlands. They were both sold out and broke club attendance records originally set by Hootie and the Blowfish. The first show on December 14, 1996, was AF, H2O, Maximum Penalty, Hatebreed and Fury Of Five, and the following day was AF, Killing Time, H2O, 25 Ta Life and Stillsuit. The shows were insane. Everyone loved hearing our old shit again. I figured it would be great to take the band on tour, but that would mean committing to the band again.

I asked Nadia if it was okay with her if I went back on the road. I had stopped playing in AF in the first place to spend time with her. It was an unspoken promise I made, and I wasn't about to break my word. If she got really upset by the thought of me going back to the band, I probably wouldn't have done it. At that point Nadia was seven-and-a-half years old.

"What do you think about Daddy playing in a band again?" I asked her one morning after breakfast.

She thought about it and then gave me a very mature answer: "Yeah, Daddy. That's what you like to do. Do it."

I wanted her approval more than anything, and thank God I got it. She was in a good place and she wanted me to be happy. Nadia and I always had a wonderful relationship. She's almost 30 now and she's in California, but we're still very close and talk all the time.

After Nadia gave me her blessings to tour, Agnostic Front went to Europe. The gigs weren't advertised as having the original *Victim In Pain* tour lineup, so people thought we were going to continue where we left off and do stuff from *One Voice*. That would have been impossible since these guys were never part of the *One Voice* era and playing like that is not their style. We delivered what we did best: *Victim In Pain*, *United Blood* and a medley of songs from *Cause For Alarm*. We only did a medley because guitarist Alex Kinon and drummer Louie Beateaux, who did that album with us, weren't there. Kabula played a major role in *Cause For Alarm*, but Colletti had nothing to do with it. It wasn't his thing and didn't play to his skills.

In June 1997, Denise and I got married. Part of the reason was because I knew AF were going to tour a lot and being married would show her that we were still together even when I was away. For our wedding, we rented a loft in Long Island City and had a big Wicca ceremony, which was written up in the *New York Post* as one of the oddest local weddings. I didn't know what this Wicca thing was all about, but she was into it. Some people think Wicca is about witchcraft, and it sort of is, but it's not about hexes and evil spells. It's about the power of nature and the transformative strength of the female. It's white witchcraft, not black witchcraft. The pentagram faces up, not down, and even the rituals are holistic and crunchy-granola.

During the ceremony, I gave her a knife and she gave me a magic spell in exchange. We drank a love potion, which tasted horrible. Then we jumped over a broom. Hoya from Madball was staring at me and it looked like he was going to burst out laughing. I felt like the whole New York hardcore community was going to make fun of me for the rest of my life, but I didn't care. Everyone was there from the NYHC scene, including photographer Ran-D. He brought a book of his classic NYHC photos, which we all marveled at. It was hard to believe we were the characters that lived between the front and back cover of the book, frozen in time. Freddy was the DJ at the party, and he was banging out the tunes.

It wasn't long after the European tour that Agnostic Front decided to make another record. I was excited about what the songs would be like with Kabula and Colletti pitching in, and I hadn't felt that way in a long time. I was really stoked when songs like "Gotta Go," "Do or Die" and "Blinded" started coming together because nothing was over three-and-a-half minutes long. Most of the songs were around two minutes and were totally old-school NYHC. That was especially cool since no one was doing that anymore. Everyone wanted to sound like Madball and—as much as I love my brother's band—I felt like we could really stand out from the pack again. We weren't trying to sound old-school. We were playing to the strengths of the *Victim In*

*Pain* lineup.

It wouldn't have sounded right if Kabula, Colletti, Stigma and I tried to do any-thing different. That's why the *Cause For Alarm* medley we played live sounded a little weird. We only had one guitarist, which toned down the sound, and the drumming didn't fit Colletti's style. But that wasn't a limitation; it gave us a game plan. We wrote a batch of angry, energetic songs that came pretty quickly and had a good time writ-ing them.

Recording them was another story. We tracked *Something's Gotta Give* with Billy Milano in Hoboken, New Jersey, mainly because Billy was an old friend. He was in Hinkley Fanclub with Kabula before replacing me in the Psychos. There was a time when Billy was managing artists, including myself, Madball and the Step Kings. Then he started getting into recording, so we asked him if he wanted to produce the album.

We did it at his Xplosive Sound Studio and it took months because Billy was learning how to use the sound board. Every time we went in, we had to re-record something because he forgot to push record or his cat stepped on one of the control buttons and accidentally deleted a track. At least that's what Billy told us!

After Billy finished recording *Something's Gotta Give*, we took it to Big Blue Meenie Recording Studio, which was owned by Tim Gilles, who worked with Vision of Disorder and S.O.D., and he fixed the flaws. We re-recorded some parts there with him. In the end, it sounded really good and featured some of my favorite songs since *Victim In Pain*.

As much as I still like that record, there's one song on there, "The Blame," that's bittersweet for me. I wrote it with Raybeez back in 1983 and he was supposed to come into the studio and do vocals with me. I'd seen him at my wedding and he looked okay. But he died before we got the chance to record the song.

The medical report listed the cause of death as advanced pneumonia, which caused acute liver failure. Raybeez was like a cat with nine hundred lives. He'd always get into death-defying situations and pull through. Maybe he lived that 900th life and that was it. But one of the saddest days for me was September 11, 1997, when his girlfriend, Leslye, told me Raybeez was dead. I loved the guy. He was manipulative, crazy and dangerous to be around. But there was never a boring day with Ray. He was my true and only blood brother.

Jimmy Gestapo wound up singing "The Blame" with me in tribute to Ray.

We also had a song called "Gotta Go," which Colletti wrote with his other band, Zombula 451. It was five or seven minutes long and it had three or four guitar leads. Billy Milano and I made it shorter and it sounded much better. It was tighter and there was only one lead. I came up with a "Gotta Go" intro chant for Raybeez: "From the East Coast to the West Coast / True sounds of a revolution!" It was a reference to lyrics Raybeez wrote for Warzone, and I felt like he was looking over my shoulder and guiding my hand when I wrote it. Colletti said I ruined the song with the intro and outro, but people loved it. It became a huge NYHC anthem and our first truly popular song. Epitaph Records liked it so much they put it on some of their CD samplers.

We sent a tape of the finished album to Epitaph owner Brett Gurewitz (also a songwriter and guitarist for Bad Religion). We didn't hear back, so I sent it to Hellcat Records, an offshoot of Epitaph run by Rancid guitarist Tim Armstrong. I was better friends with Tim than I was with Brett. Tim loved the record and wanted to release it. We were all set to go with Hellcat, but then Brett must have heard about it from Tim, so he dug through his pile of demos and found it. He listened to it and liked it, so he told Tim he wanted the record to be on Epitaph. Since Hellcat was a part of Epitaph, Tim backed off, which was lucky for us. I was more of a fan of the bands on Hellcat, so I was thrilled that the other band I eventually started, Roger Miret and The Disasters, wound up on Tim's label.

But in the mid-to late '90s, Epitaph was a great place to be. They had signed all the big punk bands—Rancid, Offspring, NOFX, H2O. When I went to California to visit, Brett gave me the keys to his house and invited me to stay for the weekend. He liked AF and he was very supportive. Most big Epitaph bands left the label because they had gold or platinum albums and were lured away by big offers from major labels. This was back when everyone wanted a major label deal since those companies had money to throw around. Now, thanks to the Internet and piracy, no one has any money to sign bands and gold and platinum records are mostly a thing of the past—especially in punk rock.

# CHAPTER 36

**B**y the time AF started touring for *Something's Gotta Give*, I was the only one that was married. Jimmy was married when we worked on the record, but then he got divorced, so there was nothing to keep him from cutting loose. Even so, everyone was pretty tame. There was a lot of drinking and joking around, but I never saw any hard drugs. Most of us outgrew that back in 1987 when we did the Cause For Alarm Tour coked out of our minds. The shows were different than the ones we played in our glory daze. There were skinheads in the crowd, but they were a new breed of skins. They wanted to look different and act different, just like we did, but the element of danger was no longer there. Punk had become safe. We always talked about that.

"Fuck, these guys never would have survived a show at A7," I said.

It was almost too easy for them because they could be a part of the hardcore scene and not be exposed to all the violence and chaos that was second nature for us. They didn't get picked on for being different because being different had become the norm. It seemed like a safer, no-threat era. Bands like Cock Sparrer started getting super popular, and these kids from a safer punk scene got into us, Dropkick Murphys and U.S. Bombs. The shows were loud and storming, but no one was getting his ass kicked. It was kind of strange, but I didn't complain since I didn't want any more violence at our shows.

I'm the same way today. I want people to come out, drink whatever they want, enjoy themselves, go back home and feel good about the show. The new crowd mentality was beneficial for us because I didn't have to worry about watching my back, getting in fights, bomb threats or cops. Playing music became less a vehicle for rebellion and more of a business.

For the first time in our career we could make few bucks on tour, too! It took almost 20 years to get there, but we were finally at a point where we didn't have to print our own shirts. We didn't have to worry about someone stealing the shirts after we printed them. We didn't have to load our vans with records that would get warped, broken or scratched. We didn't have to worry about crazy security or horrible fights. Nobody got stabbed, and nobody got beaten up. It was a win-win. When I was an angry kid it was good to be in a whirlpool of insanity. I felt more alive when I was dancing hard, stomping on people and getting into fights and bleeding. Before I had Nadia, I didn't give a fuck. I was ruthless. I was that guy out there trying to prove how street he could be. I didn't care if I lived or died. I was pissed off at society, angry about my upbringing and mad at Reagan. And what the fuck did I know about Reagan? I didn't read the paper or follow politics.

When you're older and you have your own wife and kids, you think about them all the time and that makes you more empathetic. I thought about these kids who were coming to our shows and I wanted them to have a positive experience. I didn't want some young punk to be all excited about coming to see us and then get his ass kicked. Three of the guys in the band were parents, and, it's crazy to say, life had mellowed us out. Now I do give a fuck what happens in the world and at our shows, and I want to be around to see my own kids grow up. Practically the only thing that makes me crazy today is the thought of something happening to one of my kids. That's why I relate so much to the parents of our newer fans. I'll see some kid swinging his arms around at a show, and if he punches a girl or a young kid and hurts them I'll get really upset. And when someone jumps off stage I watch them and make sure they get back up. I used to jump offstage feet first. I didn't give a shit. I used to walk on people's heads. Now I feel like my own daughter's out there. She's not, but somebody's daughter is and I want her to be happy and safe.

We promoted *Something's Gotta Give* by launching our own tour, which we called the Unity Tour. I have to credit Billy Milano for that. He figured that a punk package tour could do well. We went out with Dropkick Murphys, U.S. Bombs and Maximum Penalty. We did 78 dates in America and another 70 shows in Europe (without U.S.

Bombs). Although it was a huge success for the band, the Unity Tour was the nail in the coffin for my marriage with Denise.

For a while, Denise and I were a good couple. We met during a time when I wasn't playing music, so I was around for her whenever she wanted to be with me. We had fun playing with the band we formed, Lady Luck, but then I started working more with Agnostic Front on our second album for Epitaph, *Riot, Riot, Upstart*. I felt as if Denise got jealous and competitive about my success. When I was touring, she started teaching yoga, and that became her full-time job.

I was happy she had found something to keep her busy while I was away. I hoped that would make her happy and that we could regain the warmth and affection we once had for each other. But Denise seemed resentful when I was on the road with AF and that drove a huge wedge between us. The fact that I was focusing my energies on Agnostic Front and couldn't help her with Lady Luck made her angry. I felt as if she was always angry and that she wanted me to pay more attention to Lady Luck than I was paying to Agnostic Front, which was an absurd idea. Not only was Agnostic Front my first love, it's my main source of income. The money I was making from AF kept us afloat. That didn't seem to matter. It got to the point where the only time we weren't arguing was when we weren't together.

We became increasingly distanced until it became clear that it wasn't going to work out between us. She got offered a job in London teaching yoga and accepted it without consulting me. She knew I couldn't go to England with her because of my immigration status, but that didn't seem to bother her. She found a place to live and made all the arrangements to move there without asking how I felt about it. She decided to leave me then and there, and that was the end of it. We officially divorced in 2006, and to this day she's still in the U.K. We were married for seven years. And then we weren't.

Amy and I had our ups and downs, but she was a strong woman. When I was in prison she stood by me, and she raised Nadia while I was away. We drifted apart, as couples often do, but she was always a solid person. Denise didn't have the same kind of tenacity.

There were a lot of red flags during our relationship. Even before we got married, we started seeing a family therapist. I went along with it, and I actually liked it—not because it was helpful but because it was entertaining. These group therapy sessions were filled with people who had crazy problems with infidelity, alcoholism, intimidation and verbal abuse. It was like a live gossip show. I'd walk out thinking, *Everybody's all fucked up and I'm normal!*

We really chose a winner for a therapist. He had been married around six times and was earning a living trying to get other unhappy people to stay together. How hypocritical is that? Denise and I had a good reason to be in therapy. I couldn't admit it to myself at the time, but we weren't right for each other. I was in a touring band and needed someone who could hold down the fort when I wasn't there. That wasn't Denise, and I think I knew it from the start.

Right before we got married, I had cold feet. I told the therapist I didn't know if I wanted to get married and the only reason I agreed to it was because I was about to tour the world and being married would make Denise feel more secure. He talked me through my insecurities and convinced me to go through with it. He said having cold feet was natural for people who have had failed relationships in the past, so I took his advice.

One day, after everything was over between me and Denise, the therapist surprised me with a call and asked how things were going.

"Oh, Denise and I separated and I filed for divorce."

"I knew it wasn't right for you," he said. "She was still in love with her ex-boyfriend."

"Well, if you knew that, why the fuck didn't you tell me this before I married her?"

He had no problem taking my goddamn money when he was counseling me, and now he was telling me it wasn't right to begin with. I hung up the phone. I was pissed. But then I looked back at my history with this guy, and I realized he was a fucking snake. One day while I was there, a woman came in with her daughter, who was having second thoughts about marrying a guy she was engaged to. The mom was there for support, and they thought the good doctor would counsel the girl through the situation.

Not only did he fail to provide quality therapy, he talked the daughter into dumping the man she was unsure about and hooking up with the good doctor instead. Soon after, the two of them got married and now they have kids. The craziest thing is that he was married at the time. He had to divorce his wife to marry this young girl. He was like Barry White. He told this chick exactly what she needed to hear to get her into bed. Some women are so fragile that if somebody just gives them a little bit of love and attention, they melt. At the time, I thought this psychiatrist with a high falutin degree was a playa. Now I realize I was played.

Even though I was frustrated and depressed that my second marriage was almost over, I had a great time working on *Riot, Riot, Upstart*. Lars Frederiksen from Rancid came down from California and stayed with me in Long Island City, New York, where Denise and I moved after we left our 10<sup>th</sup> Street apartment.

Lars was gung-ho to be our producer and wanted to help us make a rowdy, ripping album. He was really involved in the process. He showed up a couple days before we recorded and wanted to learn every song so that when we recorded the album he had a complete feel for the material. He had great suggestions for arrangements and song-writing enhancements and became like a fifth member. He even helped me out with the lyrics, which made a song like "Bullet on Mott Street" especially meaningful. I dedicated the song to Richie Backfire, a good friend that had just passed away. Richie had been in a Dutch band called Backfire, became severely depressed and took his own life.

We went through the songs in the studio, but we didn't want to polish anything. Lars liked to keep a harsh, midrange sound. Brett Gurewitz flew into town to hear what we were doing. He sat down in the control room at Big Blue Meanie and listened to the mix. He didn't seem that thrilled with it, and that made Lars uncomfortable. We asked if there was something wrong and he didn't say anything. Brett is also a producer. Maybe Lars did it differently than he would have done it. We didn't share Brett's concerns. We were really stoked with how it sounded. Tim Gilles, the studio owner, mixed it and he did a great job as well.

*Riot, Riot, Upstart* came out September 7, 1999, at a time when records sales were collapsing across the board. File sharing services like Napster were exploding, and there were no consequences for illegally downloading music. These kids wouldn't walk into a store and steal a pair of jeans, but they didn't think twice about logging onto their computers and hitting "download." Now there is a nation of kids out there who grew up in the age of Napster and Pirate Bay. They never went to record stores, barely know what vinyl is and seem to think that anyone who puts out a record is rich as fuck and doesn't need royalties or publishing. For bands like us, making money on a record after receiving the advance didn't happen anyhow. But the fewer copies of an album you sold and the more kids downloaded it illegally, the less promotion and tour support you'd get from your record company and the smaller advance you'd receive for your next record.

We did a sold-out record release show for *Riot, Riot, Upstart* at Wetlands and gave away a single called "Police State" to the first 500 people who showed up. The single was on red vinyl and had a picture of New York Mayor Rudy Giuliani with his face crossed out.

We planned to follow up the first Unity Tour with Unity Tour II in 1999, but that became the Epitaph Punk-O-Rama tour. They took our lineup—H2O, U.S. Bombs, Straight Faced and Union 13—but booted us off the bill. We had the promoters in place and all the bands lined up, and at the last minute someone pulled a switcheroo. Next thing we knew we weren't scheduled to play. We were replaced by Bouncing Souls.

Billy Milano was really bitter about that. We showed them how to do a punk rock package tour, and then they used what they had learned from us to do it themselves. As pissed as we were, we licked our wounds and moved on. We played five East Coast Warped Tour shows. It was a chance to perform for a new audience that grew up with bands like Green Day and NOFX. The shows went well, and we were asked to do a sixth date in Buffalo, New York. But when we got there we found out we were booked to play a side stage that faced the catering. I don't think the promoters were being malicious or trying to diss us, but hardly any of the fans got to see us that night. Some of the bands who were chowing down in catering seemed to enjoy the show.

We got invited to play the Punk-O-Rama tour in 2000 with Straight Face, Voodoo Glow Skulls and All. That was an olive branch that Epitaph offered us for stealing our idea for the Unity Tour. We accepted it, and we were surprised by how they had turned it into a big tour machine. There were sponsors and tents. It developed from a homegrown package to something far more financially motivated. It generated so much money that they gave buses to the bands. We had done the Unity Tour in vans. For Punk-O-Rama we drove our van to the first date in Seattle, but we left it there and took the bus. We figured we'd be coasting in luxury. They didn't tell us we had to pay for all these hidden costs—gas, compressor fees, bed sheet changes, driver fees and the costs for his hotel stays. We ended up losing all our fuckin' money!

We shared the bus with Straight Face, and that's where we met our good friend Amanda the Commanda. We felt bad for her because she was working for the tour and following the whole damn thing with a van. We told her to leave the van behind and come with us on our bus. We had an extra bunk. From that point on she became our tour manager. She was smart and funny and knew how to keep us organized.

# CHAPTER 37

I started my side band, Roger Miret and the Disasters, in 2000. It began as a bunch of songs I wrote for Agnostic Front but weren't right for the band. They were a little too street rock 'n' roll, but I liked them. Since I didn't go out much, I spent a lot of time in my room with an electric guitar and a Boss recorder and just wrote. After a while, I had enough material for a whole album. I ran them by my friend Al Barr of the Dropkick Murphys, who really liked them and told me I should make a record. He suggested I get in touch with Johnny Rioux, who had been in The Bruisers with him, so I called him up. Then I was introduced to a guitarist named Rhys Kill, who was visiting from New Zealand. He was only in the U.S. for a week. I gave him a tape of the songs for what would be our self-titled first album, and he really liked it so he was on board. Rhys, Johnny and I banged out the six-song demo with Matt Kelly from the Dropkick Murphys on drums.

To this day that material remains unreleased, but it sounds really good. When Lars Frederiksen heard it, he loved it and gave it to Tim Armstrong, who asked if he could put it out on Hellcat. Since Agnostic Front was already signed to Epitaph, which distributed Hellcat, it made perfect sense. We recorded the self-titled Roger Miret and the Disasters album in August at The Outpost in Stoughton, Massachusetts with Jim Siegel, who tracked and mixed. By that time I got Johnny Kray (The Krays, New York Rel-X) to play drums since Matt was busy with the Dropkick Murphys. We had two rehearsals and then went straight into the studio to record in a few days. We self-produced and the rough-around-the-edges vibe gave the songs character. The record came out on Hellcat Records in 2001.

Since then, Rhys and I have done four albums with different bassists and drummers. I play guitar in the band, which is a nice change of pace for me, but what's really cool about the Disasters is that the band's lyrics are mostly inspired by my teenage years and the early days of Agnostic Front. It is a personal diary of the magical time when I was living in the streets of New York. The music is influenced by my early favorites, like The Clash, Stiff Little Fingers, Buzzcocks, Ramones, Sham 69, The Dictators and The Business. Since the band was a side project, I didn't feel like I had as many eyes on me as I do when I work with Agnostic Front. I wasn't under the microscope. I was creating strictly for the joy of making music and I think it showed. More importantly, I wasn't self-conscious about the lyrics. I felt safer with this new little band, which eventually became respectable. The whole thing was refreshing and invigorating.

While I was working with The Disasters I was also laying the groundwork for Agnostic Front's third Epitaph album, *Dead Yuppies*, which we shouldn't have put out with Epitaph after they left a bad taste in our mouth with Punk-O-Rama. That wasn't the only weird shit going on with Epitaph. It was junior high school stuff. It started when Billy Milano got a call from someone at the label saying they got a fax from someone in New York—so they assumed it was us—showing how to get to Brett's house and blow it up. That put Brett on the defensive, which I didn't understand since he had so willingly let me stay in his home. We had always gotten along and had great conversations about our favorite bands. What followed was a comedy of errors and misunderstandings.

There was a band from Boston, Kings of Nuthin', that I liked a lot and wanted to help out. Their singer, Torr Skoog, got in touch with me.

"Roger, how can I get someone at Hellcat to listen to our demo?"

"Send them a promo package and include a note with it that mentions my name and tell them I told you to send it to them," I said. "That way they'll be sure to listen to it."

It was all simple and innocent enough. Then I got a call from Chris Losaw at Epitaph.

"Hey, what's up with this big, giant box that just got delivered here? It's ticking."

"What the fuck are you talking about?" I said.

"It's got your name on it."

I didn't know why he would be fucking with me and I didn't appreciate his tone. "You know what? I didn't send you any box. I don't know what the fuck it is. If you want to open it since it's got my name on it, okay, but I don't know what it is. And I didn't send it."

"C'mon, Rog. You gotta tell us. This isn't cool. Everybody's freaking out in the office. They want me to call the bomb squad."

"I don't know what the fuck you're talking about? I didn't do anything. I didn't send anything."

I hung up with him and within the next fifteen minutes, Torr called me up.

"Did they get the package?"

"What package?" I replied. I still hadn't put two and two together.

"I sent the piano we burned onstage last night and the live footage of us burning it!"

This guy had sent Epitaph the remnants of the piano they torched in an effort to win them over. That's what was in the box. The broken strings and keys must have made ticking noises when they moved. It was an incredible stunt, and in the end the label didn't even fucking sign the band. If I worked there I would have signed them just for their effort. When Epitaph figured out what had happened with the piano and Kings of Nuthin', they called me back and apologized. But the whole situation was really fucking weird, and nothing seemed right between us and the label after that.

Tragically, Torr committed suicide in 2013 by jumping off a cliff at the Quechee Gorge in Hartford, Vermont. When shit like that happens enough times to people you know, it's no longer shocking. It's just sad. He was a good guy. It's too bad he never got a break.

When it was time to do our third record, we were expecting a decent advance. That was the way Epitaph worked. They'd sign bands to three-album deals. The first two albums would earn a band okay money, and then on the third they rolled out the red carpet and showed their gratitude. At least that's how the legend went. Later I found out that never happened for any of their acts, which might explain why a lot of them moved to different labels. There was a guy there named Andy Kaulkin who called all the shots for the label. He called us a week before we went into the studio.

"Well, we can't do this record with you," he said. "We're having some financial problems,"

Epitaph always had some bullshit excuse. Of course, you'd have no leverage and you wouldn't want to set up a whole new deal with another label since you were ready to go into the studio. All the cards were in their hands.

Then they'd deliver the line that saved them millions of dollars over the years, "Well, if you're really ready to go, I guess we can pay you what we did for the first two and we'll just put it out."

They acted as if they were doing us a favor. It was a really sleazy move. We got pissed and figured if that's their attitude, let's just get in the studio and get it over with. It wasn't a well-conceived plan. At that point, Colletti was doing a lot of the writing while I tried to deal with my crumbling marriage. Plus Kabula wasn't with us anymore. We basically ended up with a glorified Loved And Hated record. That was Colletti's solo band and they were really good, but they weren't Agnostic Front. I was okay with that because I wasn't mentally fit to write. I was still pissed about being fucked over by Epitaph and I couldn't clear my mind enough to inject myself into the songs. I didn't become a major part of the process like I should have, and since we didn't have that magical spirit in us—that yearning to create something new and different—it messed up our mojo. We weren't trying to get back at Epitaph or anything, but we were uninspired and it showed.

*Dead Yuppies* was Mike Gallo's first record with the band, and since he had just joined in 2000 he didn't have any input on the songs. Jimmy was a good songwriter, but without someone to collaborate with and bounce ideas off of, the music was one-dimensional. In the end, we went with what we had. We thought we could change things in the studio, but we weren't really feeling it so we just recorded the songs as they were.

It was our last record for Epitaph. They knew they'd make their money back so long as they had an album with our name on it, and we'd part ways after it was over. But our fans didn't really like it and the reviews weren't great.

The timing of the record couldn't have been worse. In August 2001, Epitaph put together a phenomenal promotional video for *Dead Yuppies* that looked like someone falling through the air. Then he landed and you saw the tape outline from the *Dead Yuppies* art work, which resembled a chalk outline of a dead body at a murder scene, except the victim was holding a briefcase. I thought it was awesome. Then 9/11 happened and everyone at the label freaked out.

They didn't want to release the album with that artwork because lots of people jumped out of the World Trade Center to escape the inferno.The idea of a dead yuppie made them think of all the businessmen in the Twin Towers who died. They were getting ready to pull everything.

"No, what are you talking about!" I said when they told me they couldn't release it. "Just put a sticker on there to explain our position. We back up our record."

In the end, that's what they did. The sticker read: "Agnostic Front is an American working class band that does not support or condone any type of extreme terrorism or mindless acts of terrorism. Our hearts go out to all those who have lost loved ones in the World Trade Center disaster.—Agnostic Front"

Epitaph never ran the advertisement of the yuppie falling. That's understandable. But for anybody who took a minute to think about it, *Dead Yuppies* was recorded four months before the terrorist attacks. When you finish an album, there's always a waiting period while they set up the album and put together a marketing and promotional campaign. There was no tie-in between the artwork and the terror attacks—none whatsoever.

# PART VIII

## Family Matters: The Search for Stability and the Endless Pursuit of Infamy

# CHAPTER 38

I met my current wife, Emily, on February 9, 2002, while I was on the last Unity Tour, which we played with TSOL, the Casualties and Rise Against. We were at a club called the Starlight in Fort Collins, Colorado, which was where she was from. I was killing time before we had to play, so I was hanging out with a girl who played bass in a local band. We went up to the bar and saw Jimmy Colletti and Mike Gallo talking to Emily and her friend. I was immediately struck by how entertained she was by the guys. Jimmy was telling her about the time he got shot in the stomach, lifting his shirt to show her the scar.

Jimmy got shot prior to one of our Unity tours in Europe. Here's how he tells it— and it's a good thing for him that a fact-checker can't disprove his claim. According to Jimmy, he got out of work and went to cash his check in Jamaica, Queens. When he left, he was held up by three Hollis hood kids on bicycles.

"Give us your money," they said.

"I ain't giving you shit!" he replied, and one of them shot him.

That's *his* story. We think he got off work, cashed his check, went to score and tried to roll the kids on the bicycles, so they shot him. I can't prove it, but I have a good bullshit detector, and Jimmy's a master at slinging shit.

One thing's for sure. Jimmy was definitely shot, robbed and fooled, and he was treated at a hospital in Queens. I was working at Reggie Pink Harley Davidson in White Plains, and when I found out what had happened, Vinnie and I went to visit him. We walked into the room, and he's wasn't in bed. He was in the bathroom in a hospital gown, with a machine and all kinds of tubes connected to him—and he was smoking! At least he wasn't smoking crack. We were booked to start a tour the next week and were in full panic mode, so we had Will Shepler fill in until Jimmy was well enough to play.

Emily didn't hear the whole story about Colletti until much later. Because of her small town upbringing, she was amazed by the crazy things these New Yorkers were telling her. It was the kind of stuff she had only heard in movies. I watched her laugh while she was sitting at that bar. When she smiled, her eyes gleamed. She was so beautiful and so genuine.

I half-expected her to do something that would ruin this image of perfection that I had. But that was not in the cards. The longer I watched her, the closer I felt to her. It seemed like I was meant to meet her there and the scene was playing out like a movie with a satisfying ending.

When I played cowboys and Indians as a kid, I was always the Indian. She's Native American, so she was the Indian princess I would have imagined myself being with. I felt like Tonto. I've always been attracted to exotic women. She was stunningly exotic and she was at a punk show. How could I ask for more? It was love at first sight.

Before I got the chance to interact with her, the girl I was hanging out with said she wanted to use the restroom and made me go with her. So I went into the ladies room and stood by the sink waiting for her while she peed. I didn't notice that Emily had gone in after us. Suddenly she was coming out of a bathroom stall. Even that was sexy. She went up to wash her hands at another sink, then turned and asked me, "Do you need anything?"

I said "a kiss." She planted one right on my lips. She had no idea who I was until after we played that night. It was just a small kiss, but suddenly I felt alive again. I felt passion and inspiration and wanted to see more of her. As it turned out, she was there to watch TSOL. She didn't even know my band. When we went on, I was onstage screaming and I saw her again. She wasn't covering her ears or heading for the bar. She was standing just beyond the pit, smiling.

I found her after the show and she told me she was going to be in Phoenix in two weeks, at the same time we were going to be there. I invited her to our show at a club called Bostons. She said she'd see me there, but I didn't know if she'd come. The night of the show I was anxious thinking about her and worried that she wasn't going to be in the crowd. But when I stepped into the place that afternoon, there she was at the bar waiting for me.

We went to a restaurant nearby and hung out for hours, talking and laughing. When it was time to perform I didn't want to leave her. Amanda the Commanda started teasing me. "Oh, boy, Roger you're in trouble. C'mon, man. You have to play the show."

Amanda tried to drag me out of the restaurant and to the venue. I struggled with her, so Emily said, "It's okay. I'll go with you." That's the only way I would leave and play the show, and she stood on the side of the stage for the whole concert. I was so pumped up that I performed with an amazing energy. At the same time, the gig seemed to take forever because I wanted to be with her again.

At the end of the night we exchanged email addresses and went our separate ways. We flirted with one another via email, and every time I knew I was going to be in town I emailed her to let her know. She came to one of our shows in Colorado and we got ripping drunk with Vinnie. We were at a club called The Aggie Theater in Fort Collins, and we had a crazy bartender, who was like someone from *Fear and Loathing in Las Vegas*. The guy was giving us shots of everything for free—tequila, whisky, vodka—and after each shot, we shouted and smashed the shot glasses against the brick walls. They exploded into dangerous slivers and shards. We laughed with every destructive crash—and he kept giving us more. When we were sober, many, many hours later, we realized the guy must have been trying to get fired. After 15 or 20 shots we were so drunk we couldn't possibly drink anything else, but the bartender kept pouring the shots so we took the glasses and dumped them over our shoulders and then threw them against the wall. The whole place was smashed up by the time we left.

We walked over to the van and as we approached it, the door opened and Vinnie fell face-first onto the street. He didn't even put out his hands to break his fall. His face just bounced off the concrete. He busted his nose, but he didn't feel it. Emily and I started laughing again like we had just seen a hysterical slapstick comedy sketch. We felt a strong connection, but we lived across the country from each other, so for the time being, we accepted that it wasn't practical to be more than close friends.

I drove out to Hadley, Massachusetts, in January 2004 to meet Hatebreed front man Jamey Jasta at Planet-Z recording studio. It's owned by Zeuss, who has worked with Hatebreed, Soulfly, Suicide Silence and tons of other bands. Jamey and I wrote together and Zeuss hung out with us and offered his advice. We didn't want anyone else around because we felt like the two of us could feed off each other's creativity to capture the vibe needed to write a powerful follow-up to Jamey's favorite AF album, *One Voice*. Hatebreed drummer Matt Byrne laid down six beats. Then Jamey took out a guitar and riffed along.

Jamey is best known as a fierce hardcore screamer, but he's a great guitarist and he easily comes up with ideas. He has what he calls his "vault," which consists of files filled with different parts for songs that he hasn't used. We pulled shit out of the vault, took riffs he came up with when he was playing to Matt's beats and I wrote some stuff. It wasn't long before we had 15 or 20 songs we really liked. Then we put the lyrics together. We purposely wrote the most ignorant, lunkheaded lines, cracking each other up until tears were streaming down our faces.

In "Still Here" I tried to be almost a caricature of my former self: "I'm not in this fight alone / Still in your face, still fucking here / 'Til my last dying breath / Hate! Hate! Hate! Hate!" For "Take Me Back" I ran out of words, so I started shouting out the names of influential old-school NYHC bands: "Cro-Mags, Warzone, Murphy's Law / Agnostic Front, Sick of It All / CBGB's where it all began / The music, the lifestyle we represent / Demonstrate your style!"

We were having a good time writing the record, which wasn't about anything heavy or serious. It was just fun. After we finished the demo we played it for Mike Gallo, Steve Gallo and Vinnie, and they loved it. So we started to shop it around to find the right label. Almost immediately the owner of Nuclear Blast, Markus Staiger, expressed interest. He was a clean-cut German guy who looked like a high school teacher and used to run a fanzine called *Graffiti*, which covered punk and hardcore. Back then he had long, spiky blonde hair. In 1987, he started his record company, which, over two decades, grew into a huge, influential metal and hardcore label. And he was a huge Agnostic Front fan! I remember him from the shows we did in Germany, dancing hard and freaking out.

One day he called me and said, "Roger, I really want your band to be on my label! It's my dream. I wanna come to the show and talk to you about it."

Not only did he come to the show we played in Stuttgart, Germany, he brought the entire Nuclear Blast staff. He introduced me to every person and told me what his or her job was. He was so gung-ho and determined for us to sign with him. I had never seen that kind of enthusiasm from someone at a record company. It was the beginning of a great relationship that continues to this day.

We didn't have a second guitarist when we did the demo for *Another Voice*—it was just Jamey and me playing everything. After we finished the demo we continued working on the album with guitarist Lenny DiSclafini, who had just joined (and stayed with us until Joe Joseph joined in 2005). We wanted to make the record a continuation of *One Voice*, so we invited Matt Henderson, who had played on *One Voice*, to be the guitarist and called it *Another Voice*. Matt liked the idea and wrote a couple more songs. Then we sent everything to Matt and said, "Don't follow Lenny's guitar tracks. They're just there as a guide for the demo. Do your thing, Wildcard."

"Wildcard" was a nickname he earned at one of his very first shows with us on tour when, out of nowhere, he knocked a dude out with one solid punch. It was like something out of a John Wayne Western movie. The dude flew through the air and landed right on the merch table.

Matt scrapped all the guitar parts and laid down his own tracks, which were signature Wildcard magic. They were totally killer.

It was 2004 and technology had advanced way beyond the point it was at when we did *One Voice* thirteen years earlier. Musicians didn't even have to be in the same room to record an album. Matt sent us a lot of his final guitar parts via e-mail. Zeuss was a magician with all the tracks and made everything sound amazing. *Another Voice* came out great, especially considering how fragmented we were when we made it. I was on tour with The Disasters when the band tracked the album. Then I got home and tracked the vocals.

There were things we liked about the demo. It's almost like Zeuss and Jamey predicted that would happen, so they recorded all the demo songs at certain tempos. When I was in the studio to do vocals, we took parts from one session and moved them to the other session. We cut and pasted different parts. We started off as an unruly punk band that hit record and relied on adrenaline, anger and excitement to bash out flawed but furious tracks. It was cool to examine music from a new angle, relying on precision and technology to create a different kind of art.

Jamey had a lot of clout in the metal community since he was the host of the revised *Headbanger's Ball* and Hatebreed were doing well. He used his rep to get us noticed by some people who had never heard of us. Not only did he mention the record in a lot of interviews, he actually took us on a world tour with Hatebreed. In our history, he was the only one to do that. Since we started, there were bands that we had done so much for and given gigs to when they needed them, but no one has come back to us later and said, "Hey, thank you for what you did for us. Now it's our turn to help you out."

There's a weird mentality in punk rock where bands say, "Oh, man. We can't have you open for us. You're our idol! It would be too weird." That's a total copout and a terrible attitude to have. If you like and respect a band and you're in a bigger band in a position to help, you can give them a chance to play for your fans and help them use that platform to build their following. It's like payback. That hardly ever happens. I'm grateful to Jamey and Hatebreed for helping us out. We toured all over the world, including South America, which, as I explained, has the most insane crowds and had an amazing time.

As 2004 melted into 2005, Emily and I became a lot closer. In November 2005, I was writing an online diary called "Tales from the Road" for AF's website. One day I wrote that I was pretty ill and then sent in the post. Minutes after the diary entry went online, I received an e-mail from Emily asking me how I was feeling and hoping I'd get better soon. I felt so alone and worn out, and her message was sincere and uplifting. She was a true friend and was genuinely concerned about me. Even though we were far away from one another, she took the time to show she cared and try to raise my spirits. It worked better than she had planned. I knew at that moment that I wanted to be close to her, so I invited her to New York for a few days in April 2006. She accepted.

I picked her up in my 1932 hot rod coupe and gave her a grand tour of New York City. I focused on great restaurants, great attractions and really good elementary schools. I was already thinking about settling down with her and starting a family in New York, so I wanted to show her the best the City had to offer. During dinner I planned to talk more about New York and point out that growing up in Manhattan is culturally fulfilling and promotes diversity. That's when Emily told me she was moving to Arizona in August. I immediately got upset and blurted out, "I'm not even gonna fuck with you then," which made the next several days incredibly awkward.

On the last day of her visit, I arranged a big dinner with all of my friends. I told Emily that I loved her and wanted to go with her to Arizona. She looked at me and kissed me softly on the mouth.

"You are welcome to come and visit me any time you want to," she said sweetly. "But I absolutely will not shack up with you."

The next day she went back home to Colorado.

I was devastated. I had laid my feelings bare in a way I rarely had done before and got rejected. She wasn't mean; she was as kind as ever, which made her decision harder to live with. I poured my heart into the Disasters song "Emily" for the 2006 album *My Riot*. The song sounds like the Buzzcocks crossed with the Beatles. It was an odd combination, but still punk—not hardcore at all. It's very much a love song with some heartfelt lyrics. If the 18-year-old me saw the lyrics, he would have called me a pussy, taken off his chain belt and beaten some sense into me. But that guy is gone and I didn't have to hold back.

"With you my life is so complete / Daylight breaks the gloom, the flowers start to bloom/ How I wish that I could be / With you, the one I love, the only one for me / Wait for me, wait for me, wait for me, Emily."

When I was done with the song, I was sad she wasn't there to hear it. I decided I was through with New York. I needed to follow my heart and move to Arizona to be with her, even if I wasn't invited. I flew to Colorado and showed up on her doorstep unannounced.

I proposed to Emily on Father's Day, 2006. She said yes and I was overjoyed, but we didn't have much time to celebrate. A day later, I had to leave for an 8-week European tour. I missed Emily, so I invited her to join me the last week in Europe. Then we took a pre-wedding honeymoon in Greece.

When we flew back to New York, my friends had arranged a surprise bachelor's party. They didn't know Emily was with me because she wasn't scheduled to be there. My dumb ass brought my fiancée to my bachelor party! My friends were so pissed. They had to send home the strippers. To this day they still ridicule me.

We got married on August 16. I wanted everything to be traditional. I've always had an old-fashioned side of me. I've just rarely gotten the chance to express it. Finally, I fell in love with a woman that valued tradition and wanted the wedding to be done right. We got married in a church in Fort Collins, Colorado. We arranged the low-key ceremony ourselves and the only people that attended were from our families. There would be no cold feet this time. Emily and I were meant to be. After the wedding, we packed up her most personal belongings, which we fit into three crates, and drove to Phoenix.

# CHAPTER 39

needed a change. I was over New York and needed something different. There were ghosts in that city. It wasn't my riot anymore. My time there was through.

Nadia was in college in California. Freddy was always on the road with Madball, and the rest of my family was in Florida. I was wasting my time and money. The rent was super-high, and I was keeping my car in a garage for $1,000 a month. You can rent a nice apartment in a lot of places for that kind of money. I've always loved Arizona, so it wasn't a crazy idea to move there. The weather's great, everything costs half as much as it does in New York and the lifestyle is way more relaxed. At first, we were only going to move to Arizona for a year while Emily finished her studies at Arizona State University. She had left school years earlier during her senior year when she went back home to Colorado.

I still had the New York apartment that I got when I was with Denise, but she was in London and we were renting out the place. I could have moved back there with Emily, except that after we had been in Phoenix for a month, Emily got pregnant. Having a baby in Arizona was a breeze compared to raising a kid in New York. We got comfortable, and I realized I could still do everything with the band without being on the East Coast. There's an international airport in Phoenix, so I can get on a plane at any time and go anywhere. Besides, it's beautiful out here. There's a vibrant art community and a lot of good hardcore, punk and Oi! bands. If you're a musician, it's fairly easy to find people to jam with.

When I found out Emily was pregnant, I wanted to cut back on work and spend more time with her. That meant I had to be less hands-on with Agnostic Front, which was hard because I've always been the guy who's in charge of everything. I had to figure out how I could focus on being a dad again and scale back AF.

We thought about our next record, and we decided that since we had such a good time with Zeuss, we should work with him again at his studio in Massachusetts. Freddy wanted to get into producing, and I wanted to help him out.

I liked the idea of Freddy working on a record with us. It was the perfect fit because nobody knows Agnostic Front better. He's been with us through thick and thin. He was there in 1983. He knows everything about our history, and we've always been his favorite band. He went onstage with us before he started his career, and when Madball started they were basically Agnostic Front plus one. He was practically in the band already.

It was a great way for us to reconnect. At that time Freddy and I weren't seeing much of each other. He spent most of the year on the road. I was looking forward to having him involved.

A lot of the songwriting process for *Warriors* happened via files sent back and forth between me, the Gallos and Joseph James, who had recently joined the band and was a close friend. They emailed me music and I wrote down lyrics. Then Mike Gallo showed up in Phoenix a week before we started recording. We quickly whipped the songs into shape. We also wrote songs on the road for the first time because we needed more material and had nowhere else to work.

When we were in Japan on a three-week tour, we wrote the title track "Warriors." It was a surreal experience. Most people go to Japan for a week. We were booked for three weeks. We had the craziest itinerary. We didn't play Budokan or the Fuji Rock or Summer Sonic festivals like so many American bands that travel to Asia. I think we played everybody's rehearsal space between Shikoku and Tokyo. We'd drive from one town to the next, and there'd be a band rehearsal space that held about 50 people.

I can't say the shows were bad. The people in the audience were revved up to see us and were literally bouncing off the walls. Our friend that booked the tour, Uzi, asked me to do a song with his band Aggressive Dogs, who were on tour with us. He wanted me to sing about a Samurai. The Japanese hardcore community is very into the spiritual side of their culture, and Uzi thought I would be honored to do a song commemorating the great warriors. When he asked me, I assumed the song was already written. It wasn't. He wanted me to write the lyrics on the spot! I wrote the song in English and it had to be translated into Japanese.

That track gave me inspiration to write our song "Warriors." It all came from that Japanese Samurai spirit. During a flight from Japan to Australia, I thought about the lyrics and how we, too, had been warriors from the streets of NYC. I scribbled down some new words and hummed a different musical idea into a recorder.

After we checked in at the hotel, I turned to Joe, Mike, Steve and Vinnie and said, "I've got this song. I want you to listen to it." We unpacked our gear and I played the song. They loved it and that theme about warriors—street warriors from the Lower East Side—turned into "For My Family," which became one of our signature songs.

After I got home from the tour, Emily had the baby almost immediately. Havi was born on June 2, 2007. She was an instant favorite among the nurses who had seen this beautiful Pocahontas princess with a full head of jet-black hair. I was immediately in love with her. From the get-go, she was so smart, striking and exotic—like her mommy. Havi is a complete sweetheart.

Since I was at home helping Emily take care of the baby, Freddy and the guys flew up to Zeuss's place a week before I arrived. I trusted Freddy, so I was okay with him getting things started without me. When I arrived, I listened to what they had done and it was great. Zeuss and Freddy got amazing performances from the band and I sang all the vocals. Then I realized "For My Family" wasn't there.

"What happened to the song? Where is it?"

"Oh, we just decided it wasn't that strong so we didn't do it," Freddy said.

The other guys in the band agreed with him, including Vinnie. They were all unsure about the song.

"Are you kidding me? I don't know what you could be unsure about. When this came into my head I heard it as a giant singalong. Everyone's gonna go nuts when we play this!"

They agreed to give it a shot. They had worked on the original demo version but never completed it.

"Go in there and finish the song," I told them.

Freddy and I redid the vocals and it became a powerful anthem. It was important to have that song on the record because I was speaking to people who were with me when we started the NYHC scene and who, sadly, are not with us today.

"For all those that we lost / This is a message, this is for you / Never forget the Lower East Side crew."

It struck a chord with me and contained some of the most meaningful lyrics I had ever written. Freddy was part of that Lower East Side crew, of course, so I was shocked that he, Vinnie and everyone else didn't want to do it. It turned out to be the most important song on *Warriors*. It's one of our biggest songs, with over five million views on YouTube. If I hadn't been so persistent, it wouldn't have gotten finished. I did it for the LES warriors.

It was similar to what happened with "Gotta Go," when Jimmy Colletti hated the intro and outro. If it hadn't been for that intro and outro, I don't think that song would have struck people the way it did. Our fans love to chant that part.

I kept doing the band while Emily stayed home to care for our daughter, but AF did shorter tours. Now we go out for a week or two and we only tour every two to three months, except during the European festival season.

I started doing more electrical work. My friend Mike Oxley, who sings for The FatSkins, operates an electrical business in Phoenix called Oxley's Electric. He grew up on Agnostic Front, and we met in 1987 in Tucson, Arizona, as part of our Liberty & Justice For... Tour. When he introduced himself, I was strapping up for another one of those faceoffs with the enemy. Boy, did I judge that one wrong! As soon as we started talking we got along like old friends. Now we are old friends. When he found out I was in Arizona, he said, "I've got some work for you!"

Over the years I've done some big jobs with him. It's great because he owns the business and understands my situation. He knows how much AF means to me, so he's cool with me going on tour. He likes having me around because he knows I'm a good electrician and a hard worker. Plus, we get to shoot the shit about the old days and talk music. What's better than that?

For a while, I had pretty steady work with him. Then I'd get ready to put out a new album and suddenly I didn't have as much work. In January 2016 we were supposed to work at Cardinal Stadium, which I was looking forward to. Since all the permit releases had to be approved and signed, the work didn't begin until August. One day

Mike said, "Okay, everything's signed. We're ready to do it."

"Oh, shit, I'm getting ready to leave on tour tomorrow," I said.

"Okay, when you come back we'll finish it."

When I got back a week later, it was done. I missed out on a big job and a nice paycheck, which would have helped out in between tours. That's the situation I'm dealing with. I want to make everything a priority, and that's just not possible. It's like trying to be in three bands at one time. One is always going to get the short end of the stick. Luckily Mike understands, and we just regroup whenever I'm around.

Downsizing our tour schedule came with its drawbacks. It hurt the band's income stream. Most of the guys were okay with that. I'm in Phoenix and doing more electrical work, so I've been able to earn enough to be comfortable and provide for my family. Vinnie has a rent-controlled apartment, and Mike Gallo was cutting hair and living with Vinnie. Joe was doing stagehand work and living with his wife, Sammy, who was a film major in NYC. Unfortunately Steve Gallo was going through a lot of personal and financial issues and needed more security than we could offer him. We amicably parted ways, and Leeway drummer Jimmy "Pokey" Mo joined the band. He brought back some of that old-school flavor that compliments the band, whether we're playing stuff from United Blood or brand-new songs. Pokey was the perfect fit, and once again we were unstoppable.

Emily and I have been married for ten years and we've had a second child. My son, Desi, was born on May 29, 2009. My wife was content with just one baby, but I always wanted a son named Desi. That was enough to convince Emily to give it another try. Even if she gave birth to another girl we would have been happy, and we had another name picked out just in case.

The gender of the baby was supposed to be a surprise, but the doctor spilled the beans to Emily and she couldn't resist telling me. I was finally going to have a son. From the time he was in the womb, he was special to me—so special that I wrote an odd country song for him that came to me in the middle of the night. I called it "JR" and recorded it with The Disasters on our 2009 release, Gotta Get Up Now. I did a video for the song featuring Havi and Desi, which the label posted on YouTube. The song actually hit the country charts and was played at AMC bowling alleys nationwide. Desi is reserved but caring. He can be really emotional, and he has a great sense of humor. He's a big-time jokester just like his daddy.

I still tour with Agnostic Front several times a year all around the world. When I'm on the road I never worry about my wife and my children. Emily is a strong woman who keeps me focused and steady. I have taken my family on short U.S. tours with me a few times, but it was only because I missed them, never because my wife felt neglected or resentful that she was left behind. Emily supports me completely, and most importantly, respects and loves me. I love my family more than anything, and I am so glad I took a chance and asked my wife for that kiss back in 2002.

What I've learned from the past is something I never would have understood when I was a teenage runaway. Family comes first. For the first time in my life I feel super-grounded. If I dropped dead tomorrow—which I don't want to—I'd be at peace. My life is good, my kids are fine and I know my wife can handle the family with or without me. Of course she wants me around and I want to be here, but that's how strong she is. I can't say that about most of the women I had in my life.

# CHAPTER 40

**S**ince we had so much fun recording *Warriors* with Freddy, we brought him back four years later for *My Life My Way*. He brought even more to the band this time. Freddy had lots of musical ideas, and he often asked us to change a part or try something he came up with. A lot of his musical and lyrical suggestions stuck, and when we tried something out that didn't work as well, he was cool with us returning to our original idea. He supported whatever worked best for the song, no egos involved. He had grown up a lot since his teenage tantrums.

Even though we were still writing heavy songs, we decided they needed more melodic parts. We wanted to bridge the gap between *Warriors* and what we had done with Epitaph, and with Freddy's help we pulled it off. Some of the songs on *My Life My Way* are aggressive, heavy and mean, but then we also have sing-alongs, like the title track, which brings listeners right back to the infectious immediacy of something like "Gotta Go." We recorded the album in Tampa, Florida, at Mana Recordings Studio with Erik Rutan. Erik is a death metal veteran, who was in Morbid Angel and has produced a bunch of wild bands, including Six Feet Under, Cannibal Corpse and Goatwhore. Together, Freddy and Erik gave the album a raw, ripping yet organic sound.

"A Mi Manera" was the first song we approached in Spanish from the ground up. We didn't write it in English and then translate it, which we did when we were on Epitaph. The European version of *Something's Gotta Give* had three bonus tracks for Spain, with "Gotta Go," "Believe" and "Voices" in Spanish. I always wanted to do something like that to honor my Hispanic heritage. We wound up releasing a three-track single of the Spanish songs on Hellcat Records called *Puros Des Madre*, and it was a huge success across Spain and South America. Whenever we go to South America we sing "Gotta Go" in Spanish and they go crazy. Freddy thought it was so inspiring that he recorded "100%" with Madball as their tribute to the Latin hardcore community.

"A Mi Manera" means "My Way" and has the same message as "My Life My Way," but the riffs and tempo are completely different. Freddy and I traded off vocal parts, which he has done on every Agnostic Front record since *Live at CBGB* in 1989. "A Mi Manera" was the heaviest song on the album, and when Nuclear Blast heard it they made it the priority track from *My Life My Way*. That didn't make sense to me since the majority of their market speaks English, but Markus loved the song so much he said it would transcend language barriers. He was right. It became a big hit in Spanish-speaking countries. We go to places all over the world, and audiences sing along to the chorus in Spanish even if they don't know the language.

When 2015 rolled around, we decided it was time to do another AF record. I thought of producing it myself because I wanted to approach it differently than anything I had done. It was kind of a split record. There were seven traditional songs that we wrote as a band on the road. They were tight and to the point, and they were each between two and three minutes long. We practiced them, and Freddy offered his input and finished molding them into solid Agnostic Front tracks.

There were another 10 songs I didn't let anyone hear. I demoed them myself with my former drummer from the Disasters, J.P. Otto, and my good friend Rich Labbate, who's in a straight edge band called Insted. I have a side band with Rich called The Alligators. Over the years, we've released two singles and a full-length. As much fun as we've had making music together, we've never played a show. In late 2014, I arranged to do some Alligators songs with Rich, but when we got together I flipped the script on him.

"Rich, hear me out," I began. "I'm recording a new record with Agnostic Front. And a lot of people have come up to me who love the Alligators. And I think I want to do these songs, not as Alligators, but with Agnostic Front."

"Oh, cool. I'm in," he said.

We got together in Phoenix to write the songs. I brought them to J.P. He had just one chance to listen to them and then record them. We went right in to do the vocals. We demoed 10 songs. I let the band hear some of the material, and they fuckin' loved it. By that point Craig Silverman had joined the band on guitar, replacing Joseph James. I let Craig and Mike Gallo hear it.

"Holy shit! This is the kind of stuff I love to play," Craig enthused.

The element of excitement in those songs is the same that we had in the beginning with Agnostic Front when it was all about chaos and insanity. Everything was new, fresh and bleeding when we did *United Blood* and *Victim In Pain*, and we just went in and tore shit up.

That's the way The Alligators worked. When Rich wrote a song, nobody would hear it. He would present it to the musicians and they'd have one chance to listen to it and two chances to practice. The third time you played it, you recorded it, and whatever went down was what we kept. The songs are simple. Any decent musician can pick them up quickly. What we needed to capture was the element of urgency—the offness that happened when everything wasn't exactly in tune or unerringly precise, that off-the-rails chaos within a band that is true fucking punk! The same went for vocals. I wasn't allowed to see them until it was time to record. I got to hear it and try it twice, and the third time we recorded it. There was a lot of spontaneity—crazy screams, out-of-time tempos and raw explosiveness. Not being able to polish those songs made them stand out. That's what keeps *The American Dream Died* sounding fresh and unpredictable. There'll be a song like "Never Walk Alone," which is structured and tight, and then all of a sudden "Enough Is Enough" rips through the speakers. None of the songs I did with Rich were over 1:50. It's such a genuine and relevant record, and it rumbles with raw rebellion. The lyrics, which challenged a crippled and crippling justice system, complemented the insanity of the music.

Even though he was the producer, Freddy never got to hear those songs before we recorded them. He only knew the other seven cuts. We were ready to go to California to record with Paul Miner. We picked his studio, Buzzbomb Sound Labs, because it was the same place I had recorded with the Alligators. I wanted to capture that magic on the record and share it with our fans. I wanted to shove it down their throats and make them love it like I do. That's why everyone that bought *The American Dream Died* got a free download of *Time's Up, You're Dead* by The Alligators. We were saying,

"If you love these songs, you gotta hear this!"

Although Freddy was credited as the producer of *The American Dream Died*, he wasn't there because Craig Silverman had another commitment and we had to reschedule the recording sessions. It wasn't a problem for anyone in the band, but it was during a Madball tour. Freddy was bummed, but we moved forward.

"Freddy, don't worry about it," I said. "We already did a lot of work together. The guys know exactly what you want to do. We can work with you over the Internet."

Every time we recorded a song we sent it to Freddy, and he came back to us with suggestions. We were able to do seven songs with him digitally, and they sounded killer.

But he never heard those magical 10 extra songs we did. Rich "Insted" Labbate was the exclusive producer for those, though he didn't want credit on the album. He just wanted to help out and hear AF play and record the songs. It went both ways. The guys loved the songs and couldn't wait to play them, but I didn't tell them they only had two chances to practice and one take to record.

They were, like, "What? I gotta do that again." And then it was, like, "Nope. Next song." You don't get the chance to polish your turd over here in Alligator Land. It's a turd and that's the way it stays. But it's a fuckin' gritty hardcore turd. It's raw, it's furious, it's genuine. And if you take those 10 songs and pull them out of that record, it's really mind-blowing.

After we finished *The American Dream Died*, I sent the songs we did with Rich to Freddy. I explained where they came from and how we recorded them.

"Holy shit!" he said. "This is the stuff people fuckin' love about AF from the very beginning!"

# EPILOGUE

The purpose of sharing my life story is so that the younger generations can have some insight as to where my music came from. Life was completely different. I put a lot of thought into telling certain stories and paid close attention to the people from my past that were involved in certain situations. Some people were not comfortable with sharing their truths.

There was a time in the early '80s when I took a garbage can and I threw it through a McDonald's window in broad daylight just to rail against the system. I was a stupid, violent, live-fast-die-young kid. I didn't think there were any consequences for my actions even after I went to prison. I did things that I am embarrassed about.

Today, I think differently. I have kids. I don't want to live too fast and I'm too old to die young. I dream about living to see my grandchildren. I love to see my kids in a stable, loving environment, and it fills me with warmth to see them enjoy the simple pleasures in life that my siblings and I never had growing up. If I never shared these stories, my children would have no idea what struggle is like. My children have a beautiful, safe life. My children don't have fear, they don't have uncertainty and they don't have struggle like I had. My wife and I both had very hard childhoods, but she didn't live on the streets and raise herself like I did. Some of my stories are difficult for her to hear, but we are honest and open about everything we have lived through. I want to teach my children that, yes, I made some bad choices, I had the potential to ruin my life and I had to take extra steps to change my life because of it. It took a lot to become the man that I am today.

But inside, I'm still that rebel. I still think a little bit differently. If I really wanted to take a stand against McDonald's or make a political statement today, I wouldn't throw a garbage can through a window. I'd approach it differently. I'd wait until the evening, put a little glue in the lock of the front door and put a toothpick in the key hole. That would prevent people from using the door, and it's as far as I would go to upset the system these days. A real anarchist would think that's pretty lame. They'd be right. I'm not out to destroy the system anymore. I've done that crime and done the time, and now I'm free.

Looking back at all the fights, riots, fires, arrests and brushes with the law I've had over the years, it's amazing I lived long enough to see the death of cassette tapes, let alone the resurrection of vinyl. I probably won't be back in prison, and I'm not likely to plant roots in Alphabet City again. That's because, just like I say in my lyrics, if you look at the Lower East Side today it just doesn't add up—at least not for someone like me.

Those were different times. When we ran the streets, there were no rules. Chaos reigned. I lived fast and many of my friends died young. But it's no longer my party. It's someone else's party and their time to live in the bowels of New York City. Without the element of danger, the nihilistic bliss and the abundant creativity that were as strong as the smell of burning tires, I can't see why kids today would want to commit themselves to life on the streets. It's impossible to squat on the Lower East Side now when every building is worth millions and even kids with decent jobs have to share tiny apartments to afford the rent. It's another world out there now—one I didn't grow up in and can't begin to relate to. So I won't even try.

When I walked out of that prison gate, I vowed never to return. I haven't. I vowed to be a better person. I have. If you met me today, you would never think I lived through such a wild time and relished every hazard along the way. I can honestly say that the crazy life I led and all my mistakes made me who I am today. A baby needs to fall to learn how to walk. I've taken my falls and gotten back up. I've talked the talk and I've walked the walk, and it has taken me to where I am today. And now I'm just gonna put one foot in front of the other and keep walking.

# ACKNOWLEDGMENTS

**From Roger Miret**

Love and respect to my family, friends and band members past and present.

Never forget the Lower East Side Crew.

Thank you, Jon Wiederhorn.

**From Jon Wiederhorn**

Nancy Wiederhorn (I will never forget you), Sheldon Wiederhorn, Elizabeth Kaplan, Joshua Wiederhorn, Chloe Wiederhorn, Miriam Rust, Hap Rust, Carole Kaplan, Frank Kaplan, Jacob Hoye, Michael Croland, Howie Abrams, Ian MacFarland, all the friends who have been there for me through the decades, the editors who have given me work over the years, Charlie, Vinnie Stigma, and last but not least, Roger Miret, who entrusted me to help tell his amazing story.

# PHOTOGRAPHY

Amy Keim: Pages 4, 11, 47, 53, 70, 80, 81, 93, 97, 127, 144, 189, 250,
Insert Pages 1, 2, 3, 4, 6 (Top), 7, 8

Drew Carolan: Insert Page 5

Rod Orchard: Pages 229, 296

Dave Brown: Insert Page 6 (Bottom)

Brooke Smith-Lubensky: Page 180

Jessica Bard: Pages 61, 62, 121

Rene Mannich: Page 219

Ken Salerno: Page 172

BJ Papas: Page 256

Sponge: Pages 287, 288–289

Roger Miret: Pages 21, 23, 78, 173, 181, 273

TRAITOR
DISCRIMINATE ME
UNITED AND STRONG
FIGHT
LAST WARNING
FRIEND OR FOE
NO ONE RULES
POWER
UNITED BLOOD
TIME WILL COME
VICTOM IN PAIN
CRUCIAL CHANGES
BLIND JUSTICE
IN CONTROL
SOCIETY SICKERS

# ABOUT THE AUTHORS

**Roger Miret** is a pioneer of the New York Hardcore scene. The Cuban-born singer joined Agnostic Front in 1983, and the seminal group released classics like *United Blood*, *Victim In Pain* and *Cause For Alarm* over the next several years. Miret also fronts his own solo group, Roger Miret and The Disasters. He lives in Scottsdale, Arizona.

**Jon Wiederhorn** is the author of *Louder Than Hell: The Definitive Oral History of Metal* (with Katherine Turman) and the co-author of *Ministry: The Lost Gospels According to Al Jourgensen* (with Al Jourgensen) and *I'm the Man: The Story of That Guy from Anthrax* (with Scott Ian). He has written for *Rolling Stone*, *SPIN*, MTV, *Guitar World* and *Revolver*, among others. He lives in Montclair, New Jersey.

Made in the USA
Monee, IL
11 March 2025

13868894R00184